There's no need to shout!

The Secondary Teacher's

Guide to Successful

Behaviour Management

There's no need to shout!

The Secondary Teacher's
Guide to Successful
Behaviour Management

David Wright

Published in 2005 by:
Nelson Thornes Ltd
Delta Place
27 Bath Road
CHELTENHAM
GL53 7TH
United Kingdom

05 06 07 08 09 / 10 9 8 7 6 5 4 3 2 1

A catalogue record for this book is available from the British Library

ISBN 0 7487 9361 5

Illustrations by Clinton Banbury
Page make-up by Florence Production Ltd

Printed and bound in Spain by GraphyCems

Dedication

This book is dedicated to my family, Maureen, Sean and Jamie, for their patience and support while I was writing it.

I would also like to express my thanks to David Brunwin who put his faith in me, gave me a chance when I needed it most and has continued to support me ever since.

CONTENTS

ACKNOWLEDGEMENT

Page 125: Assessment Framework from *The Framework for the Assessment of Children in Need and Their Families* (Department of Health, 2000). Crown copyright material is reproduced with the permssion of the Controller of HMSO and the Queen's Printer for Scotland.

PREFACE

Scarcely a week goes by without some reference to the increasing problem of the behaviour of young people. Communities are becoming blighted by the anti-social behaviour of youths on the streets and teachers are finding that the same is happening in schools. Ofsted have highlighted the problem, and politicians and other interested parties have contributed their concerns. The disruption caused by minorities of unruly students is becoming more frequent so we as teachers need to act decisively to curb it.

Too often the title of a book seems to promise so much but the content does not live up to expectations. This book has been written by a skilled teacher whose job is to help some of the most challenging children turn their behaviour around. It does exactly what the title suggests. It is not an academic text. It is a no-nonsense, practical book packed full of advice and suggestions based on the real experiences of the author and his colleagues. The main aim has been to equip teachers with the skills and knowledge necessary to manage behaviour in a positive, assertive way and to inspire confidence in tackling and dealing with disruptive children.

The methods are based on one principle and that is that children should take responsibility for their own behaviour. This can be achieved by offering choices and the expectation that they face the consequences of their decisions. An assertive style, together with a consistent approach, will eventually lead to the children making the right choices and you will have no need to shout.

INTRODUCTION

I get calls from head teachers about students who are becoming so challenging that they are nearing permanent exclusion. The class teacher has tried everything she can think of. The educational psychologist has offered advice and suggested reasons for the child's behaviour and the behaviour support team has been in and worked with the staff, but none of the interventions seemed to have worked. The parents are at their wits' end. Home life is in turmoil, with chaos and disruption virtually every night. It is a plea for help and the head teacher is desperately hoping that I will be able to provide a solution. I take children that are very challenging and try to 're-engineer' their behaviour. For some of the children, success is hard and no matter what we try to do to help, it doesn't happen. My team of staff are not magicians.

The children's emotional difficulties are so complex, ingrained and interlinked to wider issues within the family and the community that we can only scratch the surface and make a little progress. Children who have experienced significant traumas such as sexual abuse, domestic violence or neglect or who are victims of war will develop barriers in their minds that have far-reaching effects on their ability to function normally. Most schools will have some children with these kinds of experiences. The children will be on the far end of the behaviour spectrum and will create enormous problems for their teachers. The classroom can become so distressful and unbearable that the teacher begins to feel they cannot manage. Help is often too slow in coming or too little to have any real effect.

This is not the case for the majority of teachers or children but I feel it is important to make it very clear that there are vulnerable children in mainstream schools and we are not always successful in helping them. When a difficult child finally leaves a class and is referred on to an agency or another educational provision in an effort to help them, the teacher will feel a great burden lifted from their shoulders. At the same time, they may also feel that they have failed and that is why it is important to recognise that we cannot get it right with every child.

Today's schools can be challenging places to work in. They are very different to the schools of my youth in post-war Britain. For decades, teachers were regarded as pillars of the community, professional people held in high regard. If you stepped out of line in a lesson, a wooden board rubber would come flying across the room and just skim past your head, hitting the wall with a chilling thwack to remind you of who was in charge. Be caught messing around and you might find your ear being held and twisted while you dangled from the hand of the teacher scolding you. The really naughty kids would be publicly punished with a sharp swipe of the slipper, T-square or board ruler. The ultimate punishment was a caning from the head teacher. Many believe that those days were good and claim that it never did them any harm. I am not going to take up that argument here. It was a different era and things have changed.

The rock and roll years of the 1950s heralded the arrival of the teenage phenomenon. The war began to fade into the past, along with the austerity of rationing and making ends meet. Increased production required larger labour forces that in turn led to people having surplus spending power and manufacturers looking for new markets. For the first time in our history, young school leavers discovered they had money to spare. The manufacturers were quick to identify them as a potentially enormous market. The 1960s became a decade of wealth and consumption and the teenage market became a major force because young people did not have financial responsibilities. Teenagers in Britain and the United States did not have the demands on their income that their parents or grandparents had endured. By the end of the decade there was a general feeling of being well off, which brought with it a sense of freedom that was typified by a tide of liberal opinion sweeping the nation. Old values were questioned, challenged and rejected. Social rules and class divides were disintegrating. The strict Victorian attitudes towards sex and marriage that had pervaded began to disappear with the emancipation of women in the workplace and the home.

The advent of the contraceptive pill liberated women and allowed them to decide who they would have sexual encounters with. The sexual revolution enabled men and women to become more sexually active before marriage. This in turn led to the questioning of the value of marriage itself and young people began to take partners and even live together outside of marriage, something that would have been unheard of a decade earlier.

Children were encouraged to question the way things were. They were allowed to be freer. In school the move was away from the strict regime of didactic teaching in classrooms with rows of desks. Examinations divided children into 'those that could' and 'those that couldn't'. Primary education became experiential. Teachers encouraged children to discover and learn for themselves through project-based activities. Subject boundaries started to get blurred and lesson structures faded as the children were given opportunities to see what they could find out about a topic. Interestingly, secondary education did not go down that route of educating the 'whole child' using the new, quite innovative but untested methods.

It was not only the curriculum that changed. The architecture of the primary school evolved to accommodate the new liberal approaches. Walls were knocked down between classrooms and corridors. Movable tables and chairs were arranged in islands rather than rows and replaced traditional fixed desks and benches. Children were even given the freedom to move from one area to another. Carpet time was introduced so that the class could sit round the teacher for some activities to offer a more homely or relaxed experience.

In the 1970s the political trend was towards more central control. Governments began to recognise the economic value of education. A chilling realisation dawned that the population as a whole was not being well educated. Levels of numeracy and literacy were poor, which led to significant changes that have put their stamp on the contemporary landscape of education.

The high regard that the profession was held in by the general public has been undermined by the teacher-bashing activities of the popular tabloid media. Attacks on teachers are commonplace whenever standards drop, yet when they rise it is because the tests are allegedly getting easier, not because the teaching and preparation have improved. The regular negative reporting about teachers in the 1980s and the early 1990s has opened the floodgates for criticism at all levels. Now it is considered acceptable for parents to speak to teachers rudely or threateningly when they feel their child has been treated unfairly. I do not support unprofessional or poor practice but equally I believe that teachers have rights like everyone else and there are proper channels that can be used. The harm is done when a parent decides to launch into a tirade of shouting and abuse in front of the child. This undermines the teacher's position with the child and condones shouting and abuse. The repeated talk of student and parental rights coupled with the complaining, compensation culture must have had a detrimental effect and harmful influence on the teaching profession and a teacher's ability to do the job.

The second major change has been the programme of educational reforms. This includes the introduction of the National Curriculum and testing, GCSEs, the reduction of local education authority powers, Ofsted, and numeracy and literacy hours. More recently, it includes workforce reform in the shape of *Excellence and Enjoyment*, which is almost a government U-turn back to some of the thinking behind the liberal approaches of the 1960s, and wrap-around schooling to enable working parents to access childcare. The effects of these changes remain to be seen as longitudinal studies are still incomplete, but from a personal perspective the continual removal of power from the profession as a whole can only lead to deskilling. If a government repeatedly puts out publications that direct teachers on what to teach and how to teach it, it will inevitably end up with a compliant, servile workforce. The problems occur when a government changes its mind, which seems to be quite often. This destabilises the system. Teachers begin to think they are wasting their time, because as fast as they understand the latest initiative, a new one replaces it. Planning the curriculum has become an annual task because teachers never know whether it will be the same next year.

Uncertainty leads to problems elsewhere. Teachers who are desperately trying to keep abreast of the curriculum and new initiatives will find that their lessons are not as good as they could be, because they do not have the opportunity to review and evaluate them as they would like. Their time is eaten up with research and reading and then incorporating the new government guidelines into their lessons. Behaviour of the students becomes an afterthought and lessons may not be as good as they could be, so students get bored and switch off.

Change is necessary and in most cases has benefits, so we should embrace it. We have an excellent track record over the past two decades for doing just that, maybe more so than any other profession. Change also brings with it disadvantages that need to be managed and solutions found. The major difficulty many teachers are currently experiencing is the issue of inclusion. I do not know anyone who would argue against the idea, because everyone has the right to be a member of the community, to contribute to it and to benefit from it. Our job is to find ways to include everyone in the mainstream education system as long as it is in their best interests.

Teachers are struggling with problems caused by students behaving in ways that could have been avoided. They call me in to help and what I invariably see when I arrive is a child unable to cope because the teacher is not using an effective method of classroom management.

The idea for this book first came to me near the start of my career in education. I entered teaching after a number of jobs. I began working in further education colleges teaching photography and video. The principal asked me whether I would like to take a class of 15 year olds and teach them video production. They were all truants and many had not been to school for over a year. The local education authority had set up a Back to Education course for them. It had six modules consisting of numeracy, literacy, IT, business, video plus art and design, and science. The principal was very honest with me. She told me all about their backgrounds. I knew exactly what I was letting myself in for. These guys would be difficult. They did not view school as useful and teachers were not on their list of people to respect. They had reputations on the streets and could not be messed with.

I was really into my subject and just wanted others to get the same amount of enjoyment from doing it as I did. The project we did included paper engineering and programme making. The kids learned how to make pop-up cards and then produce a short piece for a children's television programme on how to make them.

The attendance for my sessions was a hundred per cent over the eight weeks. I later found out that the other teachers had not had such a good response. One of the reasons behind my success was the intrinsically interesting nature of the subject. The other reason was good teaching combined with well-planned activities matched to the abilities of the class.

Several months later I began to think about that class of kids and started wondering what would have happened if things had gone differently. What if the behaviour had deteriorated in the lesson? What would I have done? I realised then that I hadn't got a clue. I would have had no idea how to handle things and would have probably ended up with a riot on my hands.

Later I moved into the secondary sector and the rude awakening that many of the students were not going to behave without some kind of intervention by me. Suddenly I was in the front line of mainstream education and the daily problem of maintaining order. I had not been trained to deal with recalcitrant children.

The years have passed since those early, quite frightening days and I have learned a lot. The ideas and methods in this book are the product of learning the hard way. The case studies that I have used have either happened to my colleagues or me and provide a wealth of material to analyse and evaluate in an effort to find solutions.

The ethos behind the methods described in this book is simple and easy to understand: (1) the children take responsibility for their own behaviour; (2) this is done by helping them recognise that they have choices and are in control of them. Everything that I have suggested stems from these guiding principles and the aim is to help the children reach them. Gender references are used simply to enable the text to flow. Boys and girls are equally capable of behaving in ways described in this book. All names used in this book are fictitious to protect the identities of individuals featured in the case studies.

1 WHAT KIND OF TEACHER DO YOU WANT TO BE?

The teacher holds a powerful position. You can shape and influence the hearts and minds of your students by what you say, what you do and how you do it. Your expectations can ignite a passion for learning in a child that can determine their life chances and launch them on to great things. Alternatively, you can extinguish their enthusiasm, dampen their hopes and dreams and turn them off the path of learning. Such power to influence and motivate has been recognised for centuries, which is why the teacher holds such a revered position in many societies. Good teachers are respected in a way that other professionals are not.

The learning process is a complex one. How it takes place is becoming better understood in terms of what can be done by the teacher and the student to make it more efficient. For example, adopting a particular teaching style or linking information to familiar objects or ideas can help the student make better sense of the new and remember it over time. What is only just starting to be understood is how the brain functions during the learning process. We know little if anything about how we comprehend and process something like $2 + 2 = 4$.

Recent advances have pinpointed where in the brain the activity is taking place when we try to learn something. We are also aware of which areas of the brain have become specialised for specific kinds of learning, such as visual stimuli and physical skills like playing a musical instrument or executing a complicated movement.

One of the most important factors in the learning process is the mental state of the student and this has been known for some time. It is obvious really – if we are not ready to learn, we won't. So what are the barriers to learning that students experience? How do they arise and how can they be overcome? Maslow's hierarchy of needs (Figure 1.1, overleaf) offers us a model that represents all our individual needs as a pyramid, with the essential physical needs at the base (Maslow, 1998). These must be satisfied before we are able to consider others. Next comes our personal safety. If we are under threat, the body's biological defences are activated, producing hormones that prepare us for either fight or flight. Once safety needs have been satisfied, we can begin to consider ourselves and our position within a group or community.

The classroom environment can be matched against the pyramid. If a student is not secure in the lower levels then the higher levels, including learning, will become difficult. There can be many barriers to learning. Here are some examples:

- The room is too cold, hot or cramped, so the students cannot apply themselves to anything other than the discomfort.
- The student is thirsty, hungry or ill, so they need to do something about their physical needs immediately.
- There are distractions such as noise or something unusual or interesting inside or outside the room.

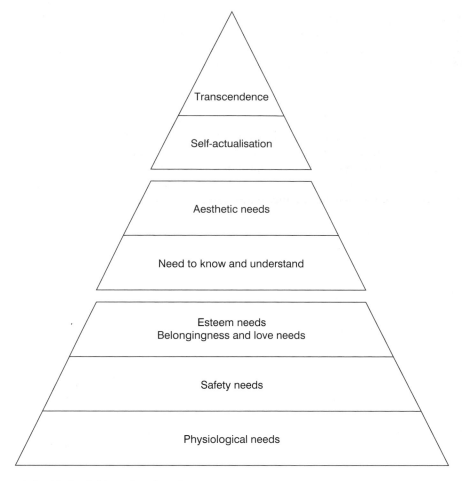

Figure 1.1 *Maslow's hierarchy of needs*

- The teacher has made the student feel scared, angry, embarrassed or useless in the way they have spoken or acted.
- The teacher's expectations are unrealistic or too low and the student feels unable or unwilling to try because they feel unsupported.
- The student may be experiencing some kind of difficulty outside the classroom, such as bullying, or at home, such as parents arguing, divorcing or being violent. There may be illness, crime or poverty in the family or they may be moving home.
- Another student or group of students in the class may be putting an individual down every time they try to answer, speak or do something in the lesson.
- The student may have difficulty concentrating due to a medical condition called attention deficit hyperactivity disorder (ADHD), which is characterised by an overactive brain.
- The student may be on the autistic spectrum and find it impossible to move on from a problem because they cannot bear to have an unresolved aspect of the subject they are studying.

The teacher has to be sensitive to the needs of the students. This means assessing whether barriers exist and, if so, helping a student over or around them. As you can see, some of the barriers can be caused by the teacher, so care must be taken to prevent them. Many teachers are skilled in avoiding them and newly qualified teachers need to develop these skills.

Many of the barriers to learning are due to incidents and events happening beyond the classroom and the school. The ones within the school can be avoided. Your presence in the classroom will determine how successful you are. Your ability to manage the students, the resources and the room will be the important factors. Teachers do this by being reactive, proactive or inconsistent in their style. The reactive teacher can be aggressive, domineering and oppressive or the exact opposite by being weak, passive and lacking authority and presence in the classroom. The proactive teacher will pre-empt problems and plan for good behaviour by using an assertive style backed up by fair rules and a consistent approach. The inconsistent teacher is perhaps the hardest one for students to work with, because they veer between being reactive and proactive.

REACTIVE STYLES

The aggressive teacher

Characteristics of the style

The aggressive teacher (Case Study 1.1) very rarely teaches the students how to behave. They take on the responsibility for student behaviour, as they believe a good teacher is one who has complete control over the students and can command a healthy respect from them, based on fear. The students will do exactly what they are told because they know what is coming if they don't. They do not make any real attempt to involve the students in constructing the rules. The students are there to do as they are told.

Case Study 1.1

'Line up properly, and you two big oafs can get to the back. One day you will learn to act your age!' The class shuffled into position but one of the boys tried to slide into a place so two others squirted him back out. 'Come here, Brown.' Brown turned and walked sheepishly up

to Mr Clark. He knew what was coming and his heart started to beat quickly. 'Get over there and get that shirt tucked in. There's always one. Well I'm not prepared to have it in my lesson!' He turned to Brown, 'Face the wall, I don't want to look at you. You think you are all such clever dicks and can do what you want.' He leered at them with real disdain. 'Right! I want the whole class to go into the room in silence. Brown, you wait till last.'

The class filed into the room in total silence with their eyes down so as not to attract Mr Clark's attention. As Collins walked past Brown, he smirked sideways at him and the teacher caught sight of his gesture. 'You think it's funny do you, Collins? Stand aside and wait with Brown.' When everyone had gone in, he turned to them both and released a torrent of abuse. The rest of the students strained to get a view of the entertainment. He stood inches from their faces as he bellowed at them and finished by giving each of them a full lunchtime detention to teach them to behave.

The style is one of a bygone age of corporal punishment and military-style oppression. It has been caricatured in countless books and films and is typified by Wackford Squeers in Dickens' *Nicholas Nickleby* and Ms Trunchbull in Roald Dahl's *Matilda*. Thankfully the teaching profession has moved on but there are still teachers making use of this style in our schools today. They get their results by the use of fear and oppression. Their authority is rigid and unquestioned. The classrooms and the school are battlegrounds where daily skirmishes are fought with insubordinate students who, they believe, don't know how well off they are.

Their style requires a considerable amount of shouting and bellowing of orders and a significant investment of emotion, usually in anger or contempt. The teacher believes he has the right to get what he wants but has little understanding of the rights of the students. In fact, he believes they should not have rights, because it will lead to discipline problems. The students have to know who is in charge and nothing should be questioned. They have several ways of dealing with students who break rules or question their authority. They show their anger, and short of getting physical, they will shout, threaten and abuse them, using a raised voice until the student backs down out of fear about what might happen. This also sends out signals to other students that should they misbehave it will be at their peril.

The teacher may resort to sarcasm in an effort to force the student to back off by making them appear stupid in front of their peers. They use phrases like these:

'It's about time you finally started acting your age.'

'Are you going to behave like an imbecile for the rest of your life?'

The other students may laugh, but they also know that it could be them next and so the atmosphere is not one of relaxed humour, more nervous laughter.

Belittling the student is a very common ploy of this teacher. The object is to make them a target of ridicule, but the result will be to seriously damage their self-esteem. This is where the aggressive teacher runs into difficulties. Fifty years ago he would have got away with it. The students would have accepted their fate and not questioned it. They may have expressed their dislike within the confines of their own peer group, but they would never have stood up to the teacher. Times have changed and everyone is far more aware of their rights. Students have become used to expressing their views publicly and teachers have had to come to terms with this.

The aggressive teacher does not seem to have evolved with the times and he believes students should not answer back. When they do, it is perceived as a direct challenge to his authority and leads to a conflict situation. In many cases the challenge develops into a battle of wills and becomes an issue connected to secondary behaviour rather than the original incident (Case Study 1.2).

Case Study 1.2

Two girls are looking at a magazine when they should be completing the geography task. Mr Cartwright spots them giggling and calls across the room, disrupting the whole class and making the thing public. 'Put that away and get on with your work, you two. What do you think this is, a shopping mall?'

'No, Sir,' said one of the girls giggling, 'there's no shops.'

'Don't be clever, Carly, your brain won't cope,' retorted the teacher. Carly looked very cross with his reply and kissed her teeth in his direction.

'What was that? Who do you think you are?'

'It was nothing, Sir!' she replied arrogantly.

'Yes it was, you kissed your teeth. You know the school rule on that,' he shouted, looming over her in a threatening way.

'No I don't and I didn't do it anyway. I was just moving my brace because it was hurting my gums.'

'A likely story, anyway that's a detention at lunchtime for you, Madam!'

The teacher managed to move the attention from something low-level like being off task to a major battle over a secondary response. He mishandled the situation by giving a heavy-handed response to something quite insignificant.

The aggressive teacher does not consider giving the students the opportunity to take responsibility for their own behaviour. He retains control, offering little or no choice, only ultimatums. The decision about what happens next remains with the teacher because he believes he can control the class and make the students do as they are told. He is confident that he can force the students to follow his directions because he backs it up with threats and punishments. The students resent this kind of treatment and some retaliate. What ensues is a power struggle, and in a battle of wills the teacher knows he must not lose face at any cost. It will be a win-lose battle, fought for high stakes. The students will lose because he regards them as the underdogs and employs his full armoury of sarcasm, aggression, abuse and physical presence to ensure he triumphs. On no account can there be a win-win situation. The students will not be given a means of saving face. The only result for them will be damage to their self-esteem caused by the humiliation they will suffer. It may come immediately or it may be via a threat of revenge in the future (Case Study 1.3).

Case Study 1.3

'What's that you've got there, Watson?'

'Nothing, Sir, I was just getting a sharpener out of my pencil case.'

'I am not stupid, Watson, you had a mobile phone didn't you?'

'Yes, Sir, but it wasn't switched on.'

'I don't care. Give it to me.'

'No, Sir.' Watson did not want to part with his phone because he'd just got it for his birthday the day before.

'Give it to me now!'

'No, Sir, I don't want to.'

'Give it to me now or else!'

'Or else what? You can't make me.'

'Oh yes I can and I will. Then you'll be sorry.'

Many teachers do not want to be aggressive but feel they have no option, especially when things start to get difficult. They have little experience of dealing with non-compliant students in any other way than to exercise their status in a forceful, threatening manner. When they do, the relationship in the class changes quite dramatically. Teachers who use these tactics on very rare occasions do not usually experience any problems, because the students recognise that they have pushed them too far. They are not normally aggressive. After all, it is sometimes necessary to show you have teeth, so the students know you are capable of something more that you keep under control. Overuse of it will end with the students fearing you, making it impossible to develop a positive, productive relationship with them.

The effects of this style

The most significant effect of this style is the absence of respect. Obviously the teacher does not respect the students and they do not respect him. His negative expectations rub off on them and they end up acting in the same way. They believe that they are not good enough and that it is not worth making any effort, because the teacher will not notice. The message he sends is that he does not like them.

Students who misbehave become his targets. He puts them down with his actions and communicates to everybody else that they are in the wrong. He will blame the students, parents, friends and other teachers for the poor behaviour. In fact, he will blame just about everyone except himself. He will go through his career with this fixed view and will be unable to contemplate the idea that he is wrong and there could be another way of managing behaviour that does not require an aggressive stance.

Teachers who use aggressive tactics may end up feeling guilty when they lose their temper. The process is self-destructive because once they show they are aggressive, the students put up their guards and become wary on future occasions. It will be very difficult for them to develop relationships with the teacher if they are always suspicious and on edge in case there is another outburst.

A teacher who is continually aggressive in his approach will be regarded as an enemy by the students. They will see him as unfair and resort to illicit means of coping with his lessons. They will lie, cheat and make up excuses to get themselves off when he blames them. They will feign illness and make up appointments to get themselves out of the room and away from him. In the end, they may even vent their frustration on their own classmates by passing the blame or bullying. The net result will be a climate of fear and the students will become completely turned off the school. They will go home and tell their parents of their grievances. Then the parents will side with them against the staff unless the trend is reversed.

The passive teacher

Characteristics of the style

The passive teacher (Case Study 1.4) is generally uncertain about his role. He understands the importance of being the adult and leader in the classroom but confuses the various qualities that a good teacher needs to have. For example, the purpose of the teacher is to teach. To teach is to help and he believes those in need of help will naturally welcome it. In reality, those in need of help may not realise it and may regard themselves as beyond helping or see the offer as an insult.

The passive teacher lacks the self-belief that he can lead and manage groups of students. He is aware that there are teachers with different styles to his own, teachers who seem to be far more extrovert and have the knack of getting the best out of their students. This awareness has an oppressive effect and renders him helpless to change. He will readily acknowledge that he is not in the same league and resign himself to the fact that he cannot perform any differently. He puts the abilities of more successful teachers down to some kind of natural, innate gift that he has not got and cannot learn.

Case Study 1.4

Derek didn't normally have trouble controlling classes, but he'd been lucky and had always taught well-behaved classes. His Year 9 maths set was a great group and a real joy to teach. Then one afternoon he had some boys from the other group sent to his room because their teacher was off sick and the deputy had split up the class. They were all right for the first ten minutes then one of them started shuffling around. Derek couldn't see what was going on but knew they were all involved.

'Stop that, you are disturbing the others who want to work.'

'My hand slipped,' said Aaron. His mate, Ryan, sniggered.

'I really want you to get on with your work.' This is a poor comment because Derek was not specific in what he wanted them to do.

The two boys made like they were getting down to work, so Derek left them and went to one of the other students who was waiting for help. A few minutes later a paper pellet flew across the room and hit someone sitting by the window.

Derek turned to the same two boys. 'Look, I know you don't like this work, but you need to do it otherwise you won't do very well in the exams.' Aaron shrugged his shoulders and muttered that he didn't care. 'Now I would be grateful if you got on with your work before it's too late.'

Derek is losing it now because the boys are not interested in his gratitude. Derek's attempt at challenging the boys was ineffective. He did not give clear directions and when they ignored him, he failed to give them a consequence. He should have been far more assertive, reminded them of the rule and redirected them to the work he wanted them to do. And how did Derek know that Ryan and Aaron didn't like the work?

Some teachers are confident in what they do and get satisfaction from doing the job well regardless of whether they will be popular. They do not seek acknowledgment or favour from the students. What usually happens is the students recognise they have a teacher who is supportive and who is encouraging them to be individuals and take responsibility for their own learning and development. They understand that order is part of the process and that the teacher is in charge. This gives them a feeling of security, so they feel confident to extend the boundaries and push themselves beyond their own limits. The passive teacher does not possess a very good sense of self-confidence. He is at heart insecure in what he does and so he seeks recognition and affirmation of himself as a person rather than from the job he is employed to do. He needs to be liked and seeks popularity by avoiding making unpopular or difficult decisions. He will shy away from confrontations and be cautious about challenging students when they misbehave. He will endeavour to ingratiate himself with the students, staff and parents rather than be assertive when a boundary is under pressure, a decision is in question or an action is disagreed with.

His feelings will be fragile and exposed in his quest to be accepted and liked. The slightest criticism will cut deeply. The need to be liked will become the priority and he will be quite hurt when a student makes a remark like these:

'Oh, Mr Sachs does it a different way and it is really good.'

'You're not as good as our usual teacher.'

'Ms Donaldson is much better than you at explaining things. They always seem so easy to understand.'

Such remarks are often a ploy by the students to manipulate the teacher to get them to do things that they want.

The passive teacher reacts to situations. He does not proactively work to control or use them. He does not pre-empt situations by planning how he will manage behaviour, yet he will plan lessons in detail. He may even have a behaviour code but he will enforce it poorly. He will probably miss incidents or only become aware of them once they have happened. He will be unclear about how to deal with them and appear erratic because of his lack of preparation. Most people who face new situations without having prepared themselves beforehand will be anxious and have to think on their feet. The passive teacher will feel threatened by misbehaving students, because he has not worked out his response. He will let incidents go unchallenged because he is afraid he will make himself unpopular. Students who get away with behaving inappropriately once will start to get confused. They will test the boundaries to try to find out just what they can and cannot do. The passive teacher will find that incidents increase and he will feel that he is fire-fighting all the time. His opinions about the students will be tarnished because he believes that they should respect him, even though he does little to command it.

A great deal about a person is communicated by their tone of voice. It is not what you say but how you say it. If you sound like you do not really mean something, then people will ignore you. There is a difference between quietly asserting your will and being timid and shrew-like. The passive teacher will endeavour to persuade, request or plead with his students. The way you look conveys meaning too. A resigned expression, outstretched arms and a detectable stoop are the body language of a defeated person. He will use phrases like these:

'That's not fair.'

'That's not what I would have expected from you.'

'I would have liked you to . . .'

'If you cared about me, you would . . .'

His efforts to appeal to the students' better nature may work with some but not all. Many will be ready to exploit this weakness once they discover it.

The passive teacher will assume the role of the victim when things go wrong. He will wonder why it always has to be him. The other teachers do not seem to have the problems he has. He may feel isolated during stressful times and the result will eventually be an outburst of emotion. If it comes as aggression, he will immediately feel guilty and wish he hadn't lost control. The students will be confused because he will not tell them why he is angry. He will harbour aggression until it has to escape somehow and when it does, it will be unrelated to the original reason for his feelings.

The students will quickly get the measure of this kind of teacher. They will realise that he has weaknesses and some will even try to dominate him. The room will become a place for slanging matches between the students and the teacher. When students do behave for him, it will be because they choose to, not because the teacher is asserting his will. The class are in control and free to change their behaviour in an instant.

So where does the passive teacher go wrong? He fails to assert his presence and status as the adult in charge. He confuses the students with directions that are unclear and he is erratic in dealing with them when they break the rules. His fear of the students not only prevents him from challenging them at the time but also stops him following up at a later point. He is easily swayed and gets drawn into secondary issues. His overriding hope is that they will be better next time.

The effects of this style

There will be a growing resentment between the teacher and the students. The teacher will resent the students because they do not behave responsibly and of their own accord. The students will resent the teacher for his failure to keep order and manage the class. The students who are behaving well will despise the teacher and feel they are losing out. They will also be frustrated because the recalcitrant students are getting away with things. They will want the help of the teacher but it will be taken up by the disruptive students. Eventually they will realise that the only way they can get the teacher's attention is to misbehave as well.

Praise is sometimes used as a bribe along with the rewards already available. The passive teacher will give the least deserving students rewards in an effort to curb their poor behaviour. The better-behaved students will see this as unfair because it undermines the behaviour code and devalues the rewards at the same time. Some of the students will feel that their efforts go unnoticed because only the most able and the poorly behaved get rewarded.

The passive teacher's style does not result in the students learning to make choices about their behaviour. They are not helped to develop their own internal checks and accept their responsibilities. Ultimately the teacher's abdication of this key role becomes the students' loss. Furthermore, if the teacher does not change and push back, he will find himself retreating into the corner, failing in his efforts to teach and going home feeling more and more stressed. When a teacher reaches this point, depression and illness eventually become the outlets for their feelings. Patchy absence and a tired, washed-out view of the profession develop.

THE PROACTIVE STYLE

The proactive teacher (Case Study 1.5) is assertive and able to get what she wants in the classroom. She is confident of her ability to manage the students and is committed to creating an environment that will help them feel safe, secure and liked. She states what she wants using unambiguous directions and communicates her expectations clearly to the students. She will back up what she says with appropriate actions, reassuring those who lack confidence, praising those that do well and challenging those who try to test her boundaries. She recognises her right to teach the class and achieves it through the creation of a learning climate that is in the best interests of the students.

We can choose which style we want to adopt as teachers. The positive, assertive teacher makes the effort to communicate to her students that everyone can succeed if they try. She knows it will not be easy and some students will find it harder than others but she will do her best to help when things get tough. She will be pleasant, kind and understanding and at the same time provide very clear guidance on what is acceptable behaviour. She will exercise her right to lead and teach in a friendly but assertive manner without resorting to threats. She will not need to shout, because the students will know that if the task requires them to talk, they can do so in a normal way. When a group of students start to raise their voices, she will check them in a firm but friendly way and if they go off task, she will bring them back by redirection and reminding them of the rule for group work.

Case Study 1.5

Helen's Year 8 class were working on a short piece of drama about friendship. She had organised the students into groups of five and their task was to decide the context and characters for the plot. The groups engaged enthusiastically with the task and were aware that they had fifteen minutes to produce a rough outline that could then be worked out during the following lesson. They were directed to stay in their group areas and keep their voices down. Helen would give them a warning two minutes before it was time to stop.

She spent the time moving around the groups helping and encouraging them in their ideas. She would scan the room keeping a watchful eye on their behaviour, even while she was talking with individual students. She was experienced in this kind of work and knew that the groups could get carried away if allowed to. There were one or two students in the class who could start to be silly and would need a close eye kept on them.

After a while one of the groups began to get louder, so Helen went over to them. 'Have you agreed on an idea, Peter?' she asked, picking on the student who'd been making the most noise.

'Yes, Miss.'

'Good, what's the plot, Mike?' directing her question at the other loud member of the group. He briefly explained it to her and she listened intently, nodding, smiling and affirming her agreement and support of what they had decided. She asked a few questions to clarify some points then concluded, 'That seems a very good idea, perhaps you could work on the dialogue now,' redirecting all of them to the task. 'I want to remind you to keep your voices down, because you were getting rather loud and disturbing the others.' Helen reminded them of the rule and finished with a smile.

'Okay, sorry, Miss.'

Helen made a point of talking to the whole group but addressing her comments at the two loudest. She cleverly refocused them by skilful questioning, listening intently to their replies and then reminding them of the directions in a calm, assertive way.

The low-level disruption in Case Study 1.5 calls for a different level of assertion than would be needed to remove a very disruptive student from the room. Keeping response levels in proportion is essential. Careful modulation of the voice will communicate your expectations. Teachers who use their very assertive voice for the small things like wandering, being off task or chattering will find it harder to deal with extremely stubborn behaviour.

The proactive teacher will establish her behaviour code by first agreeing a set of basic rights for staff and students. Everyone will be aware that it is their own responsibility to reinforce and support those rights. Fairness is one of the key factors of a positive, proactive style. The proactive teacher will ensure that she is consistent in the way she deals with all her students. She will help them make their own choices but will not try to persuade or influence them. She will explain the consequences of their actions and then it must be up to them to decide. In this way, she will be helping them learn to make their own decisions. Eventually all the students will know where they stand, that the rules are fair and that their actions will be followed up by the teacher.

No one can be right every time. We will all have our off days. It may have been a late night or a domestic crisis, but whatever the cause, there will be times when our patience is short or our tolerance levels low and then our ability to handle students is impaired.

The proactive teacher knows her students will not always be able to behave well. She also understands that there will be incidents she has not experienced, so she will plan for them by considering her response in advance. She will work out what she says and does for a range of incidents to ensure she is fair and has no need to shoot from the hip.

The proactive style is based on the recognition of good behaviour. The saying 'catch them being good' is a useful one because we should try always to be on the lookout for students doing the right thing rather than just reprimanding those who cannot follow the good example set them. Praise is essential in building self-esteem so the more we can give, the better (Case Study 1.6).

Case Study 1.6

Ibrahim was a very difficult student to manage. He was diagnosed as having attention deficit hyperactivity disorder (ADHD) and was on medication but could still be abusive and get distracted quite easily (see Chapter 8). Susanna had been working with him throughout Year 7 and had learned how to keep him focused by giving him short achievable tasks and checking his understanding regularly. He had been having trouble recently at home, which had affected his behaviour at school, so she had met with him and agreed some strategies to help him stick to the task and stay in his seat during lessons.

The next time she had him was for science. The class were working in groups of three, carrying out an experiment to find the pH of a range of substances. She noticed that he was recording the results of each test for the group and hadn't wandered off since the start of the task, nearly ten minutes ago. As she moved from one group to the next, she kept him in her sights. When he looked up from his work and noticed her, she gave a discreet thumbs-up

sign to him, smiled and then moved on to the next group. He beamed at her then went back to his work. At the end of the lesson, the students filed out and as Ibrahim passed her desk she called him aside.

'You did well this lesson, Ibrahim. I noticed you were recording the results and you stayed with your group the entire time without getting up.'

'Yes, Miss. I didn't know that lemon juice is an acid. It must rot your guts!'

'You bet, and your teeth if you drink too much. Well done, Ibrahim.'

Her brief exchange and praise sent the message that he had done well and she was pleased. They were also able to share what he had learned in a friendly way that reinforced their relationship.

The proactive teacher uses non-verbal communication to send signals to the students that she is in charge but not a threat. She does not point her finger at students. She respects their personal space, except in extreme cases (Case 8.7). Her posture is open and she will speak to her students face-to-face in a relaxed way. Her expression will convey the calm of a person in control through a smile and direct eye contact. Her tone of voice will reinforce her position and convey warmth that students will interpret as friendly and helpful. Cold, curt, aggressive remarks will not feature in her repertoire of day-to-day comments. When there is an opportunity to use humour and find something funny, she will use it to defuse difficult situations and restore calm.

Her overall presence in the room will convey to everyone that she is in control and well organised. She will be smart and well groomed, decisive in her actions and her classroom will reflect these qualities in its orderliness and stimulating resources. None of these qualities will be accidental or innate. She has worked hard to develop them and she will continue to hone them as the students change and bring new challenges.

Putting it all together

Think first. The best way to manage is to plan your approach, work out your responses and pre-empt potential problems by communicating your expectations to the students and by teaching them how to make good choices. When you direct a student use *I* statements like these:

'I want you to stay in your seats during this activity.'

'I am the adult in charge in this room.'

'I want you to follow my directions.'

Be clear about what you want and state it:

'Stop talking and look at me.'

'In two minutes you will stop the discussions and go back to your own seats.'

Say the student's name so they know you are addressing them:

'Errol, I would like you work with Alan.'

'Sally, all four legs on the floor, thank you.'

'Kallum, nice work.'

Avoid getting caught up in the student's own agenda through getting sidetracked by their secondary behaviour. Refocus them on your original direction.

A common mistake that teachers make is to ask a question that has no connection with what they want the student to do:

'Why are you talking?'

'Why are you out of your seat?'

'What are you doing?'

Each of these questions can be rephrased in a way that is far more direct and prevents the student being cheeky or arrogant:

'Put your hand up if you have something to say.'

'What was the direction for this task?' 'It was stay in your seats.' 'Good, then go back to your place and raise your hand if you need something.'

'I can see you haven't made a start?'

Some rule reminders are best phrased as questions, such as the student out of his seat. It helps the student to focus on the original direction or rule and not get into explanations about why they are not doing what they are supposed to.

'Martin, what is the rule about Walkmans?'

'No Walkmans during lesson times, Mr Wright.'

'Good, put it away in your bag or on my desk, thank you.'

Finally, do not confuse your opinion of the behaviour with your opinion of the student. It is the behaviour you do not like. Make a point of saying that to the student. We need to reassure students that we like them as people. That way, we are able to support them. If a student feels you hate them, they will not make the effort.

The effects of this style

The classroom will reflect the proactive teacher's personal views. It will be orderly in its layout of desks and furniture. Getting this right is fundamental to the effective management of behaviour and delivery of the curriculum. The resources will be carefully organised and stored in a way that gives the students access. The wall space will be used to display work in progress as well as supporting material to stimulate the students. The displays will invite interaction through questions, puzzles and hands-on exhibits. The work on display will be a celebration of the achievements of everybody in the class.

Eventually the students will get used to a culture of respect that has been cultivated by the teacher. They will defend the rights of everyone and in doing this they will create a room where they can all feel safe, secure and able to learn together. The whole class will know what to expect from the teacher and what they are expected to do and how to behave. The teacher will have worked on building their self-esteem so that they value themselves and feel confident. With confidence will come the ability to accept responsibility for their own behaviour. The proactive teacher does not try to control the behaviour of her students. She helps them manage it. Her goal is for them to grow into responsible people. In adult life they will need to be independent, so they will have to make responsible choices. She will guide and support them in this journey.

The proactive teacher tries not to react to situations, especially new ones she has not encountered before. When she is in doubt about what to do next, she does not act. She will tell the student she wants to think about the incident before coming to a decision. This will serve several purposes. She will have time to calm down if she has become stressed. The students will also calm down. She can mull over the facts and seek a second opinion if she needs to. The students will have a higher opinion of her because she obviously wants to make the right decision and is prepared to take time to do that.

FOOTNOTE

There is another teaching style, probably the worst for students to experience. The teacher is inconsistent and does not adhere to any particular way of working. One day he will be assertive and seem very fair and in control. The next day he may be assertive and fair again or he may have changed and be very aggressive and snappy or very weak and passive, letting all sorts of behaviour go without comment. The students will become so confused that they will keep their heads down. Any chance of a productive relationship will founder. They will become defensive and uncertain.

This book is about acquiring and developing the skills to become a proactive, assertive teacher. The methods and procedures are used to create a positive atmosphere where students and teachers can do their best, learn without limits and feel safe and secure. The starting point will be your own perceptions and expectations. The next step will be to create a learning environment where your expectations can become a reality. Good management of behaviour is crucial in this process. It does not necessarily come first but needs to be perceived as having equal importance as the teaching of the curriculum. The two go hand in hand. Students who can behave well give themselves the best chance to get involved in their learning. Interesting lessons engage the students and then they will not feel the desire to misbehave.

SUMMARY

- Barriers to learning can be caused by the teacher within the classroom. It is in their power to make the classroom a positive learning environment.
- Teachers can be reactive or proactive in their style of behaviour management.
- Aggressive teachers and passive teachers generally have reactive teaching styles. They tend not to plan ahead but respond passively or aggressively to incidents as they occur.
- The proactive teacher adopts an assertive style to uphold their own rights and the rights of the students.

- The assertive teacher ensures that she is the leader in the classroom and teaches the students the boundaries of acceptable behaviour.
- The assertive teacher communicates her expectations to the students.
- Self-esteem and confidence are important and nurtured by the assertive teacher through praise, positive reinforcement and choice.
- Students learn that with choices come consequences. They know that when they make a poor choice there will be a consequence to it. The teacher does not try to control or persuade the students to behave, because she believes they need to learn to be independent.
- The proactive teacher plans ahead so she is prepared to deal with problems in a rational way rather than reacting to them as they occur.

2 THE FOUNDATIONS FOR GOOD BEHAVIOUR

The room is full. There are thirty-one adolescent teenagers occupying it. They share the space with a teacher, seventeen tables, thirty-four chairs, as many bags and coats all hemmed in by piles of textbooks, several computers and an atmosphere of excitement, hormones, heat, hunger, humour and for many a desire to be somewhere else, somewhere freer. This enforced captivity will end in about fifty minutes when they are finally released by the school bell and the conclusion of the school day. The experience of school is over five hours of this kind of existence punctuated by movement from one room to the next, another teacher, another subject and another challenge to get through without too much hassle.

It's unnatural, yet we put our students through this day in, day out with the hope that they will get an education, some qualifications and a chance of a career at the end. For some the journey is fraught with obstacles. They not only have to survive the daily routines but also the added problem of fear. During their school life, some students will be bullied and oppressed by teachers and their peers until the experience of school becomes unbearable and they seek a release. It may be truancy, school phobia, aggressive behaviour and, in the most extreme cases, self-harm or suicide.

The timetable of predominately language-based activities such as reading, writing, copying from the board, dictation, note-taking and written examinations and tests forms the backbone of the curriculum; it does not suit every student. Alternative approaches based on visual, auditory and kinaesthetic (VAK) teaching methods may well suit a large proportion of students much more than linguistic methods. Teachers who understand this will plan lessons to accommodate a variety of styles and will probably find they have more success and fewer problems with behaviour than those who do not. The experience of school becomes less mundane and those students likely to encounter problems with behaviour, learning or both will be less likely to end up turned off by school or in trouble because their boredom has led to incidents in lessons.

It is not surprising that behaviour becomes an issue for many teachers. Students and parents no longer regard the teacher as a paragon of society, someone to hold in high esteem and respect. Forty years ago teachers had a control over students that was not questioned. When a student was disciplined, the parents would support the school and not question the authority or decision of the teacher. Things have changed. Students feel they can answer back and parents feel they can go to the school and dispute the action taken by a teacher. We now need to be very careful how we respond to students who behave inappropriately. Teachers who use a coherent set of rules and directions backed up by rewards and consequences that are administered in a fair and consistent way will find that they can explain their actions confidently and clearly to parents and students who feel the need to challenge decisions. Teachers who act irrationally will find themselves on shaky ground because a parent or a student will spot the inconsistency and argue strongly. Eventually the teacher will have to concede because they will know they do not have a watertight case to fall back on.

Establishing a strong foundation for your behaviour plan will be a vital first step. Rogers (1994) outlines four elements that contribute to a well-balanced system that goes beyond simply managing behaviour in the classroom. These elements form the cornerstones to a means of developing responsibility, respect, self-esteem, confidence, fairness and opportunity for all the students in the group:

- Prevention
- Correction
- Consequences
- Support.

You will need to get the balance right between all of these if you are to manage and develop responsible behaviour within your groups. The only way is to roll up your sleeves and assert your position as the teacher in order to establish yourself and be able to introduce your methods. The students will not give up their position freely, so you cannot expect to just walk into a new class and get started. You will have to show them that you are in charge and expect them to listen and act responsibly. Many students will do this and accept your behaviour code willingly. Those who do not will become the focus of it. So what is involved in each of these cornerstones?

PREVENTION

Many teachers will argue that it is natural for teenagers to test the limits of authority. Part of growing up is a desire to be independent and to break away from parents and the rules and systems imposed by adults. They need to find their own identity that separates them from their parents. The uncertainty that comes with the changes at the onset of puberty causes adolescents to look to their peers for support, so they feel a strong sense of belonging to that group. Children are maturing earlier, and as a result, all of these changes are happening at a much younger age.

The order and authority that might have existed in schools several decades ago is now one of the targets to be challenged. Teachers need to be far more active in putting preventative measures in place to help children learn the limits of authority in a safe way. Their search for an identity should not be crushed in an aggressive regime. It is possible to let them develop their own personalities by firmly asserting some boundaries that should not be transgressed, while allowing less important ones to be crossed for the sake of their learning. Mistakes are part of this process and need to be made in a supportive culture so the benefits can be gained without damage to the child's confidence and self-esteem.

The most irritating distractions for teachers tend to be the low-level, minor ones that occur regularly. More serious disturbances are less common but do need to be prevented as well. Therefore the first step is to list the most common disturbances and sort them into minor and major ones. This can be done as part of in-service education and training (INSET) by having a session to develop a behaviour plan for the whole school. Here are some of the minor disturbances you might come up with:

- Calling out
- Leaving their place and wandering around the room
- Note passing

- Arriving late
- Not bringing the correct books and equipment to lessons
- Eating or chewing during lessons
- Not wearing the correct uniform
- Wearing jewellery
- Wanting to leave the lesson early without a note or permission
- Chatting during silent work
- Being too loud during group activities
- Bickering while entering the room
- Taking another student's things
- Kicking and throwing bags
- Writing on the board
- Sitting in the teacher's chair
- Defacing displays and writing on desks
- Wanting to go to the toilet during the lesson
- Feeling sick
- Passing wind
- Mobile phones going off in the lesson
- Loud noises in the next room
- A wasp in the room
- A student outside the room distracting your lesson
- Forgetting homework or not doing it.

And here are some major disturbances:

- Swearing directly at a teacher
- Swearing at another student
- Hitting a student
- Hitting a teacher
- Having a tantrum by throwing things and shouting
- Making sexual or racial comments or being abusive
- Theft or alleged theft
- Leaving the room without permission
- Bringing a knife or other weapon into school
- Smoking, drinking or taking drugs during school time
- Vandalising school property
- Vandalising property outside school during school time
- Bullying.

The aim is to draw up plans that will minimise the effects of these disturbances. Some preventative measures will be outside the remit of the class teacher, but thoughtful and careful planning will reduce the likelihood of most of them occurring. This is achieved by establishing a behaviour code with the help of the students. It should contain rules that will apply at any time, one of which should be 'follow directions'. It should also detail the rewards and consequences that you are going to use.

Another useful exercise for an INSET session is to consider what questions a newly qualified teacher might have about classroom management in the school. Preparing a list of questions will enable you to put together guidance on how to prevent obvious problems in a practical way. For example, too often teachers have not considered whether they trust students or they have felt students are trustworthy and then found their valuables have disappeared from an unlocked drawer or bag. It is far better to remove such temptations to begin with. So what are the questions? Here are some that staff may come up with:

- Should the students line up outside the room or go in and wait until I arrive?
- Should the students stand behind their chairs and wait until I tell them to sit down?
- Should the students sit where they choose?
- Should they call me Mr Wright, Sir or by my first name?
- Should I allow them to go to the toilet during lessons?
- Should I give out the books or let a student do it?
- Should I be in a classroom or storeroom on my own with a student?
- To set homework, should I tell the class, write it on the board or give out a sheet?
- What will happen if some students arrive late?
- Should the students leave as soon as the bell goes or should I dismiss them when I am ready?
- Can I trust the students or should I lock my bag away?
- Should I use physical force on a student?

Some of these questions will almost certainly involve putting together a set of directions. Activities like getting changed for physical education (PE), doing group work and taking examinations all require sets of specific directions (Chapter 4). It can be extremely useful to work out sets of directions in advance so the problems can be anticipated and preventative measures planned. Similarly, problems may already exist and need a solution that can be found by working through what you want the students to do (Case Study 2.1).

Case Study 2.1 *Andrea*

I came to the school with mixed opinions. My experience of faith schools was of orderly, well-behaved children with a sense of right and wrong. Yes, of course there were incidents of high jinks and the occasional kicks at the system but overall the students knew how to behave and would respond well to the directions of most teachers. I had also worked in several large comprehensive schools located in the tougher parts of London and knew that the kids could be challenging, to say the least! But this school was a real eye-opener. It had over fifteen hundred female students and a mixed sixth form. The standard of behaviour was terrible, partly due to the lack of experienced teachers and an endless chain of supply teachers, but mostly because of the atmosphere of aggression, fear and bullying that came from the top. Teachers kept themselves to themselves and did what they could to stay clear of the tyrannical head and deputy, who subjected teachers and students to a regime of criticism, aggression and calculated put-downs. Some of the teachers treated the students in very similar ways. The result was an oppressive regime of unhappy students, some cowering under the strain and others continually looking for ways to buck the system.

I didn't know how I was going to make a difference in such a difficult environment. My responsibility as assistant head included behaviour and 'discipline' for Key Stages 3 and 4. I knew what should happen but I felt the odds were stacked against me. There were girls smoking in out-of-the-way corners. Many of the rooms had girls standing outside, put there because they had misbehaved. Students were wandering the building without permission, bunking off up the shops or going home early. The toilets were vandalised and covered with graffiti and the playgrounds were jungles inhabited by the wild and the timid. I vividly remember when I realised things had to change and it was because children's lives were at risk.

It was my first day and I was on bus duty after school. The bus stop was three minutes away from the school, on a dual carriageway leading into the heart of the city. As I walked out of the school gate with the other members of staff on duty, I noticed several large groups of girls, probably Year 10 or 11. There were gangs in the neighbourhood and I later learned that some of our girls belonged to them. The bus stop was located on the other side of the road. The public were often swamped by a hundred and fifty or more girls, who pushed and jostled to get to the front. When the bus came into view, they would barge harder and those in the front would end up in the road. The double-deckers would career past the stop, their drivers weary of having to avoid the girls. They would then pursue the bus like a horde of banshees, shouting and swearing in a very dangerous way. We had no chance of controlling them or rescuing any students who got in the way. There was no system, the staff just stood and watched. This needed to change and quickly.

The trouble with the school was that the head didn't use systems; she had expectations that she tried to secure by bullying. When students found they had some freedom because of the lack of strong teachers, they acted without thought or care for others and seemed incapable of making responsible choices. I knew they needed to be taught how to behave and that meant taking the job on myself. I began by tackling every student who broke a rule. I didn't get into conversations, just reminded them of the rule, took their name and gave them a consequence that I personally administered.

After a few weeks there was a noticeable difference. A number of teachers must have realised I was prepared to challenge every student, even the tough ones, and eventually they began to follow suit. The students started to get better behaved, at least while I was around, and the teachers started sending the harder cases to me. I knew I was getting a reputation among the students as someone to avoid and the staff were telling me about the improvements they had noticed. The head and deputy didn't seem to like what I was doing. Perhaps I was a bit of an embarrassment to them, because I was getting results without resorting to aggressive methods.

Back to the bus queue problem. What we needed was a system that any member of staff could manage and what I wanted was a safe, orderly queue of students standing in pairs at the entrance to the bus stop lining up along the fence. I wanted members of the public to have free access to the seats at the stop and to be able to get on and off the bus with ease. I also wanted the students to line up on their own in case the member of staff on duty was late. The stop was a fair distance from the school and I had already witnessed a number of disputes and fights between the rival groups, so I felt that the staff should have mobile phones in case of emergencies.

I arranged some meetings with the staff that did bus duty and we put together a list of features for an ideal situation. Then we worked on the directions that staff would give to the students. These included where and how to queue, what to do when the bus arrived, how to treat members of the public and what would happen if a student failed to follow any of these directions. We arranged a special assembly where we briefed students who caught the bus. I explained why we needed to make the changes and took them through the consequences if they failed to follow the directions. I told them I was sending a letter to their parents and would also be informing the bus company of the changes.

The new system worked well. The students stopped rushing and crushing when the bus arrived. The members of the public using the stop seemed happier and one man who regularly caught the bus remarked on how well behaved the girls had become. I also noted that the new routines were becoming a habit and when staff arrived late one day, they found the students waiting in an orderly queue for the bus without being told. All the students needed was some order imposed on the chaos. Of course, some of them tried to subvert it by dodging queues, pushing in and nipping round the front but they were dealt with swiftly and firmly. Eventually it settled down. I had succeeded in my efforts to manage the students in a fair and systematic way without resorting to the overbearing methods of the head teacher.

Thinking through how to respond to the minor disturbances will also help you. You will grow in confidence and your lessons will run more smoothly. This takes time but is a sound investment, especially if it's shared. An interesting activity for staff meetings can be to set aside some time on a regular basis to discuss responses to particular incidents. These can be compiled into a school behaviour management manual that provides invaluable guidance on how incidents can be dealt with using positive, proactive methods. You will need to nominate a group leader who is responsible for timing the session, noting down the suggestions and writing them up afterwards. They should be a keen and experienced member of staff who can separate the suggestions into those that could be useful and those that are not useful. Scenarios 2.1, 2.2 and 2.3 give some examples.

Scenario 2.1: Refusing to begin the task

'Okay, everyone, you have twenty minutes to draft your response to the letter. Remember you are writing because you are dissatisfied with the company's service and expecting them to give you a refund for the loss of enjoyment you have suffered on your holiday due to the accommodation being below the standard advertised in the brochure.' The class got started but Joe just sat at the desk scowling. He was often like this. Getting going was difficult for him but he would do it once he realised you were not going to budge. He knew that if he didn't do the work now, he would have to do it at lunchtime. 'I haven't got a pen, Miss!' he said in a cocky way.

How not to deal with this

- 'Get on with it, Joe, or I will make you do it in detention!'
- 'Start work now or you'll have to go and see the head of department!'
- 'You're always trying to get out of doing the work, Joe. Will you ever learn?'
- 'Stop staring at the desk, Joe. The work won't get done by itself.'
- 'What's the matter, Joe? Are you lost for words for a change? You are normally very good at complaining.'

And this dialogue:

Teacher	Get on with it, Joe.
Student	I haven't got a pen!
Teacher	How many times have I told you to make sure you bring one. You can sit there and think for now. Come to me at lunchtime and I will lend you one so you can do it then.'

These responses will almost certainly result in the student challenging the teacher and then the low-level incident will become a high-stakes, win-lose battleground that could have been avoided.

The positive, proactive approach

'You haven't started yet. Do you need some help, Joe?' The teacher makes a friendly offer of assistance to ascertain whether the student is having problems understanding what he is required to do. He declines the offer, so the teacher leaves and expects him to begin but he doesn't.

'I see you still haven't started yet, Joe.'

'I need a pen, Miss,' he said smirking. He is trying to delay by finding an excuse that could waste more time or draw the teacher into an argument over the lack of equipment.

She ignores this and holds out some pens, smiling at him. 'Choose a blue one or a black one.' She has refocused him with a limited choice that prevents him thinking up another excuse.

Once he has chosen a pen, she redirects him back to the work. 'Now you have a pen, let me just remind you of what you have to do.'

Then she follows through with a rule reminder in the form of a direction. 'Okay, so you have until 10.45. That's just over fifteen minutes to complete the task.'

Finally, she repeats her offer of support in a friendly, helpful way. 'Off you go and remember if you get stuck or need any help, just raise your hand and I will come to you as soon as I can.'

The whole chain of events takes less than a few minutes but results in the student getting down to work and doing as instructed despite his attempts to delay things and cause a disturbance in the lesson.

Scenario 2.2: Arriving late to a lesson

A student arrives late and the lesson has already begun. The teacher has introduced the lesson and is engaged in a short warm-up activity with the whole class.

How not to deal with this

Teacher	Oh hello, Lauren, (*sarcastically*) it's nice of you to join us. What time do you call this?
Student	I'm sorry, Mr Brown.
Teacher	You are over five minutes late and this is not the first time!
Student	Sorry, but . . . (*beginning to cry*).
Teacher	Well, what's your excuse this time then?

The teacher has stopped midway through the warm-up activity, which disturbs the whole class. Every student will lose out and become an audience for the incident. Students love a spectacle and will enjoy the show even more if the teacher is the object of derision or ridicule. Conflicts like this create unnecessary difficulties for the teacher, especially as he seems to have assumed the student was deliberately late and not bothered to ascertain what the reason was. Furthermore, students do not view teachers kindly if they use sarcasm.

Some students use lateness to gain attention and cause a great deal of disruption.

Student	Sorry I'm late, Sir. I forgot my bag and had to go back and get it.
Teacher	That's okay, Bobby. Try to be on time next lesson. Now go to your place and take out your books.

Bobby swaggered across the room, kicking bags as he went and then sat down, loudly scraping the furniture. The teacher resumed his lesson and was immediately interrupted again by Bobby ripping open the Velcro flap of his bag.

Teacher   Can't you do that more quietly? You are disturbing everyone and I am sure they would prefer not to have been given this exhibition of juvenile behaviour.

Student   I bet they would, Sir. Shall we ask them?

The teacher let Bobby disturb his lesson by being late. Directing him to his usual place allowed him to cause further disruption. Bobby's attention seeking was finally successful when the teacher responded with a rhetorical question rather than redirecting him. Bobby took up the gauntlet at the end by suggesting that the rest of the class should be asked whether they wanted to be distracted or not. The teacher seemed to have lost sight of the fact that his lesson had been disrupted and the student had gained control of what was happening.

Some teachers invest too much time on lateness, showing that they are more concerned about punctuality than about the students.

Teacher   You're late, Collins!

Student   Sorry, Sir, I had to see Mr Stenner.

Teacher   Well I've just about had enough of this. You lot don't seem to realise how important it is to be punctual. Furthermore, you are wasting valuable time and we have got a syllabus to get through. I am going to have a word with Mr Stenner and you can stay back at break to make up for the wasted time.

Once again, the teacher is adopting a confrontational stance that is totally unnecessary. He is showing the whole class that he can get wound up by a student being late. He is overly concerned with telling them about his problems covering the syllabus and seems oblivious to the fact that the lateness may not have been the fault of the student. He has not checked the excuse for accuracy and has given a punishment that really may not be fair.

The positive, proactive approach

Students arrive late for all sorts of reasons. Some are legitimate and some not. Whatever the reason, it can be disruptive and waste valuable time. Students are expected to be on time and that may actually be very difficult if they have come from a room at the other end of the school. We have two objectives: to find ways of incorporating latecomers into our lessons without disrupting the flow of a lesson and to establish the reason for the lateness so the necessary action can be taken.

Most students have their places in the room. The teacher may allocate places or they may choose where they will sit. A late arrival will interrupt things if they have to cross the room to get to their usual place. To avoid this you may be able to leave a couple of spare seats near the door. When a student is late, direct them to the spare seats as unobtrusively as possible.

Student   Sorry I'm late, Miss.

Teacher   Good morning, Jane. Please sit there for the time being (*pointing to the seat near the door*) and you can tell me why you are late at the end of the lesson.

Do not attempt to find out why the student is late, because the rest of the class are waiting for the lesson to resume. A simple greeting followed by a direction and a request to see you later are all that is required. You can find out the reason for the lateness after the lesson and take any action then if it is necessary. Do not prejudge the student; assume they have a legitimate reason for being late, welcome them into the class and then forget about it until the end.

Scenario 2.3 A student passes wind during a lesson

The class have been working on a report based on their geography field trip. They have been working silently for ten minutes and doing well when suddenly the silence is broken and one of the boys passes wind loudly so everyone can hear. Boys can be quite crude at times and events like this are extremely hard to avoid. When they happen they cannot be ignored. They usually prompt a wave of laughter and feigned asphyxiation. There is little chance of it going unnoticed by the rest of the class, who will take the opportunity to stop work and engage in humorous and silly behaviour. Preventing the problem is very difficult. It is not easy to raise the issue in a serious discussion and you can hardly have a rule like 'no passing wind in lessons'.

How not to deal with this

- 'Who did that? Stand up immediately.' This is unlikely to get a response and will lead you into deeper conflict if it is pursued.
- 'Stand up or I will keep you all in after the lesson until someone owns up.' A whole class detention will always cause problems and you will be seen as grossly unfair.
- 'Whoever did that must leave the room immediately.' You will probably not even be heard as the class will be laughing and your irate, serious response will become the target of their ridicule. Either way, you will be on the losing end. You cannot get a child to own up and take you seriously, because they will not want to submit to you. You will need to be cleverer than that.

The positive, proactive approach

There are some preventative measures you can try for these kinds of incident. Teaching social skills like politeness will provide a way in and can be done during personal, social and health education (PSHE) lessons or in form time through discussions about the kind of behaviour that is acceptable in your classroom. Unsociable behaviour could include sudden outbursts, silly noises, humming, tapping and clicking sounds. The mention of belching and passing wind may provoke a few giggles but at least you will have made your point. Older boys will pass wind loudly to gain attention. The reaction from the other students will be about the smell and will be overexaggerated. Your response should be quite decisive and as unobtrusive as possible.

Teacher   Alan, that was very rude. Pack up your things and go to . . . (*choose from your class time-out area or another class you have agreed*).

Student   But, Sir, I couldn't help it.
Teacher   Maybe you couldn't and we will discuss that at the end of the lesson. Now go and I will come and see you when the bell goes.

The student will have to negotiate his return to the group with you and agree to observe the behaviour code in future. Do not enter into any discussions or arguments during the lesson. Alternatively, you may feel you do not want to take it this far, so a simple response with a deferred consequence could be used:

'Alan, that was very rude. See me at the end of the lesson.'

Then turn away. Do not respond to any reply, just continue with the lesson.

Sometimes you will not be able to discover the culprit, so your response should be minimal. Open the windows and tell the students who are overreacting to stop being melodramatic and continue with their work.

Students who cannot be sensible and quieten down will need to be given an activity that demands attention and concentration such as a short period of note-taking. There is nothing like copying a few notes down from the board to get the class back under control.

Student   Phew! What a stink.
Teacher   I'll open some windows.
Student   You pig! That was evil.
Teacher   Right, this seems to be a good time to make some notes of the key points. Take out your pens and start copying from the board please.

Alternatively, you could try humour as an effective means of taking the heat out of the situation. The students who overreact are obviously not really suffocating, so you could play along with the gag:

'It's windy in here today!'

'Someone overdid the beans at lunchtime!'

'We really must have a word with cook about the dinners!'

'Whoever did that trouser puff is in dire need of some serious dietary advice.'

This will probably defuse the situation, put an end to the play-acting and give rise to general laughter that can then be allowed to die down. You can get the class under control more easily because they will not find your quips as funny as their own show of amateur dramatics. You will still have to deal with the incident if it occurs again but by showing you have a sense of humour you won't have students deliberately doing it to wind you up.

The point of working through incidents like this as a staff is to develop uniform responses that are positive and assertive. Staff with less confidence will feel better prepared and not have to work out what to do at the time. The students can be taught the sets of directions for the activities to eliminate the disruptions that are often caused when changes occur during lessons. They will become second nature as the students internalise the routines. You can then concentrate on rewarding the majority for getting things right rather than spending too much time on negative behaviour with the minority of students.

CORRECTION

When incidents do occur, they should be dealt with fairly by being consistent and challenging all students who fail to comply with your directions. This can be very hard for a variety of reasons. The hurly-burly of being a teacher often prevents us from paying attention to the small things students do that could have the potential to quickly escalate into larger problems.

Some teachers find certain students hard to challenge because of their size or demeanour. It seems unfair to correct a student who usually behaves very well, especially if a consequence is due. Surely a student should be allowed to make a mistake. Being fair to everyone involves treating all the students in the same way, to avoid accusations of favouritism. Corrective measures should be as unobtrusive as possible and consist of the following four things:

- Rule reminders
- Questions about the work or the behaviour
- Redirections with choices
- Support and encouragement.

These can be given using diversions and humour to take the heat out of the situation. They should be made in a calm way with a lowered voice, employing privately understood signals where appropriate. The aim is to help the student understand what they did wrong by using coaching methods to help them avoid the same mistake in the future. Sometimes words are unnecessary because you can correct the student simply by looking at them in a certain way, at the right time. Scenarios 2.4 to 2.9 give some examples.

Scenario 2.4: Students talking during lessons

Lauren was teaching a Year 10 science group. The students were working in groups of three on an experiment as part of their coursework. Several students were taking advantage of being at the back of the lab and were having a bit of a chat. The third girl in the group was trying to do the work on her own.

How not to deal with this

- 'Oi, you two! Cut the chatting and get back to work or I'll put you in detention.'
- 'I presume you two have finished. If so, I'll give you some more work.'
- 'If you want to chat, you'd better come to my room at lunchtime and you can chat in your own time!'

All of these ways disrupt the whole class and provide them with a show. They will also embarrass the students and prevent them from appreciating what they did wrong.

The positive, proactive approach

Lauren noticed them and stopped talking to the group she had been helping. She caught the eye of one of the girls who was chatting and gave her a very serious look that said, 'I am aware that you are chatting. I do not approve, so stop now!' The girl was transfixed for a few seconds. The other girl realised she had stopped talking and followed her gaze to the teacher. She could see that Lauren was not pleased and was looking at her friend very sternly. They both turned to the third member of the group and asked her what they should be doing. The whole incident took only a few moments but was an example of how an authoritative look can speak volumes. Another method of getting students back on track is by proximity. This involves moving near to them so they know you are watching what they are doing. Your closeness does not require anything being said, so other students will not be distracted.

Scenario 2.5: A student is off task

The Year 8 technology group was always a little bit noisy but things got done and the students enjoyed the lessons. James had an easy-going style suited to the nature of the work. He expected the students to get the work done but did not insist that they worked in silence. Only when a student stopped work and carried on chatting did he step in, and it was usually done in a very quiet way. You would never hear a raised voice in his room. He knew when students were having problems and he helped them overcome the barriers so they would gain success. He had a way with the class that was based on the belief that everyone was going to do the work he set. Some might do it better than others but they would all do their best. He made sure the students knew this. One student was supposed to be working on his waistcoat but was tangling the cottons into a bit of a mess.

How not to deal with this

The temptation is to tell the student off for making a mess rather than correct him by refocusing him on the task. Here are some typical negative responses:
- 'You can come back after school and untangle that lot!'
- 'That's school property you're ruining. Do you have to make such a mess?'
- 'I have been watching you waste your time for the past five minutes and I can't understand why you do it. You must be some kind of idiot. This is a secondary school and you'll be taking your GCSEs before you know it. You haven't got time to waste.'

The teacher will not get very far with responses like these. Stressing the value of time to Year 8 students will not have much effect. They are unlikely to be thinking about careers yet. The concept of school property being of value is also difficult for some students to comprehend, so a wanton waste of resources will not concern them much.

The positive, proactive approach

James spotted the boy not getting on with the project he had set. He sauntered over to the area where he was working, checking the progress of various students as he went. He walked up to the boy and stood close to him but looked away at what some other students were doing. The boy felt his presence and realised he should stop what he was doing. He looked up at James, who was still looking in another direction, then picked up his waistcoat and started tacking the seams with darts ready to machine them. James registered his return to work and turned and made a comment about the position of the hem. He gave the boy a few reassuring words about the quality of his work before moving to the other side of the room, where another student was also going off task. Groups of students can be remotivated in a similar way (Scenario 2.6). A direct intervention is required and the ringleaders should become the target of your attention.

Scenario 2.6: A group of students are off task

It was a beautiful summer day, so Anna decided to move her Year 7 art class outside and do more perspective drawing of the school grounds as they had been working on this for several weeks in the studio. The students were instructed what to do, given boards and materials and then off they went to their various positions in the field. Anna toured the groups to check progress and give advice and assistance where necessary. She noticed a group of four students who did not seem to be engaged in the work.

How not to deal with this

Teachers often feel they are doing the students a favour by letting them go out to the field to draw. The students do enjoy it but some will take advantage of the freedom and misbehave. The teacher will then feel betrayed and respond in an emotional way:

- 'Right, you four, pick up your stuff and go back into the class. I'm not having you wasting time misbehaving out here.'
- 'I don't get it with you lot. You never do as you're told. I give you an opportunity to do something different and you take advantage and spoil it for the rest.'
- 'Show me your work. You haven't even started. How do you expect to complete the work this lesson with half the time gone already?'

And this dialogue:

Teacher	Okay, you four are in detention for mucking about!
Student	But we don't know what to do, Miss.
Teacher	Of course you do. We have done perspective before. It is exactly the same.
Student	That was in class and we did it from imagination. This is the real thing and you can't see the horizon.
Teacher	Stop making excuses. I have been watching you and you haven't even made an effort.

The positive, proactive approach

When Anna got to the students, she directed her first question at John, the boy who had clearly done the least.

Teacher	John, where are you going to put the horizon line?
Student	I was thinking of here, Miss. (*John draws it lightly.*)

Teacher	That's probably a good choice, because there is more above the line of interest than below from where we are sitting. Now work out where the vanishing point is and let's see if you can start to rough in the verticals for each building.

She guided him back to the task with some specific questions and useful tips. Then she turned to Paul, who had been throwing grass.

Teacher	Paul, you have your vanishing point but no detail yet. Show me where the roofline will run for the hall. (*Paul draws in a construction line.*) Do you know how to construct the front of the hall, Paul? Remember things on the horizon line near the vanishing point will not have much of their sides showing.

Anna had Paul engaged. She continued with the other two boys then returned to check how John was getting on. Once she was satisfied they could all do the work, she reminded them of the target for the lesson and told them she would be back later to see what they had managed to do.

Careful correction combined with support and assistance had been all the boys needed. She did not need to resort to scolding and reprimanding them for not doing their work. All they needed was the personal touch. They were still finding the work difficult but when she showed them what to do they settled down.

Directing questions at students who do not seem to be giving their full attention invariably wakes them up and forces them to refocus their minds. It will also jolt other students whose minds were wandering, because they do not want to be caught out with a question they cannot answer.

Scenario 2.7: A student falls asleep during the lesson

The Year 9 history class had just finished watching a video about the causes of the Second World War. Some of the students were sleepy by nature. Rob knew they stayed up late at night and were slow-witted in the lesson the next morning. He was drawing their attention to the main points in the video to make sure they had noted them down, when he noticed a boy slouched in his chair with his head down. He was not looking at the front or taking notes. It was hard to tell whether or not he was asleep, but it was clear he wasn't paying attention.

How not to deal with this

Many teachers will just move in and disrupt the flow of the lesson. They will probably feel indignant that a student seems to be falling asleep in their class. They will assume this is the reason without attempting to find out.

- 'Wake up, boy! This is not a bedroom. Go to bed earlier.'
- 'Would you like me to dim the lights and get you a pillow, Martin? You look very uncomfortable trying to get to sleep like that.'
- 'Come on, Martin. I don't want you falling asleep in my lesson, it can't be that boring.' This comment will probably give the student an opportunity to tell you it is, even if other students don't find it boring.

The positive, proactive approach

Rob was very good at handling whole-group activities. His use of open questions combined with reassuring comments helped him bring everyone into the discussion. He would carefully structure his questions in a way that would enable any student to answer at their level of understanding. If a student was not particularly knowledgeable, he would begin with a fairly basic question and then get the student to amplify what they had said with further probing questions rather than ask a different student the next question. He believed that getting one student to talk about something for several minutes aided their understanding and the rest of the class also benefited by listening. They knew their turn would come eventually and everyone got used to it.

Rob ended his explanation about the Treaty of Versailles and its punitive effect on the German economy after the First World War then directed a new line of questioning at Martin.

Teacher So, Martin (*pause for Martin to lift his head and give his attention*). You remember the point that was made on the video about the British government appearing to appease the Germans? Can you name the British prime minister who was in office at the time?

Student (*woken up and ready to answer*) Chamberlain, Sir, Neville Chamberlain.

Teacher Well remembered, Martin. Can you describe what Chamberlain did, using that analogy of the bully in the playground?

Martin went on to show what he knew about the British appeasement. Then Rob moved on to another student to get him to describe the errors of Chamberlain's actions. His strategy had got Martin back into the lesson without having to break the flow of thinking in the rest of the class.

Sometimes it is necessary to challenge the students to help them back on the correct path. A break or distraction is unavoidable but it serves another purpose. It shows the rest of the class that you do mean what you say. The procedure of correction should aim to help the student recognise where they are going wrong, and you may not always have to give a consequence; a small reminder of the rule may be sufficient to refocus them on the task.

Scenario 2.8: Students calling out during lessons

Terry liked the students to contribute to the lesson but had difficulties with them calling out rather than waiting to be invited.

How not to deal with this

The aim is to keep control without crushing students who are trying to participate. Avoid statements like these:

- 'Put your hand down, Steven. We know you know the answer.'
- 'Stop calling out, Michael. You are preventing the others from answering.'
- 'If you call out once more, Sajit, I am putting you in detention.'
- 'For goodness sake, Ollie. If you are going to call out the answer, make sure it's right.'

The positive, proactive approach

The objective is to control the situation as soon as you begin asking questions. This is easily done in several ways and removes any conflict, calling out or the need for put-downs.

Teacher   Michael, what do we call the movement of molecules through a semi-permeable membrane from a solution of low concentration to a solution of high concentration?
Student   Osmosis, Sir.
Teacher   Thank you, that's right.

The teacher focused the question solely at Michael, so the rest of the class knew they were not being called on to answer. Alternatively, you can begin with an instruction like this:

> 'Put your hands up and wait for me to ask you if you can tell me the main features of an isosceles triangle.'

The teacher waits for the students who know the answer to put up their hands then she selects one of them.

Teacher   Yes, Emily, can you tell me the main features of an isosceles triangle?
Student   It's got two angles and two sides that are the same.

This could be turned into a game: I am going to ask you a question and if you know the answer, you must wait and do nothing. Then when I say 'now' everyone who thinks they know the answer puts their hand up. I will pick the person with their hand up first and invite them to answer. If you put your hand up or call out before I say 'now', you will be disqualified for that turn.

Some students will still ignore your directions. It may not always be deliberate but they will need correcting.

Teacher   Can you give me one of the functions of white blood cells?
Student   (*without being invited*) To attack bacteria!

The teacher has a number of options but should make sure the student does not feel he is being put down in front of his peers simply because he was eager to give his answer. The teacher should tactically ignore him by choosing someone else with their hand up.

> 'Thank you for putting your hand up and waiting, Steven. What do you think the function is?'

The first sentence is a rule reminder. The teacher is reinforcing the behaviour she wants and ignoring undesirable behaviour. The correction is indirect but often just as powerful, because the students who are keen to answer will soon learn the right way and put up their hand. The direct approach is different in that it requires an immediate response.

Teacher   Colin, what should you do when you want to speak? (*rule reminder*)
Student   Put up my hand and wait, Miss. (*correction*)
Teacher   That's right, so in the future I would like you to do that. Okay? (*redirection*)

Student   Yes, Miss.
Teacher   Thank you. (*repair*)

Sometimes the correction is better deferred to a more suitable time when you can have a one-to-one conversation.

Scenario 2.9: The student who cannot seem to settle

Carl was finding it very hard to settle. He seemed to want to do other things. He was looking out of the window, tapping the desk, staring at his pencil and repeatedly putting his hand up and asking for paper, pencils, a textbook, a compass, etc. The teacher finally warned Carl that he needed to get down to work and stop wasting any more time. Carl returned to his work but a few minutes later he was turning round and chatting again.

How not to deal with this

- 'Turn round, Carl. I've given you a warning but you seem to be dead set on ignoring me, so you can stay in detention. You won't be able to ignore me there.'
- 'That was your last chance. You can stay in during lunchtime.'

The positive, proactive approach

The purpose of the intervention is to get the student back on task and to correct him. If he has failed to follow directions, a consequence is due but should be deferred until later to minimise the disruption.

Teacher   Carl, I have already given you a warning for chatting during silent work. What is the rule about talking? (*rule reminder*)
Student   No talking during silent work. If I need to talk, I've got to raise my hand and wait for you to give me permission. (*rule reinforcement*)
Teacher   That's right. Now, I gave you a warning for talking and you carried on.
Student   Sorry, Miss.
Teacher   That's okay. I accept your apology, Carl, but you chose to chat after being given a warning, so you know you have a consequence. We will discuss what it will be at the end of the lesson. (*deferred consequence*) Right now, I want you to get on with the work with no more interruptions. (*redirection*) Do you need my help or can you get going alone? (*support*)
Student   I think I need your help on this bit, Miss.
Teacher   Okay, let's have a look at it together. (*repair and rebuilding*)

Carl has been challenged, corrected, given a deferred consequence and helped to get back to work without wasting unnecessary time in the lesson discussing the incident.

CONSEQUENCES

Sometimes it is necessary to go further than just correcting the student, as we saw with Carl in Scenario 2.9. The student that breaks a rule will need to learn from *you* that they have chosen to do so and therefore they are choosing the consequence as well. This is an essential area of your response. The proactive teacher sets out to help the students learn to manage their own behaviour. Part of this is the understanding that when a rule is broken a consequence will follow. Consequences can be immediate such as a time-out, moving places or being sent out of the room, or they can be deferred such as detention or loss of privileges. They should be linked to the behaviour (Chapter 5) and in proportion to the incident. Scenarios 2.10 and 2.11 give two examples.

Scenario 2.10: Students damaging school property

On her way to the classroom, Liz noticed two students defacing a poster in one of the rooms. They didn't see her because she was outside the building in the playground and they had their backs to the windows.

How not to deal with this

- She could have gone in all guns blazing and rapped on the window. 'Oi, you two, cut that out and get to the head's office now!' Some students would feel intimidated and actually do what was being asked. Kids who deface displays are more likely to run for it, and then the opportunity is missed.
- She could have tried going to the room and pleading with them. 'Now come on, boys, that's not a very good use of your time.'
- 'A lot of time and effort goes into those displays, lads. You are spoiling them and probably upsetting the teacher and students who did the work.'

None of these strategies will help the students to understand that they have done wrong and should make amends. There has been no talk of consequences and putting things right.

The positive, proactive approach

Liz thought that they should make amends but she did not teach them and felt it was a hard one to prove because when she got to the room they were sitting down chatting. The school had a rule about being in the rooms during break, so she used that as her way in.

'Hello, boys, you're aware of the rule about being in the room during break?'

'No,' replied one of them cheekily.

'Well let me remind you,' she responded confidently. She went on to reiterate the rule and while she did it she surveyed the room and displays for any evidence of damage. If it had been negligible, she would have talked about the amount of effort that goes into displays. When she spoke about preventing deliberate damage, she engaged them in direct eye contact to communicate that she knew what they had been doing.

'I was walking past this room a few minutes ago and I saw you two doing something you probably shouldn't have been doing.' Making eye contact, she continued, 'It reminds me of a display that needs changing. I would appreciate it if you would both help me with it.'

Liz did not actually accuse them because she was not sure they had done any damage. Instead she chose a tack that would enable them to see how much work was involved and gave them some ownership of a display board.

When the damage is obvious you should challenge them and get them to own up.

Teacher (*pointing to the damage*) As I passed this room a few minutes ago I saw you both at the back by this poster.

Student It wasn't us, Miss.

Teacher It was someone. That is a deliberate act of vandalism. Those obscene words have been written during break. We can easily prove it wasn't either of you by comparing the writing on the poster with a sample of your handwriting and the pens that you have. Do you understand what I am saying? (*making eye contact again*)

Student Yes, but it wasn't us. We were just looking at them.

Teacher Maybe you were, so I am going to offer you a choice. You can empty your pockets and then we shall compare the pens and writing on the poster. If it proves to be yours, we shall call your parents in and discuss what you have done. I am sure they will be furious if they see what you have written. Or you can own up to it now and I won't say anything to them.

The teacher uses parental disapproval and the punishment the students may receive at home as a threat to get them to admit they did it. Once they have owned up, she can start working with them on repairing what they have done. The consequence could be helping to put up a display and then letting them take responsibility for it. In this way the consequence fits the incident. The students will have to give up their time but in return they may take pride in their work and be less likely to repeat the offence.

The essential aspects of this area of behaviour management are choice and enabling the students to realise it is their behaviour that is undesirable, not them as people. They will sometimes make the wrong choice but that does not make them bad people. We are all entitled to make mistakes and that is how we learn. It is the handling of mistakes that matters. An opportunity to help the student see where they went wrong could be lost if they are handled wrongly. Sensitive handling will help the students learn from their mistakes, the relationship between student and teacher will grow and self-esteem will be enhanced. Then the students will become more independent and responsible for their own behaviour and aware of the consequences that accompany their choices.

A sense of fairness is an important element. Students need to feel that the teacher is making balanced judgements and treating everyone in the same way. Teachers who do not do this will damage the confidence of their students.

Scenario 2.11: Fairness and consistency in dealing with students talking

Liam was teaching a group in the computer room and the students were working in pairs on a magazine layout. Two of them decided to take advantage of the teacher working on the other side of the room; they began chatting about the match they had seen the night before. After a while Liam became aware of their talking.

How not to deal with this

Liam did not want to get up and come over, so he called across the room, 'You two, be quiet and get on with your work.' The two students stopped for a few seconds then resumed their chat once he had looked away. Liam started to get angry and a little paranoid that they were deliberately winding him up and trying to test him. He stopped what he was doing and went over to them. He scolded the two students then addressed the whole class.

'I don't know what's the matter with this class today. Perhaps it's because we have moved to the computer room. You all seem unable to settle. You two can do a detention at lunchtime and anyone else who misbehaves can join them.'

The class settled back down to their work but one or two students continued talking about the match. Liam felt that they all should have stopped but he had not made that clear. Furthermore, it was difficult to work in pairs on a shared task in silence.

Liam was getting angry and confused about what he wanted. This was partly due to the difficulties he was having with the computers. Several had frozen and the printer had got jammed and he had to clear it himself. When he looked up after fixing it, several students were sniggering about something and he thought it was directed at him.

'That's it, I warned you. These two students have spoiled it for all of you. Clearly you can't get on with things on your own, so you will all stop what you are doing, log off and come and sit at the desks until the end of the lesson.'

'But that's not fair, we weren't talking,' pleaded a couple of girls who had been trying to work in silence.

'I don't care. You will have to take that up with the students who were.'

'But, Sir, you said that if we did not behave right, we would get a warning first. You didn't give one.'

Liam was on shaky ground. He could not argue because the girl was right, but he had already done it and did not want to do a U-turn. The class were very upset. They felt they had been treated unfairly and conned. Liam had introduced the behaviour code and wasn't sticking to it.

The positive, proactive approach

Liam seemed like he was having a bad day and that is when a good behaviour code usually comes into its own. It will only happen if you stick to it, but Liam seemed to have forgotten and was letting his emotions take over. It is a straightforward case of dealing with the kind of distraction that happens in every lesson. His approach should have gone as follows. He should have wound up his discussion with the boys he was helping by saying, 'Okay, lads, see how you get on with that. If you need any more help, just raise your hand and I'll get back to you as soon as I can.'

Then he should have moved on to the boys who were chatting, stood near them and given them a look to say, 'I am watching you and I expect you to stop talking and get on with the work.' If a more direct approach was required, he could have said, 'The work is to be done in pairs. I notice you are doing a lot of chatting and making very little progress. If you are stuck, you should raise your hand and wait for me to come over. Otherwise you should be working and if you need to talk, keep your voices down.'

If the students do not stop talking, he will need to go over to them and speak in a calm, unemotional way: 'I have already spoken to you about your chatting but you have chosen to ignore me, so I am giving you a warning to stop chatting and get it finished. If you continue to chat, you will be choosing a consequence, which will be to wait after class for one minute. You will also have to do the work in your own time if it is not finished.'

Notice the rule reminder about consequences. The students are given a chance to decide and the consequences are made clear. The rest of the class can carry on working without being involved. This places the responsibility with the students. The teacher, who is having a bad day, can remain out of the decision and is better able to keep calm. Sometimes students just cannot behave well. When they make poor choices, do not feel you have failed. Providing you give them a chance to decide and make the consequences clear to them, you will be doing your job well.

SUPPORT

The final area of behaviour management is support and encouragement. It is vital to the whole process because it can have a disproportionate effect on the progress of the students. Feeling that you are doing things right and well is important to everyone. Praise and feedback are important in affirming that feeling. A lack of acknowledgement can make your students feel that you do not really care or that you have not noticed their efforts. The end result will be unmotivated students. Critical feedback given sensitively can also have a profound effect in helping the students identify where they went wrong and deciding what to do next time. Giving this feedback needs care and practice. It is best begun with something positive:

'I really liked the way you got your group organised. They listened to what you suggested and that saved a lot of time that might have been wasted.'

Then move on to the constructive criticism:

'What you could do now is to try to take turns speaking. That way you'll all get a say and not risk losing any good ideas.'

The students will feel that you are genuinely trying to help and treating them in an adult way; this will contribute to fostering a positive relationship. Students who begin to experience difficulties with their behaviour will need a particular kind of support to ensure that they do not end up losing control and getting excluded. Many schools have a framework for supporting students with behaviour difficulties, and here are some of the items they include:

- Peer support
- Behaviour recovery plans and mentoring schemes
- Anger management courses.

The aim of is to curb the frequency of incidents and prevent students getting trapped in a spiral of repeating consequences where they feel they are always doing something wrong. The methods employed should be practical. The solutions are not obtained by producing a written plan with targets and dates. The students need help, not a piece of paper. The written plan is for recording what everyone agreed should happen, but it will not be sufficient on its own. Each student will need coaching in order to change habits and eliminate poor behavioural traits. Time needs to be set aside and specific methods need to be used that will include role-play, drama, empathising and customised exercises for specific difficulties. The coach will need to work with the student on a regular basis so that new ways can be properly learned and internalised. There is not enough space to describe these methods in depth but 'trust the teacher' (next section) is a typical activity and will give you a flavour of what might be done.

TRUST THE TEACHER

A common problem that exists in primary and secondary schools is the students' lack of trust in the teachers to sort out their difficulties. The usual route that students go down is to respond to an incident directly rather than take it to someone in authority. The reason is partly due to the lack of trust and also a lack of personal control. The student gets angry and then retaliates. The result is trouble for all the students concerned. In many cases the retaliation is perceived as the worse offence as it is often out of proportion to the incident that provoked it. For example, a boy tackles aggressively during a game of football in the playground. The second boy turns around and says something to him and he takes offence and lashes out. Before you know it, a fight has broken out and the boy who started it will be in deep trouble. The other boy who took umbrage gets off because he didn't start it. The aim of this activity is to help the students to understand how to deal with these kinds of day-to-day conflicts in a controlled way using the teachers as arbiters. Scenario 2.12 is an example.

Scenario 2.12: The stolen pen

The lesson had just begun and the teacher was in the middle of a warm-up activity involving a question and answer session with the whole class. Paul had taken out his pen and textbook and placed it on the desk ready. He was listening intently and raising his hand each time he knew an answer. The teacher looked in his direction and nodded for him to speak, but Paul was not sure whether it was for him or the student behind. He looked round to see and realised it was the other student. When he looked back to the front he noticed that his pen had disappeared.

Activity 1

The students tell you what they would do and you challenge each suggestion by asking them to consider what the consequence might be. Here are some questions for the class and their possible responses:

Teacher	What would you do?
Student	Call out, 'Who's got my pen?'
Teacher	What would the consequence be?
Student	I would probably get told off by the teacher for interrupting or getting aggressive during the lesson.

Activity 2

Describe how you would like them to respond and then help them to role-play it to practise their response. You will want to help them with how they report to the teacher because the obvious response from most students will be that the pen has been stolen. However, it may have fallen on the floor or in a bag. Conclude by showing them how you will respond to their report:

> 'Thank you for telling me that, Paul. I will deal with it at the end of the lesson. Can I lend you a pen or do you have another?'

This defers the whole incident until later and prevents the lesson getting disturbed. The offer of a pen ensures Paul can continue and gives him something different to think about. It is all about making good choices, and the four areas of behaviour management will enable you to support the students in taking on that responsibility.

SUMMARY

- The positive approach involves responding to the four key areas: prevention, correction, consequences and support.
- Plan to prevent conflicts and problems by communicating your expectations in advance to the students.
- Consider the whole experience the students have, including room layout, work partners, and pace of lessons. They may contain triggers for poor behaviour.
- When correcting, tackle students in an appropriate way using rule reminders and redirections.
- Wherever necessary, use assertive instructions with choices rather than emotionally driven orders.
- Consequences must follow when rules are broken. They can be immediate or deferred until later.
- Consequences must be fair and in proportion to the behaviour.
- Repair the relationship after the consequence is given.
- Coach students who make the wrong choices so they do not repeat the mistake.
- Dislike the behaviour not the student.

3 THERE'S NO NEED TO SHOUT!

Students may be used to teachers shouting at them. Most schools will have had one or two teachers who bark instructions and reprimand students in a loud voice. Some schools become dominated by that culture and the students get used to it. Shouting is not the same as projecting your voice in a loud way that allows you to be heard. Shouting above the hubbub of noise in an assembly or the dinner hall may seem the only way, and there lies the problem. Good management of behaviour prevents the problem to begin with. There is no reason why the noise level should be high in an assembly if classes are well managed by their teachers and the understanding is that the students whisper or remain silent. Equally, dining halls can be a cacophony of noise if the staff allow students to shout, call across tables and behave in ways more appropriate on a football field. Students should be allowed to relax, chat, socialise and meet with their friends over lunch but control is needed as with any activity in a school where large groups come together.

In the first chapter we looked at styles that teachers could adopt when managing behaviour. The focus of the second chapter was on the four main elements that go to make up the foundations of good behaviour management. The next step is to consider how you can develop a proactive style. This entails thinking about how the teaching space is used, personal appearance, language, and the use of humour and anger so that your interventions are positive, formative ones that enable your students to learn and grow from the experience. The essential ingredient in this process is modelling the behaviour you want to see from the students. Setting a good example through demonstration is the most effective way forward and this chapter provides useful insights into how this can be achieved. The overall objective is to manage the behaviour using positive, assertive methods so that the classroom is a calm place, conducive to learning, and you remain confident and relaxed and do not need to lose your temper.

THE TEACHING SPACE

The room where you teach, the teaching space, is like a theatre. And when you are teaching in it you need to make it yours. This can be done in several ways. The noticeboards and displays can be used to support your lessons and show your students' work, even if you are not based in the room. If the room is your own base room, you can really stamp your identity on it and present a wide variety of visual materials. Make sure you check with the teachers whose rooms you use around the school before changing displays. Explain that you need a small board for notices. Then get your students involved by putting them in charge of the boards and contributing to what goes up.

The ownership of the room is an important issue. Students know their space is at the desks and the teacher has the area up front around the board. You can subtly assert your authority in any room by changing things. This is particularly important if you are new or covering a colleague's lesson, because the students will perceive you as outside their normal group even though you are employed by the school. A useful analogy is a herd or pack of animals in the wild. The members of the pack recognise their leader, the usual teacher, and the authority he holds. They know their position in the pecking order. A new buck who enters the pack will not have any power at first.

To gain authority you must assert your position and dominate the space. When you enter a room, greet your students and start to change things immediately. Here are some examples:

- If the lights are off, switch them on.
- If the windows are shut, open them.
- Clean everything off the board and write your name.
- Move books, etc., off the teacher's desk.
- Open your bag and place your things on the desk.
- Move the teacher's chair and sit in it or put your coat on it to show it is yours.

If you can get into the room before the students, rearrange some furniture, alter the angle of computer monitors and put up one new poster. What you are doing is making the environment yours for that lesson.

INCREASE YOUR SPACE

During the lesson do what the students least expect. Make a point of walking around the room and down every aisle. Show you are not afraid to venture out from your 'teacher's space.' You are making a statement: this is my room and I can go where I like and do what I want. Teaching outside your space will increase what is yours. Move to the front desks while you do whole class activities and even conduct them from the side of the room.

Impose your will by seating the students where you want them rather than letting them choose where they want to sit. This may not be necessary if you are only covering one lesson, but any longer and it is essential. It can be done alphabetically, boy and girl or in groups to maximise cooperation. Explain you are doing it to learn their names; use it to assert yourself even though changing seats involves an investment of time. Do not respond to their protests.

The subtle signs you will give will show that you are now the authority figure in the room. This will enable you to command respect and cooperation without even needing to say anything. The signals are strong and even primeval. Our natural instincts run deep and it is worth drawing on them in situations like these.

LANGUAGE

Body language contributes significantly to the overall communication process. It can convey much more than can be said. For example, when we first meet someone new, we make immediate judgements about them from their clothes, expressions, mannerisms, facial features and posture. Much of the decoding is instinctive but it can be useful if we understand more about this means of communication. Such skills could contribute greatly to our ability to manage a class well.

We pick up visual cues about people almost instantaneously, so appearance is a vital part of our armoury. The students have expectations about what their teachers should be like and will typecast you depending on their first impressions. The male teacher who is well groomed, wearing a neutral-coloured shirt and tie, together with a suit will send out the message that he means business. He is dressing for the position he is aspiring to and recognises that others will expect him to dress in that way as well. The converse is the man who lacks confidence. He wears the right clothes but it looks like the suit is wearing him because he hunches and stoops.

The same is true for women. A smart businesslike outfit and a well-groomed appearance confers a level of status that the students expect and understand. Too much attention to fashion will distract from this image. On the other hand, do not ignore attention to detail. A teacher who stumbles into a classroom with a mountain of books under his arm and dumps them on the table only to see them slip and slide away does not create a good impression. Try not to carry too much; if you have a lot of things that need to be taken to a room, ask some students to help you. It avoids you struggling with the load and it will create the impression of someone in authority. You may need to carry a bag, so choose one that will reinforce your status such as a briefcase and do not pack it too full. Definitely avoid plastic carrier bags.

Once you are in the room, you are under the scrutiny of thirty pairs of eyes, so make your introduction count. Some teachers like to greet the class and tell them their name then write it on the board. Others prefer to write their name first. Whichever approach you adopt, act confidently and send out the message that you have arrived and the lesson is beginning.

Much depends on how you address the students and what you say. They are more likely to pick up what you are saying if you use phrases that tune into their preferred learning styles. For example, visual learners may tune into you more quickly if you use phrases like these:

'Let's have a look at . . .'

'Can you see what I mean?'

'That looks good.'

'I want you to imagine in your mind's eye . . .'

'What does success look like to you?'

'Try to picture this . . .'

Here are some phrases for auditory learners:

'I hear what you are saying.'

'How does this sound to you?'

'That rings a bell.'

'Ask yourselves what you would do if . . .?'

'Do you hear what I am saying?'

'What will people say when you get it right?'

'Tell me about your experience.'

These are some phrases for kinaesthetic learners:

'I can follow what you are saying.'

'That touched a nerve.'

'What does success feel like?'

'I want you to get to grips with this.'

'Can you change your position on this?'

'What will people do when you get it right?'

'Where do you stand on this?'

Teachers tend to talk a lot. We give instructions, directions, explanations, praise, criticism, advice, support and when there is time we chat to the kids. To get across your messages effectively, avoid long explanations just before giving directions, because students will be poised for action. When an intervention is required it is best to be brief and precise. Begin by naming the student and making eye contact with them to ensure they are paying attention:

'Chantelle, (*make eye contact*) remember the direction about walking.'

Allow a pause so the student can engage with what you are saying, then give the direction in an assertive tone. Finish with a smile and a thank you then turn away expecting it to be done.

'Peter, (*pause*) put the chewing gum in the bin please (*spoken assertively*). Thanks.'

Some students will have a tendency to switch off and go deaf when they think they are being lectured to about their behaviour, so avoid lecturing. They do not need long explanations about what they did wrong. A simple rule reminder followed by a redirection will be enough. Explanations should be left till later to avoid disturbing the lesson. Do not discuss a particular student's behaviour in the presence of the class or their peer group, because it may well fuel their need for attention. Furthermore, students love a show between a student and a teacher.

Long sets of directions can be confusing for some students. You will need to know what they are capable of and gauge how much each one can take in at a time. Low-ability students generally perform better when the task is broken down into smaller steps with discrete instructions that can be given separately. Then the students will be able to recognise when it is complete and judge whether they have been successful. Securing success is one of the keys to good behaviour. Students who feel they are failing will often become troublesome.

Ignoring the student who is behaving inappropriately can sometimes be a more powerful strategy. They will quickly realise they are being ignored by the teacher and look for reasons (Case Study 3.1).

Case Study 3.1

Teacher	I want you to put your hand up if you can tell me something about the Bayeux Tapestry. (*Joe calls out without raising his hand.*)
Joe	It shows The Battle of Hastings. (*The teacher physically changes his position and turns his shoulder towards the student. Then he points to someone with his hand up.*)
Teacher	Thank you for raising your hand and waiting for me, Luke. What can you tell me?
Luke	It is an embroidered pictorial account of the Battle of Hastings.
Teacher	Good, now can anyone tell me where the landing took place and where the battle was actually fought? (*A number of students put up their hands, including Joe.*)
Teacher	Thank you, Joe, for putting up your hand this time.
Joe	They landed at a place called Norman Bay near Pevensey and marched as far as Senlac Hill near Battle Abbey.
Teacher	That's very well answered, Joe. Thank you. (*Joe realised the teacher had deliberately passed him by the first time because he had called out instead of raising his hand, so the next time he did as the teacher asked and was rewarded by being chosen.*)

Eye contact is crucial in engaging attention. By looking straight at a person, you show that you are addressing them. Our eyes are our most important means of communicating. You can tell a lot about how someone is feeling and the sort of mood they are in by the look in their eyes. Students will read your expression and see disapproval, happiness, displeasure, humour and compassion. Learn to control and use these expressions to your advantage. Direct eye contact is essential to ensure the students pick up your feelings. Very often a student who is being reprimanded will try to break eye contact because they are ashamed, angry or trying to control the situation. When this happens, you should try to regain eye contact to maintain your authority (Case Study 3.2).

Case Study 3.2

Kirsty was deliberately trying to wind up the girl sitting in front of her. Mark saw what she was trying to do and gave a very clear warning to stop or there would be a consequence. She waited until he turned his back then started again. He guessed she would and he turned round just in time to see her kick the girl's bag out into the aisle. 'Kirsty, I have warned you not to continue with that behaviour. Stay after the lesson, I want to speak to you.'

Kirsty settled down for the rest of the lesson and there were no more incidents involving her. The deferred consequence of staying back and talking to the teacher seemed to have done the trick. When everyone else had left the room, Mark called her over to his desk and started to talk to her about her behaviour that lesson. She listened to what he was saying but averted her eyes. After about half a minute she slowly turned her shoulder so she was no longer facing him. Her body language showed she was not prepared to listen to what he had to say.

'I can see that you are not happy with what I am saying but I would like you to look at me while I am talking.' Kirsty ignored him and continued to look down. She was acting arrogantly and Mark could see she was going to be difficult unless he could get her back quickly. 'Well, Kirsty, I would like us to reach an agreement about this but I cannot continue until you are looking at me.' She still ignored him. 'I am not going to talk to your shoulder, so you need to turn and face me. I have got the next lesson free, so you need to decide what you are going to do.'

Mark knew she would eventually face him and that is why he continued with the lesson. Kirsty complied with his request, indicating that she knew she had done wrong and needed to do something to put things right. He refrained from getting angry and did not go on about it being rude to turn away from someone when they are talking. He offered her a choice and acted as if he did not mind how long she took to decide. If she had looked like she was not going to do as he asked, he would have postponed the meeting, because she had chosen not to listen to him. She would have been given a detention, put on class report and been seated in a different place away from the other girl. Her turning back and facing Mark had redressed the balance of power. Mark was then able to continue the conversation.

The tone the teacher uses can convey to the students how they feel. Try different ways of saying some of your regular directions and listen to the effect:

'Come here, John.'

'Sarah, put the chewing gum in the bin, thank you.'

You can change your tone of phrase so it is friendly, polite, angry, sarcastic, indifferent, assertive, pleading and joking. Notice how different they sound. Try to imagine someone else speaking to you in these ways. Put yourself in your students' position and consider how you would feel. How would you want to be spoken to? Most people prefer to be spoken to in a decent way. Obviously there will be times when urgency is required and a more assertive, louder tone is necessary.

The difficulty that occurs for teachers is that there is an underlying 'them and us' assumption that immediately sets up a conflict situation. It is very easy to make this assumption rather than treating people in a friendly way. Calling the register provides a simple illustration. Surnames can be used:

Watson. Here.

Willis. 'Ere.

Wright. Here.

First names can be called:

Helen. Here.

Michael. Here, Miss.

David. Here.

Or first name and a greeting:

Morning, Helen. Morning, Miss Brooks.

Hi, Michael. Hi, Miss.

Hello, David. Hello, Miss Brooks.

This way may take a little longer but it sounds friendlier and helps the students to be polite and well mannered.

Different situations need appropriate responses. A fight in the playground requires a more assertive response given in the form of a command. A fluffy, soft approach used by a teacher to offer choice is a totally impractical way of trying to intervene between two well-built Year 10 students attempting to knock the stuffing out of each other (Case Study 3.3).

Case Study 3.3

Ali was hurrying back to the staffroom for a quick cuppa at break when he saw two Year 9 students shouting at each other. One of them had made a dangerous tackle and the other lad had objected, so they were facing up to each other and tempers were rising. The boys looked like they were going to take the matter further and needed to be stopped. Playgrounds are noisy places and there was little chance of Ali being heard if he shouted at them to stop; he was quite a long way off.

He moved quickly towards them until he was in earshot then called out in a commanding tone to get their attention, 'Mark, Steven!' They stopped and looked up. 'Steven, over there!' He pointed to the far end of the playground. 'Mark, over there!' He pointed to the other end. Once separated, Ali went to Steven who was nearest to him. 'What was going on there?' he asked in a very authoritative, businesslike way.

'Nothing, Sir.'

'Okay, go in and wait outside my room and cool off. I shall be in to talk to you both in a few minutes.' Ali did the same for the other student. When the teacher got inside, he dropped the tone of his voice as a loud, assertive approach was no longer needed.

ANGER

The chief priority in any positive approach to behaviour management is maintaining personal control and not revealing emotional feelings, like anger, that will obviously occur from time to time. There will be some occasions when it is necessary to show displeasure but these will be rare. Then, when the students do experience your anger, it will have far more effect because they rarely see that side of you. Overuse will diminish the impact and change the students' perception of you as a teacher from someone who is reasonable and in control to a fierce, grumpy person who is always barking and shouting. Some teachers believe they should show their anger at least once to demonstrate they have teeth, so the students do not misjudge them as easy-going.

Anger is an emotional response and may result in negative feelings after an incident, especially if you are trying to handle conflicts in the way this book describes. Getting angry does not lead to a rational set of actions. Harassment, abuse and overreaction are the usual kinds of response, and it can be difficult to control them when you're seeing red. You may also find that not only have you said things you do not mean, you've said them in a way that is harmful. Devastating damage can be done to relationships when tempers are lost and that is why it is better to avoid losing your temper. Ask for assistance or postpone making a judgement until you have calmed down and can think more clearly.

When are we most likely to get angry? That is an interesting question and will vary depending on your personality. The common trigger is when the student becomes defiant, rude, belligerent, consistently annoying or abusive. Try to find out what makes you angry in your work and consider how you have been dealing with it. Do you get sucked in emotionally and then fly off the handle? Does your anger get directed at a student, resulting in outbursts like this?

'You make me so angry!'

'I am really annoyed with you.'

'That's it. I've had enough of you.'

This is unproductive. If you need to express your feelings, direct your anger at their behaviour.

'I am very angry because of your comments.'

'Your behaviour has made me extremely cross.'

'Calling me that has made me very angry.'

This enables the student to see how their behaviour has caused your reaction.

Anger is a powerful emotion. If you bottle it up, it will leak out eventually in a way that causes damage to people who were not involved. Controlled anger is different and can be a very potent force when used sparingly. If you do get angry, consider carefully how you plan to control it. By far the best option is to give yourself time to cool off. Things always look better the next day (Case Study 3.4).

Case Study 3.4

Alice was fed up with school. She really didn't want to be there. She had been having a hard time at home. Her mum and dad had been arguing for days now. Her dad hadn't come home last night and her mum had spent the whole night crying. Things looked grim between them and she was sure they were about to split up. Last night her thoughts were that she loved her dad but did not like what he was doing to her mum and felt she owed her loyalty to her. This was making her feel that her dad should go to hell and she never wanted to see him again. By the morning she had grown even more aggressive, partly due to her lack of sleep and partly because he hadn't returned. If he walked through that door, she thought she might

actually kill him. Anyway, her mum cajoled her into going to school with her younger sister, so off they went but she was still seething.

Jackie was Alice's English teacher. She had been teaching for just over a year and felt she was getting into it. The only problem she had was remaining calm when the kids behaved badly. She had read the books and been on the courses run by the local education authority (LEA) on behaviour management and felt confident she could manage the classes most of the time. Occasionally her temper frayed when she got frazzled but she had been developing some strategies.

Last night her boyfriend had called and wanted to take her out. They had been going steady for six months but he had got tired of her letting him down because she had essays to mark or lessons to plan. She had a pile of GCSE coursework to get through and had to turn him down. They had a big row and he stormed out saying he didn't want to waste any more time on her. He was going to find a girl who wanted to have some fun. She struggled through the essays but was really feeling down by the next morning.

Jackie didn't know what was up with Alice that morning but whatever it was, she needed to cut it out otherwise she would be in trouble. She wasn't settling and every time someone spoke to her she nearly tore their head off. She stomped around the room thumping books down on the desks, so Jackie gave her a warning. She ignored it and continued, so Jackie told her to go to the spare desk and work for five minutes. Alice didn't even look; she just spun around and lashed out as she screamed something sordid. Jackie caught the blow in the chest and it winded her. She knew she shouldn't take this but she was also too low to think straight. 'Take one more step near me and you'll wish you hadn't!' she threatened.

'Yeah, well what you gonna do, Barbie? You can't touch me.'

Jackie stood back for a few moments, paused and recognised this was one of those occasions she was not very good at. 'I am very angry because of your behaviour, so I am not going to deal with the matter at the moment.' Then she turned to another student, 'Steven, please go and get Mr Williams.' She moved to the front of the class leaving Alice staring out of the window.

A few seconds later Mr Williams arrived and Jackie was able to explain briefly that there had been an incident and a student had hit her. He told her he would cover her class while she went and reported the matter to the deputy head. The deputy returned after hearing Jackie's account and spoke to Alice, who got up and went to the head of year's office. Jackie was able to calm down and get over the shock of the incident. She was also able to discuss her next course of action with a colleague.

Alice was full of remorse and poured out her worries to the head teacher, who decided that, in the light of her difficulties, the fairest consequence should be a fixed-term exclusion but she would have to see Jackie before she returned to her normal timetable. On reflection, Jackie felt she handled the incident very well. She should not have threatened Alice and that was something she still needed to improve but when it came to withdrawing and sending for a colleague, she felt she had done the right thing.

WHEN SHOULD YOU RAISE YOUR VOICE?

When you shout you condone shouting. If you do it to get attention, that makes it okay for the students to do it. It can be a challenge to find other ways of getting attention in a lesson where a healthy level of discussion is required. There are various ways depending on the age of the students. You could count down:

'Three, two, one, stop. Pens down. Look at me.'

You could give a signal like calling out 'one minute', ringing a small bell or perhaps putting a large card on the board. Raising your voice to reprimand a student will lessen the effect when you really need to use a loud command to prevent a serious incident or break up a fight. Only use a raised voice when you really need to and then only to gain the attention of a student. As soon as you have got their attention, lower your voice back to the normal and adopt a more controlled tone.

Voice control is a useful exercise to try at home. Say something loudly then follow it with another sentence said quietly:

'Martin, put the hammer down!' (*say it loudly*)

'Now come over here please.' (*say it quietly*)

Simulated anger can have its uses in your repertoire of responses in order to emphasise a point. Again, it should be used very sparingly to maintain the effect. The secret is to raise your voice in the same way as if you are angry:

'Throwing your bag is wrong!' (*say it loudly*)

Then modulate your voice back to normal:

'Now go and pick it up and bring it to me.' (*say it normally*)

This shows that you are still in control and have not succumbed to your emotions. Teachers who have a problem dealing with their own anger will find it a useful skill to help them with their self-control. Ultimately, the aim is to use an assertive voice instead of losing your temper.

HUMOUR

Some people believe that teaching is like acting. The classroom is the stage, the lesson is the script, the students are the audience and the teacher is the actor. Collectively they become the performance. This is a useful way of viewing one aspect of teaching. The upfront, whole-class part of the lesson can indeed become a performance. This is not all that a teacher does but it enables you to develop a rapport with your class.

Humour can be a key part of the performance because it helps break down barriers. A funny story or silly sound effect can turn a mundane piece of work or potentially tricky concept into a memorable event that students will retain. A well-placed comment or joke can take the heat out of a difficult situation (Case Study 3.5).

Case Study 3.5

Cameron liked to use his break time duty to get to know some of the students in a more informal setting. He would pause and exchange a few comments about their games and find out what they were interested in. He stopped to chat to one group of Year 8 lads who were swapping cards. He leant forward to look at the cards more closely and one of the boys stood back and exclaimed, 'Phew, your breath smells evil, Sir.' Cameron was really embarrassed and didn't know where to hide his face. After a few seconds he responded in a very quick-witted way, 'I'm sorry, I was taking part in the International Curry Championships last night and some of the dishes were explosive!'

Finding humour helped to lighten the situation and showed he had the capacity to make fun of himself. It also gave him the chance to get away behind the smokescreen of laughter and he felt better even though they had levelled a harsh personal comment at him. Imagine how it might have gone if Cameron had taken offence and got angry about the comment. He might have spoken to the boy in a harsh way, told him not to make personal comments or reprimanded him for something he was doing wrong as a means of getting back at him. The boy would have felt a sense of injustice, because the teacher's breath did actually smell. What the boy did wrong was to speak to Cameron as though he had equal status.

Students tend to like teachers who can share a joke with them and are confident enough to laugh at themselves. Deliberately doing something wrong then getting the students to find the mistake and explain why, can be a very useful and enjoyable way of checking for learning. Ridiculing personal characteristics or possessions also helps to build bridges: 'Is that your old crate in the car park, Miss?' 'Do you mean the blue, metallic hatchback, 0 to 60 in five minutes, not bad eh?'

Making light of things that students do can be a good way of showing you do not get wound up by the small stuff. For example, a student aims a screwed-up piece of paper at the waste bin but misses. The teacher says, 'Let me know when you are ready for a trial for the basketball team, James. Now come and pick it up and put it in the bin, thanks,' followed by a smile.

Not all teachers see themselves in the role of the performer and capable of using humour in the classroom. You may feel your personality does not fit with the extrovert role. But you need not be an extrovert to use humour. It's about acting like an extrovert and going into a role for the duration of the lesson. It requires you to step outside your own self-image and be someone else (Case Study 3.6).

Case Study 3.6

Alex was a newly qualified art teacher. He had been at school since September and was really enjoying teaching. He was not an outgoing person but was pushing himself to try to do more teacher-led activities. He had recently read about hot seating, a method that involved the teacher going into role as a character from the lesson being taught and then answering the student's questions as that person. He really liked the idea because he could be someone he wasn't and it didn't matter. The students could get more from the lesson and he was sure they would enjoy it.

He was going to introduce the Year 8 groups to Pop Art. One of the artists he wanted to include was Jackson Pollock, the American action painter. He came up with the idea of combining action painting with music. The students would create pieces of work using the beat of the music as the stimulus. To extend the idea and give the students a multimedia experience, he decided they should film each other making their pictures and then edit the clips to produce a short film that would become the artwork. Action painting is great fun and can be exhilarating to produce and watch being done.

Alex told his students that next lesson there would be a visiting artist coming. He got himself some American-looking gear and prepared to be Jackson Pollock. He also produced a special flyer that announced Jackson Pollock would be visiting the school and named the class and the teacher. The flyer gave useful background information that the students would need to know. It also included some colour reproductions of Pollock's most well-known pictures. On the day, Alex got a colleague to begin and end the lesson so he could go and change. He made his excuses to the students and explained that he had a meeting to go to but Jackson Pollock, who was in the UK for a week gathering material for a new work, would be staying with them for the lesson. He did not tell them that Pollock was dead, because they would see it was him after a while. A few minutes later he returned to the room dressed in an old sweater, baseball cap and shades.

He introduced himself in an American accent and explained his action painting technique. The beat of the music would inspire the mark-making process. If they heard slow music, they should make lazy, undulating, open marks; with a medium tempo their marks would be thicker and more angular; and a fast tempo would give rise to harsh, jagged, aggressive lines in bold colours. He also explained the filming process and the need to download and rough-edit the pictures and sound by the end of the lesson. When he had finished talking, the class got going. At the end he set up a session to preview the film and allow the whole class to discuss the results and ask questions.

Eventually he left and Alex returned. He used the plenary to get the students to tell him what they had been doing, show their pictures and film and talk about Jackson Pollock. This worked brilliantly because the students were so absorbed. They had so much to say and none of them let on that they knew Alex was Pollock. They kept up the act and colluded with Alex. He thought that was rather nice. The lesson was a resounding success and the students said they really enjoyed it, especially doing the action painting.

Alex was pleased, as he had done something that was difficult for him. He was not usually outgoing but as Jackson Pollock he felt he had really become a different person. He had done and said things that he wouldn't have imagined doing as himself.

MODELLING GOOD BEHAVIOUR

Modelling good behaviour is a powerful means of securing the behaviour you seek and making sure the students know how you want things done. The students will use what you do and how you do it as their standard, so if you value good manners then you should demonstrate good manners. This means avoiding examples of bad manners for example:

- *Scrawling on work*: having taken a student's book to look at, the teacher might scrawl corrections all over their work.
- *Thoughtlessly changing what a student has done*: a student may have been writing a poem in a brief style to give a staccato feel when read aloud. Unaware of this intention, the teacher may tell the student to use longer, more complex sentences.
- *Touching a student*: some students may not want their teacher to touch them.
- *Ordering students around*: this is common in many schools, especially when larger numbers are involved. If a group of students are not queuing for lunch and a teacher

starts ordering them to get in line, in twos, etc., they might reply that the teacher is not being very polite. This will allow them to shift the emphasis from their inability to queue to the secondary issue of manners.

The best approach is to use basic manners with students of all ages. Model good behaviour with 'please', 'thank you' and requests rather than orders:

'Can I see how far you have got, please?'

'Do you mind if I read your introduction?'

'Would you like me to read through and make some notes on the work or on a separate sheet?'

It is well worth explaining your marking policy and how you will correct their work during the first week of taking a new group so that everyone in the class is aware of how you work. Try to draw attention to the students who are behaving in the way you want them to. Sitting, waiting patiently, putting bags away tidily, whatever it is, praise good behaviour wherever you can. Any students who are not showing this good behaviour can then learn from the situation.

PRIMARY AND SECONDARY BEHAVIOUR

The skill is to address primary behaviour and ignore secondary behaviour; secondary behaviour will draw you into side issues:

'We have a rule of following directions, Harry. The direction was only two at the sink at once.' (rule reminder)

'It is not your turn yet, so go back to your seat please.' (redirection)

The teacher turns away to attend to the needs of the other students. Harry is expected to do as he is asked and is given some take-up time, as students do not always respond immediately they receive an instruction. Some need more time than others to process the request.

There will always be some students who will ignore the redirection and answer back:

'I thought Simon had finished and was drying his hands.'

There will be the temptation to rise to the bait and over-service a comment like this, but you need to refocus the student back to your direction:

'The rule is only two at the sink. Return to your seat and I will tell you when you can go to the sink and wash your palette.'

Secondary behaviour includes the way a student acts and their tone of voice as well as what they say. An arrogant or deliberately defiant posture can be infuriating but the important thing is to stay calm and unaffected. You may think 'How dare he act like that?' or 'Who does she think she is talking to in that way?' but reacting to those thoughts will only make the incidents messy. The students will get the attention they are seeking and a shift will take place from the rules that are in your control to the uncertainties of individual personalities, which are not.

A common cause of secondary behaviour comes when a teacher is too much of an authoritarian and issues orders. Most of the class will probably follow the order but there will usually be one or two who do not like being told what to do or are looking for a means of expressing their frustrations as an outlet for other problems that are going on in their lives. They will defy the teacher in a challenging way that usually results in a conflict over their rudeness or something they said, not the original reason. The student ends up digging themselves into a hole and the teacher cannot offer a way out (Case Study 3.7).

Case Study 3.7

Julie was an uninterested Year 11 student. School was one of those things to get through. She didn't really have any time for the teachers and yearned for the day when she could leave and get a job at the superstore. She wasn't stupid, but she felt all that school stuff did not relate to her life and what she liked doing. She had just got a new coat and was wearing it to school. Her appearance was important to her. She took a pride in how she looked and that meant she stood a better chance with the fitter guys, especially the ones with their own cars.

The teacher noticed she hadn't taken her coat off and called across the room, 'Julie, take your coat off and hang it up now because lessons are about to start.' There was no way she was going to take it off and hang it on a chair to get dusty and trodden on. And she wasn't going to hang it on a peg in the cloakroom where it could get nicked. Besides, she felt cold. The stupid school heating wasn't working properly and it felt like the arctic in the classroom. The teacher reminded her again but she was annoyed by the way he did it.

'No, Sir! I'm cold, it's freezing in here.'

'The rest of the class have taken their coats off.'

'So!' she thought.

'Take it off. I'm not going to tell you again.'

'No! I'm cold and I don't want to freeze.'

'Take it off or I will send for Mrs Patel.' Mrs Patel was head of the upper school.

'Oh sod off! I said, I'm cold. Don't you ever listen?'

'Right, that's enough. You don't talk to me like that.'

'Says who?' She turned her back on him.

'Turn round and face me now! Don't be so rude. You are a very arrogant girl.'

The teacher was getting pulled into a slanging match. Julie had dug in and had no way out. Soon she would be removed and the head of the upper school would have to take some serious action, because the school took a hard line on swearing at staff. The teacher had no way out because he had taken the win-lose route by insisting the student obeyed his orders. He could have explained to her that the coat should be removed and if she insisted on keeping it on, there would be a consequence. Then he could have left her to think about her options and make up her mind. The conflict would have been avoided and he would not have got involved in her secondary behaviour. Julie may even have decided to comply once she had some time to think about it.

Take-up time allows the student to reflect on the situation, to weigh up the consequences and calm down. The time can be given freely or you can use timers. This will ensure the student doesn't use it as a means of wasting time and getting out of doing the work. Whatever method you choose, lost time needs to be made up and this is something you should discuss with the student once things have calmed down.

Take-up time also allows some space for the student to look for a way of saving face. When they choose to comply, there will be less damage to their pride because they are not being made to give in. Resolving any conflict depends on minimising damage to the student's pride. This is even more important once they move on to secondary behaviour.

WHEN TO INTERVENE

There are several schools of thought on this. One is that the teacher uses their judgement and tactically ignores minor disruptions to maintain the flow of the lesson. Praise and positive affirmation are given to the students who are behaving in the desired way at the same time as a student is being tactically ignored. The student will learn from his peers who are modelling the correct behaviour. The flaw in this method is the inconsistency. A student who is spoken to about a specific incident may plead that the teacher did not do anything when other students did the same thing.

The other option is to pick up every incident when it happens. In that way, the students will know that they can never get away with anything. The difficulty in this approach is that the teacher has to be extremely vigilant and there will be times when they will miss incidents. It is also very demanding and may turn out to be so time-consuming with difficult classes that nothing else gets done.

The decision must lie with each individual teacher. Sometimes teachers may have extra members of staff in the room with them if the class are very difficult or there are students with special needs. In this case the second method could be more advantageous. Teachers working in pupil referral units (PRUs) may also use this method because the students need retraining. For most other types of class, the teacher's judgement will be the most practical solution.

Minor distractions such as tapping, leaning on a chair, chatting and chewing should be dealt with unobtrusively to prevent the flow being disrupted and avoid attracting attention from the rest of the class. Wait for an opportune moment when the class are engaged in the task then have a quiet word with the student followed by a thank you. Turn away expecting it to be done. When words are not enough, a warning or consequence should be given with the minimum of fuss. It is very easy to get cross with a student and show you are angry by saying things like this:

'Right! That's a warning!'

It is far better to remain calm, put a tick on the behaviour sheet and address the student in a normal voice:

'Paul, you were talking during silent work, so I am giving you a warning.'

'Paul, you have a warning for talking during silent work and have chosen to continue to talk, so you need to go to the time-out desk for five minutes.'

The intervention is made in a direct way. There is no ambiguity and the student is expected to comply. On the occasions when he doesn't, the teacher must avoid the secondary behaviour and avoid saying things like this:

'How dare you ignore me!'

'Who do you think you are?'

'That's no way to speak to a teacher.'

Just refocus the student back to the rule that has been broken and remind him of the consequence for not complying. Students do not like to be threatened. Make your challenges unthreatening by being polite and assertive (Case Study 3.8).

Case Study 3.8

Sonia was very pleased with her new mobile phone. She brought it to school to show her friends because it had a built-in camera and she wanted to take their pictures. She knew the rule about no mobiles during school time, she knew she was supposed to give them in at the office and collect them at home time, but she couldn't be bothered with all that. Loads of kids kept their phones on them. Bernadette was clamping down on the mobile phone problem. Everywhere she looked girls were using them and they kept going off during lessons. She had briefed the upper-school staff to challenge every student seen with one. The students needed to know they could not continue to flout the rules. But she had not given the teachers any strategies to deal with difficult conflicts.

How not to deal with this

Bernadette had some authority as the deputy head, but the rest of the teachers found it hard to assert their authority. The students were tough and did not want to part with their phones. Gemma saw Sonia with a phone and felt she had to deal with it. She went across the room to the girl who had her back to her.

Teacher	Sonia, you know the rule about phones.
Student	No, Miss, what is it?
Teacher	They should be given in at the office.
Student	I wasn't using it, Miss.
Teacher	I saw you calling someone just now.
Student	No, Miss, I was checking it because I dropped it and thought the SIM card may have been damaged.
Teacher	I saw you talking, now give it to me and you can have it back at the end of the day.
Student	No, I don't want to. The others haven't given in theirs, so why should I?
Teacher	I'm not going to ask you again. Now give it to me!
Student	When they give theirs in. You're always picking on me. Why don't you find someone else?
Teacher	You'll have to go to the deputy if you don't give it in now.

Gemma has failed. She had got herself into a conflict and Sonia had tried to imply that Gemma was singling her out. She had to pass the matter on to the deputy.

The positive, proactive approach

Teacher Sonia, will you come here please? I need to talk to you. I noticed you had a phone. Has it got a camera in it?

Student Yes, Miss, I just got it.

Teacher Nice one, now will you put it down on the table and let's talk about it.

At this point, the student may object but you should be insistent. Explain that you are not asking the student to give it up yet, just to put it out of the way, in a neutral space. Eventually, with persistence, this will happen because the student knows she has broken the rule and you are not demanding that she gives you the phone.

Teacher Now, Sonia, what is the rule about mobile phones?

Let her explain the rule to you then ask her what she should do in the future, i.e. give it in at the office or leave it at home. Then slowly stand up while explaining the reasons why you have the rule, i.e. to prevent them being stolen, going off during lessons or becoming a distraction. Go to where the phone is and pick it up. Reassure and praise the student for getting it right and tell her that she can collect it from you at home time. This prevents a clash and is a very effective way of dealing with phones, jewellery, clothing, personal stereos and any item that should not be in school. You can also telephone or send a note home to the parents explaining the rule and what you have done and requesting their support to help avoid this problem in future.

The other important factor in determining when to intervene is whether to defer dealing with the issue. Some incidents can be dealt with by telling the student you are aware of their behaviour, noting it then dealing with it later on. This allows the lesson to continue and gives you time to think about the incident. Making a note will ensure you do not forget. Incidents that may cause serious injury or endanger another student must be dealt with immediately.

Develop a behaviour code

The scenarios included so far often depend on a well-thought-out behaviour code that includes clear rules backed up by rewards and consequences. Developing the behaviour code is the next step in managing behaviour. It should be done with the students to ensure they know why it is needed and are prepared to support it. Chapter 4 begins this process by considering what the rules should be.

Summary

- Developing a positive style involves a range of factors, including the teaching space, personal appearance, specific modes of address and non-verbal communication.

- Tailoring your language to match the preferred learning styles of the students will enable better communication and more effective learning.
- Model the behaviour you want the students to learn.
- A powerful way of teaching the students how to behave involves tactically ignoring them when they do not follow your directions and praising them when they correct themselves.
- Helping the students to build their self-esteem is very important. Giving praise and reassurance when the students are doing things right will reinforce their confidence.
- Humour can be used to take the heat out of potentially difficult situations.
- Feigning anger on rare occasions will show you have teeth and are in control of your emotions.
- Becoming a performer will enable you to adopt different personas during whole-class teaching sessions, and this will enhance the learning experience.
- Focus on the primary behaviour and do not get sucked into responding to secondary issues. Timing is crucial. Knowing when to intervene and how to challenge a student is essential in maintaining the flow of a lesson.

4 THE BEHAVIOUR CODE

WHY HAVE A CODE?

Surely you cannot plan how a class will behave? Anything could happen; a student may talk during silent work, throw something, hit someone, set off a fire alarm, etc. A badly behaved class is one of the crosses we will probably have to bear at some time in our career. Or is it? Of course, we are not able to control our students completely so that incidents like these never happen but we can reduce the likelihood of them occurring. Furthermore, and more importantly, we can plan how we will react to incidents. We can choose to respond assertively and fairly, or we can be irrational and unfair. The behaviour code is a carefully thought-out set of guidelines and responses that will help students to choose responsible behaviour leading to greater self-esteem. Just like lesson plans enable you to deliver the curriculum, a behaviour plan helps you to manage the students. It's a sort of game plan.

Teaching is a very challenging job that often requires us to make thousands of on-the-spot decisions every day. We deal with the needs of up to thirty students during a lesson as we endeavour to teach them new things. A great deal of time and effort is spent planning how we will teach particular subjects, topics and new concepts. But how much time have you spent thinking about how you will help your students behave appropriately? Have you thought about how you will tackle the disruptions and conflicts that hinder you from teaching and the students from learning? The successful teacher plans lessons with teaching styles that reinforce the desired behaviour. This is achieved by teaching the rules and positively acknowledging good behaviour through what is said, together with activities that carefully match the range of preferred learning styles of each student.

The behaviour code is a means of communicating exactly what you expect from your students and what they can expect in return. It lays down the parameters of responsible behaviour and details what the consequences will be for a student who steps over the line. The purpose of the code is to achieve a classroom that is an orderly, organised, safe and happy place where everyone can learn. A behaviour code will vary according to the groups you teach and will be the blueprint for your own style of classroom management. It will help you plan your approach in advance by:

- Being positive and using encouraging language and actions
- Sharing your expectations when you introduce it into your lessons
- Working out your responses to common problems in advance.

Thinking through each of these points and developing your own style will help your students learn to choose the right behaviour. It will also help you become more confident in what you do as a teacher.

THE SCHOOL APPROACH

A measure of a good school is the way the behaviour is managed. It may be that you work in a good school with a well-disciplined environment and the students understand what is required. Even so, you may still encounter very challenging behaviour from time to time and will need to use the procedures. Try to imagine what it would be like without a system that supports you. You would feel isolated and left to your own devices (Case Study 4.1).

Case Study 4.1

Lorna was new to the school. She had been teaching for two years and decided she wanted more responsibility, so she leapt at the chance to be head of Year 7. It was an opportunity to develop her pastoral skills with a view to an assistant head's position. She was interviewed and offered the post, starting in September. The summer months passed quickly; she was really looking forward to the new challenge and responsibility for the new students.

The first day of term arrived and the Year 7 students turned up full of holiday chatter. A brief honeymoon period passed and then she started to feel the change. She had assumed the students would behave well and hold her in awe as the head of year. But this wasn't the case. Her lessons became punctuated by her hopeless attempts to 'shush' the students. Her corridor duties were the same. She was ignored as they bustled around, oblivious to her directions. By the end of the third week, she was really fed up. She felt helpless. Students who misbehaved in her lessons found themselves unchecked because she didn't have any strategies that seemed to work.

Students who were sent to her by other teachers began to realise she was not a threat and became arrogant. Sitting at home one night talking about the day's events to her partner, she realised she was failing and started to wish that she'd stayed in her old job. Her partner could see she was feeling miserable. He had a friend who had been a teacher for years, so he rang him up. He told Lorna that good schools have an induction programme for their new teachers where they explain their systems for managing behaviour. And he thought it sounded like the teachers at Lorna's school relied on their personalities to keep order. What she needed was a behaviour code with some rewards and consequences that would work with her classes. She also needed a set of procedures to follow when teachers referred students to her as head of year.

THE CODE AND ITS OBJECTIVES

What will a behaviour code do for you and your students? It will help you establish the right atmosphere in the classroom so you will be able to teach. Young people in a school environment will often try to test the rules to find out where the boundaries lie and what they can get away with. They will put considerable thought and energy into thinking up creative and elaborate schemes to go off task or evade lessons. Read *Learning to Labour* (Willis, 1977) to get an insight into this. We need to think about how we will deal with these events in a positive, assertive way. Students should be redirected to the task in a calm, considered way. If you do not have a code, you are forced to think on your feet. You will have to decide what to do when it happens. You will find yourself reacting to the situation instead of using a preplanned set of responses designed for that incident. On-the-spot reactions may lead to inconsistencies in your approach and there is also the risk of irrational action. The students will be quick to comment on things they believe are unfair, and if they are ignored, they will become frustrated and possibly angry (Case Study 4.2).

Case Study 4.2

Kevin had been teaching science in a secondary school for one term. Things had gone quite well at first and he was enjoying what he was doing. After Easter things seemed to change. The students in his Year 9 group started to misbehave. It was nothing very serious really, just pranks. One student put too much chemical in a solution and it reacted vigorously, producing large quantities of froth. Others started chatting when they should have been listening. Kevin tried to keep order but without success. Eventually things came to a head. It began with two students arguing about a piece of apparatus. Kevin told them to be quiet and sit down. Then a boy got up, walked across the room and grabbed another boy's pencil. Kevin intervened. 'Give me that, now!' he shouted. The boy reluctantly handed it over. 'And you can take that expression off your face.'

'What expression?' replied the boy.

'You know, now sit down and get on with your work.'

Eventually the boy returned to his seat. A number of other minor incidents occurred during the lesson and each time Kevin got angrier. The final straw came when a boy got up to fetch a ruler and tripped over a bag in the aisle. He fell against another student and jogged him.

'Where are you going? That's it, you will do a detention. I will not have you totally ignoring me.'

'But, Sir, I was just . . .'

'I know what you were doing. Don't answer me back.'

Kevin was getting very impatient by now and did not like the way the boy had challenged him. The rest of the class had stopped what they were doing and were enjoying the show.

One of them called out, 'Sir, that's not fair. The others didn't get a detention when they were walking about.'

'Do not interfere.'

'But . . .'

'Right, you can join him in detention.'

The situation was escalating. Kevin was starting to act irrationally and letting his emotions cloud his judgement. His frustration was causing him to treat the students unfairly. He had not used a staged response and had no systems for dealing with their behaviour. Instead the incidents built up to the point where he snapped. The students needed to own their decisions and Kevin needed to be fair and consistent, using staged responses to avoid any possibility of overreacting.

THE BEHAVIOUR CODE WILL HELP YOUR STUDENTS TO LEARN

Students do not come to school trained in how to behave properly. Many will come from homes where the expectations are not clear. Parents have different standards and levels of authority in the home environment. Sometimes they may appeal to the school for help because their child is out of control at home. So assume that your students will need to be taught how to behave in your room. They should learn the rules and adhere to them if you are to maintain an orderly class. A well-behaved class is the bottom line. You cannot teach effectively and your students will certainly find it hard to learn if they are distracted by one or two individuals. Every student has the right to learn and when one student misbehaves, he is infringing the rights of the other students (Case Study 4.3).

Case Study 4.3

Carolyn was given the unenviable job of teaching maths to the bottom set in Year 10. Most of the class were fairly well behaved. They knew they were not high-flyers and got on with what they were told to do. But a small group of boys wouldn't go along with things. They were not completely switched off but they were heading that way and would end up very disillusioned if they were allowed to continue. Carolyn hadn't yet managed to develop any effective strategies to deal with them and found she was calling for assistance more and more. She didn't enjoy teaching them because most of her time was spent dealing with their annoying distractions.

The students in the class lacked clear guidelines. Some misbehaved and prevented the others from learning. Often her response was inappropriate and she found she was getting drawn into dealing with secondary behaviour. Things escalated and everything got blown out of proportion. The miscreants were not acting responsibly and the rest of the class were having their rights infringed. Clear rules and consequences would have protected their rights.

THE BEHAVIOUR CODE WILL LEAD TO A SAFE ENVIRONMENT FOR EVERYONE

Put thirty students together in a room and you have a potential problem. Many of them will probably not want to be there but know they have to. They will not always get on with each other and will disagree. Some will wind others up for the sport. You may not notice friction occurring until it is too late and the flashpoint has been reached. How can this be avoided? Your code will communicate the rules clearly to the students, offering them a safe, calm environment in which to learn. Fighting, swearing and bullying are unacceptable and the code will reinforce that. Your students will know that everyone's safety and well-being are being safeguarded.

The behaviour code will enable you to gain the support of students, parents and other staff. It shows you have thought how you are going to manage behaviour in your lessons. Parents will be more supportive because they will know you are endeavouring to help their children. Colleagues will be prepared to offer assistance knowing that you have exhausted your own strategies first and they will realise the situation must be getting serious.

WHAT DOES A BEHAVIOUR CODE ACTUALLY LOOK LIKE?

The behaviour code consists of three elements:

- Rules and directions
- Rewards
- Consequences.

These elements will vary according to the age of the students and the conditions you work under. However, the basic principles remain the same. Figure 4.1 shows a typical behaviour code.

Behaviour Code for Secondary Students

Rules
Keep hands, feet, objects to yourself
No teasing or name-calling
Follow directions at all times
Speak in a nice voice

Rewards
Praise
Stickers, house points, credits, etc.
First choice during free time
First in line for break, lunch, end of school
Made a monitor
Postcards and letters sent home to parents
Telephone call home to parents
Have lunch with the teacher

Consequences
The first time a pupil breaks a rule
        Warning recorded in the behaviour log
The second time
        Five-minute time-out away from the group
The third time
        Last in line for break, lunch, home or free time
The fourth time
        Stay in during break or lunch or 5 minutes after school
The fifth time
        Teacher calls parents
The sixth time
        Sent out of the room to the next stage in the hierarchy, e.g. head of the key stage, deputy or head teacher
Serious incident
        Sent to the head teacher

Isolation from class
A student who is isolated from the class must apologise and state what s/he will do to put things right and how s/he will behave in the future. A letter will also be sent home explaining why the student was internally isolated.

Figure 4.1 *Behaviour code for secondary students*

WHY DO WE NEED RULES?

Why do we need rules? The reason is very simple. Rules enable us to live in peace together. They allow us to go about our daily business, safe in the knowledge that we are free to do as we please as long as it is within the law. The rules protect our rights. The same applies in schools. Every student has the right to enter a classroom without fear of being teased, called names, racially abused, etc. The rules in your classroom protect these rights and make it clear to everyone where the boundaries are. The rules will also protect your rights as a teacher. Yes, you have rights too. You have the right to carry out the responsibilities of a teacher in safety. You have the right to teach and direct what goes on in your lessons. Fair rules are part of an orderly, well-managed classroom.

Students have their own perceptions of what is acceptable. They may differ from yours, so you will need to communicate your rules. Generally, students want to know what they can and cannot do and will respect the teachers who set fair rules and enforce them consistently. Do not assume that the students will behave when you take on a new class. They will see you as a challenge, someone to test to find out whether or not the boundaries can be pushed back. In the worst case this could develop into a battle for supremacy (Case Study 4.4).

Case Study 4.4

Margo had been teaching for over six years but this was only her second school. She was looking forward to her new job and had been given a number of examination groups. The term began and she was very optimistic as she met her classes.

Things went well at the start and she began to get accustomed to the different ways of doing things. After a few weeks, she noticed a slight change in the way the students behaved. It was more obvious in the lower sets but hard to pinpoint. She tried to deal with them by talking one-to-one with students when they misbehaved but it didn't work. By half-term she felt she had almost lost control. The more daring ones would come bursting into the room shouting, hurling their bags and putting their feet on the desks.

The maths teacher in the next room could see she was in difficulty and tried to help by telling her his behaviour code. Margo tried the consequences but gave up after a couple of lessons. She knew she was losing it and the students were taking over. The students in the adjacent room were distracted by the noise and commotion coming from Margo's class, and one boy asked whether there was a teacher in there because he couldn't believe that children could act that way during a lesson.

Margo had expected the students to behave and had not prepared herself with a behaviour code. The students were not aware of her expectations. Most behaved at first but a few wanted some sport. They spotted the gaps and moved to exploit them. They tested Margo and found little or no resistance. She had no effective strategies nor any presence in the room. Eventually other students joined in the game. The majority gradually lost respect for Margo and the lessons deteriorated into chaos. She was facing one of her most difficult challenges since becoming a teacher. Sadly, this is what happens to teachers who are not properly prepared to manage the behaviour in their lessons. Margo needed a code that included clear rules.

How do directions differ from rules?

Rules remain in force through the whole day. For example, if there is a rule of no swearing, the students must abide by it whatever they are doing. Directions vary according to the activity or context. You cannot have a rule that says 'no getting out of your seat' because it would be impossible to enforce. Students need to collect and return resources in some lessons. You need a specific direction instead, e.g. 'raise your hand and wait for permission if you need to leave your seat'. This will enable students to leave their seats and you can control when and how many at a time. Directions are given at the start of each lesson and students should learn them. One of the class rules is 'follow directions'. Therefore any student leaving their seat will have broken the rule and face the consequences outlined in your behaviour plan. Directions enable you to introduce a range of working methods and still manage the class effectively. Rules and directions used together will help your students understand the boundaries you have set.

Introducing the rules

Students should be involved in deciding the rules so they can have some ownership of them. Then they will be more likely to take responsibility for their behaviour. Rules provide a structure that can be very liberating for students. Once they know the boundaries, they can be more motivated to behave, which in turn will raise their self-esteem. Your students will be more inclined to learn the rules and use them if there are not too many. Three or four are about enough. Make sure they apply at all times and to every activity.

There are lots of rules in schools and you will adopt them in your classroom. Here are some typical school rules:

- Uniforms must be neat and tidy.
- Line up in twos outside the room.
- Walk in corridors.
- Do not leave the room without permission.
- Address the teacher as . . .

Canter and Canter (1992, p. 51) describe these as 'observable rules' because the behaviour can be seen clearly. Students who see the correct behaviour are much more likely to understand the rule and adopt it. Rules like 'no unnecessary talking' or 'be kind to other students' are very good goals to aim for but are vague and ambiguous, making them difficult to enforce.

Make the rules clear, positive and fair

Rules need to be easy to understand and not open to questioning. When you begin to write your rules, state what behaviour you want or what is unacceptable:

- Keep your hands and feet to yourself.
- No swearing.

Frame the rules positively wherever you can. 'Keep your hands and feet to yourself' means no hitting, pinching or spiteful contact.

Rules are designed to help you manage your class, but unjust rules lead to resentment. Encourage your students to suggest some rules. Many students will have a good idea how to behave and will enjoy the opportunity to contribute. Write their ideas on the board as they think of them, discussing why each one is important.

CAN YOUR RULES BE ENFORCED?

Can your rules be enforced? Of course they can, as long as you avoid rules that cannot be maintained. Teachers often start out well, helping the students put together class rules and publishing them on the wall. Then they fall into disuse because the teacher discovers they are difficult to enforce at all times, e.g. 'stay in your seat'.

What happens when a student needs to wash a brush, get a sheet of paper or compare notes with someone else? You could find yourself breaking off from an explanation with a group of students to attend to a request for something trivial. The aim is for the class to develop responsible behaviour. A well-managed class should offer students some freedom to attend to their own needs. You may want to control movement around the class during the establishment phase. Eventually the students will know what you expect and you can relax some of the directions.

Rules apply at all times so they can be consistent. So how do we deal with the specific behaviour required for certain activities?

GIVING DIRECTIONS

Directions are instructions and are specific to the activity the class are doing. They vary with the activities, so they cannot be enforceable all day. Rules are absolute and should be adhered to whatever is going on, e.g. 'no swearing or name-calling'. Directions are given at the start of each new activity, so do not assume the students will know how to behave for different activities. Give students clear instructions and keep them brief.

WHAT DIRECTIONS ARE NEEDED?

Begin by thinking about the lesson and what you want the students to do. List the routines and practices specific to the activities, e.g. a class test. You will want the students to be silent, keep facing the front, eyes on their own papers and hands up when they need something. Here are some of the activities you may want to think about:

- Teacher-led lessons where you stand at the board
- Work done in small groups
- Whole-class discussions
- Practical sessions with students working alone or in pairs
- Presentations by individuals or groups to the rest of the class
- Class tests, written and oral.

How will you want the students to behave? There are several options, so you need to take control. If you do not assert yourself, the students will. So tell them. Make it perfectly clear what you want. There are also many routines before the start of your teaching. Here is a list of things you could focus on:

- Lining up
- Coming into the room
- Getting ready for the start of a lesson
- Responding to questions
- Working with other students
- Using resources, apparatus and equipment
- Using a computer
- Cleaning up after practical subjects
- Leaving the room.

Consider every activity the students will be doing and make sure all activities are included. Your aim is to help the students recognise the need for rules and directions and then adopt them in their daily routines. Then they will be able to behave well whatever they are doing.

Keep directions simple so they are easy to understand. Have only a few directions so that everybody will remember them. Imagine you are doing the activity yourself and be alert for when poor behaviour could occur. Then spend some time listing the directions for the activity. Here are some examples.

Lining up outside the room

1. Stand still in single file.
2. Face the front.
3. Talk quietly or no talking.

Entering the room

1. Wait outside in line until you are told to enter.
2. Hang up your coats, put lunch boxes away.
3. Go straight to your place and take out books, pens, etc.
4. Sit with arms folded.
5. No talking.

Registration

1. Sit in seats facing the front.
2. No talking.
3. Answer 'good morning', 'good afternoon' or 'present' when your name is called.

Teaching an upfront, whole-class lesson

1. Put everything away except pen and paper.
2. Look at me. Silence.
3. Raise your hand and wait till I give you permission if you wish to speak.
4. Listen while I am speaking or while another student is speaking to me.

Working in groups

1. Stay in your seat; raise your hand if you need something.
2. Do not shout; talk quietly to each other.
3. When I give the signal to stop work, put pens on the desk and face the front.

Art, science or technology activity

1. Stay at your place; raise your hand if you need something.
2. Only one person at a sink, power tool, etc.
3. Clean and put away all the equipment, tools or paints you have used.

Class test or examination

1. Enter the examination room in silence. Do not talk until the teacher gives you permission.
2. Leave bags and coats outside or at the front of the room.
3. Sit facing the front, eyes on your own paper.
4. If you need something, raise your hand and wait in silence until a teacher comes to you.
5. Leave in silence.

Walking in corridors

1. Walk quietly, no running.
2. Walk in single file and keep to the left. (It could be the right in another school.)
3. Do not touch displays on the walls.

Assemblies

1. Enter the hall in single file, in silence and sit in class seats.
2. No talking during assembly.
3. Leave the hall in single file. No talking.

Changing for PE or swimming

1. Enter the changing room quietly. Put all clothes in your PE bag, put socks in shoes placed under the bench.
2. Line up quietly at the door in single file. (It could be in pairs at another school.)

After PE or swimming

1. Line up outside the changing room in single file. (It could be in pairs at another school.)
2. Enter quietly and go to your place.
3. Only n students in the showers at once. (Choose a value for n.)
4. Get dried, changed and line up before the bell.

Computer work

Schools will obviously have their own specific user instructions. These directions will ensure students behave appropriately in the room:
1. Stay in your seat.
2. Raise your hand when you need something. Do not call out.
3. Close programs, return to the desktop and log off.

PUBLISH YOUR RULES

Make sure you get as much support as you can by publishing the rules. Put them up on the wall in the classroom and draw the students' attention to them. Write home to the parents introducing yourself and enclose a brief description of the plan, detailing the rules, consequences and rewards you will use. The students should also receive a similar introductory letter for inclusion in the front of their folder or exercise book.

SUMMARY

- Rules should be posted on the wall and they are in effect all through the school day.
- Keep the number of rules to a minimum.
- Directions apply to specific situations and activities.
- Directions vary according to the age of the students and the requirements of the activity.
- Keep to three or four directions for each activity.

5 REWARDS AND CONSEQUENCES

DO I NEED TO GIVE REWARDS AND CONSEQUENCES?

Young people learn through their experiences how and why things are done. Actions that lead to pleasurable experiences are repeated. The teacher who encourages students to behave appropriately by rewarding them when they do things right will reinforce the behaviour (Case Study 5.1). Giving rewards has several advantages:

- Students are motivated to do well.
- Attention can be shifted from bad behaviour to good behaviour.
- Self-esteem can be boosted, leading to a positive atmosphere.
- Students of all abilities can gain recognition.

Case Study 5.1

Pete took up the post in an all-boys school in the summer term and the following September he was given a Year 9 group for technology. They had a reputation among the staff for being difficult. For the rest of term, the staff kept ribbing Pete saying, 'They are so wild, a real handful. No one can tame them.'

Well, Pete wasn't going to become their dinner. He spent the last few weeks of July watching them whenever he had a spare moment. He was interested in the way they behaved around the school. Yes, they were high-spirited and some boys seemed to be involved in some dodgy business around the school gates at home time, but he also saw some positive things. Several of the boys were acting very responsibly by bringing their younger sisters to school. In contrast, a couple of real tough nuts talked about their parents and how they were on at them because they were in trouble with the police, at school and down at the youth club. Pete gradually put together a plan to tame these 'wild animals'.

September finally came and Pete got to meet his class. Just like other new groups, there was a honeymoon period. He knew he only had about a week to do what needed to be done before they went for the jugular. He explained his plan to them and outlined how he was going to run things. He told them quite unequivocally that he expected them to behave and detailed what this meant. Then he threw in his secret weapon. 'If you guys play ball with me,' he explained, 'I will make a point of telling everyone how hard you are trying to change your image. I'll show them you can do well if you turn your mind to it.'

'Yeah, how you gonna do that?' asked Lami.

'I'm going to break up the two-hour lessons into ten-minute sections. If you behave and I don't have to speak to you, I'll put a tick against your name. If you have eight or more ticks by the end of the lesson, I will write home to your parents and let them know how helpful and responsible you have been in technology this week.'

'Why ain't we got to get all twelve ticks?' asked Steve.

'Good question, Steve. No one is perfect and I don't expect you to get it right first time. We'll start with eight ticks. That means you behaved well for over an hour of the lesson. That's good going but I will expect you to get nine ticks next week and ten the following week until you can get all twelve ticks every lesson.'

The boys listened and then Ryan chipped in, 'Well, I don't want no crappy letter sent home, it ain't worth a ****!'

Pete had anticipated this. He knew some of the boys would be resistant even though they desperately sought their parents' approval and attention. 'Give it a go, Ryan, see it as a challenge. I bet you could get eight ticks if you put your mind to it. I watched you play basketball the other week. You're no loser. You were six points down and the other team seemed all over you, but you weren't going to be beaten. You set up Lami to score the winning basket. Try this one, Ryan.'

Ryan shrugged his shoulders and turned away. He wasn't going to play ball this lesson. Pete carried on anyway. The lesson went quite well but not brilliantly, because a few of the lads tried to disrupt the others. Pete dealt with them by moving them to separate places. He did not have a proper discipline plan but he knew what he wanted. A few days later, several of the boys came charging up to him in the playground. 'Oi, Sir! My Dad got your letter. He was really surprised. He couldn't believe that someone was saying something good about me. He's taking me to the match on Saturday as a reward.'

Lami added, 'I never thought you'd bother about those letters. My mum was in tears when she read what you writ.' At the start of the next technology lesson there was a lot of buzz about the letters.

'My dad says if I get all twelve ticks, I can have a raise in my allowance!'

'My old man says if he gets another letter like this, he'll teach me to drive!'

Neither Steve nor Ryan received letters, but when they started to hear about the others they changed their minds and their behaviour. The following week they got their letters and, more importantly, their parents were very pleased and began to treat the boys differently.

Pete cracked the whole class within the month. He gained their respect because he was fair and did what he said he would do. The boys had become used to let-downs and were surprised that someone was taking notice instead of putting them down. He had found something they valued. Later he introduced other rewards but the most powerful one proved to be his word. He had kept his word and written the letters home. Doing this with a class of thirty is no mean feat and takes time. It will probably only be a short-term thing but well worth the initial investment.

Pete switched to rewards that were easier to deliver once he had control of the class. With the help of the other teachers, he started a way to help the boys behave better in their other lessons. He arranged some trips to a local car factory, a television studio and a motor racing circuit. He told the boys they could earn points to go on trips by behaving in other lessons. The teacher signed their reports at the end of each lesson and Pete updated their totals each week. The boys took to the scheme because they wanted the rewards. By the end of term, Pete had changed the class from hell into one of the best-behaved groups. The parents were pleased, the other teachers were impressed, and the boys continued to earn their trips well into the sixth form.

Motivate your students to do well

In Case Study 5.1 Pete knew he was going to have a hard ride, so he invested time and effort in the early stages of the relationship between himself and the class. He found out about them, read their files, watched them at play and worked out what made them tick. He got right to the heart of the problem – the boys craved attention and went out looking for it. They did not care how they got it, which usually meant they were in trouble in and out of school. Pete found a reward that they valued and made it possible for them to earn it. He explained what he expected and did not aim for perfection first time, although it was his ultimate target. He kept their interest by changing the rewards. The boys who behaved well got their rewards and this prompted the others to join in. The power of peer pressure motivated them. They did not want to be left out.

Increase your students' self-esteem

All too often we ignore students, only giving them attention once the situation has deteriorated. Do not let this happen. Get in there early; notice good behaviour, work and actions. Give out some positive recognition and praise the students four times more often than you reprimand them. We all like to be told we are doing things right. Pete began his lesson on a positive note and made it clear that the boys could earn his attention by being well behaved. When the parents received his letters they were surprised. Pete had done what he said; he had kept his word and the parents were pleased to hear some good news for a change. They supported his efforts by giving their sons more tangible rewards like driving lessons and days out bowling, paintballing and football matches. The letters helped the boys feel good about themselves and their parents' praise boosted their self-esteem. They discovered that they could get the attention they craved without having to misbehave or break the law. The outcome was a class of kids who felt good about themselves and were more likely to learn than those with hang-ups and poor self-images.

CELEBRATE SUCCESS

Make a point of rewarding students in front of others. This will be part of your overall plan to model the behaviour you want. If you acknowledge their efforts, they will do the same for each other. The result will be students who boost the self-images of others around them.

Telling students they are doing things right can be a powerful force in bringing the others in. This is useful during lessons when you want to streamline your activities:

'Well done, John, for raising your hand.'

You will need a slightly different approach with the older secondary students:

'Okay, Kang, you packed up quietly, so you can go first.'

You can even give out tangible rewards at the end of the lesson:

'Atif, you have earned twenty points, so you get your early lunch pass. Well done.'

There may even be opportunities to present rewards in assemblies.

PROVIDE OPPORTUNITIES FOR EVERYONE TO EARN REWARDS

Positive recognition is for everyone. Make it possible for all your students to succeed. Pete knew his class would not change their ways overnight, so he set achievable targets where the majority could experience success. The really difficult boys could not manage the whole lesson but were able to get it right during some of the ten-minute sessions. Pete praised them and encouraged them to try again next lesson. Eventually he cracked it with all the class.

Sometimes one or two students simply cannot cope. Do not give up on them. They probably need even smaller periods of time. Try five-minute intervals, or perhaps you could reduce the target to four ticks in a lesson. Treat behaviour in the same way as you would your teaching. Break up what needs to be learned into bits that the students can do, and their success will breed confidence.

The use of rewards needs to be balanced. It is easy to give them to the badly behaved to get a quiet class while the well-behaved students get overlooked (Case Study 5.2). They are the 'invisible' ones. Notice them. Give them praise and reward them as well; they deserve it.

Case Study 5.2

Samira was a very conscientious Year 8 student. She worked hard at school and always completed her homework. She was neat and well organised. She never caused any trouble, because she liked to get on with things. She enjoyed listening but would rarely volunteer any answers or join in the class discussions.

Her class had a group of badly behaved boys that tended to soak up a great deal of the teacher's time and energy. The head teacher was looking for ways to improve the results and decided to survey students on what they thought about the school. When Samira was asked, she revealed that a whole day could go by without a teacher speaking to her personally. She was one of a silent majority who were just there but not really part of what was going on. The other teachers were shocked when they heard this from the head teacher. Although they were overworked, they felt this kind of thing should not happen.

After a great deal of discussion, they decided to implement a range of new strategies. The teachers agreed to shift the emphasis by rewarding good behaviour much more frequently and tactically ignoring bad behaviour. Within weeks, Samira was a changed student. She was still conscientious and well behaved but she contributed much more to the lessons. Her self-esteem had grown once the teachers acknowledged what she'd been doing all along.

Not all students are ready to behave and do as you say. Motivating the switched-off students is becoming more and more difficult. If you have any in your class, you will really have to work with them. A positive approach is worth trying. Some students have little or no respect for teachers and harbour serious hang-ups. You will probably benefit by getting professional help in dealing with them, but your average 'bored with everything' student is likely to respond to praise and rewards.

Positive recognition and a reward system that is valued by the students will help to reduce behaviour problems and enable you to establish good working relationships with them. By raising their self-esteem, students will become more self-confident and take risks with their learning. They will offer more answers to questions, safe in the knowledge that it will not hurt if they get it wrong. They will also ask more questions and engage with their subjects, rather than being passive spectators who will only give answers when called on. Follow the rule of praising four times as much as you reprimand.

WHY DO TEACHERS FOCUS ON NEGATIVE BEHAVIOUR?

A teacher's worst nightmare is the class from hell. Have you seen it? Have you been there? If not, have you ever thought about it? Imagine. You walk into a classroom and you find kids sitting on desks chatting with their backs towards you. Several are sharing the earplugs of a portable stereo. Some are playing catch. One student is sitting in the teacher's chair going through the drawers of her desk, and swearing is coming from a group at the back. You try to call them to attention but there is no reaction. Faced with such a prospect, it is hardly surprising that teachers get anxious about some of their classes. Anxiety is part of the job and we need to manage it. So how do we do it? Have a look at Case Study 5.3.

Case Study 5.3

Janice had been given a Year 10 English class to cover because a teacher was absent. She hadn't taught the students before but she knew about their reputation. They were the bottom set and many had statements for behaviour and very low ability. As she approached the room, she could hear the racket through the open door. Suddenly something flew out and landed at her feet. She ignored it and went in as a boy was just about to leave. She put her arm across the doorway and blocked his way. He looked at her and muttered something. Janice ignored it, gave him a stern look and pointed to the seat. He turned around and swaggered off. This wasn't going to be easy.

She closed the door and calmly walked over to the desk. The noise continued and the class ignored her; one or two looked up to see who had come in. She composed herself then looked straight at a small group in the front. 'Raise your hand if you can hear what I am saying,' she said in a voice just loud enough for the students at the front to catch. A number of them heard and put up their hands. She smiled and immediately cast her eyes towards another group, on the right of the room.

'Raise your hand if you can hear what I am saying,' she repeated. They promptly put up their hands and so did one or two others in the front rows. By now there were about eight students with their hands up looking questioningly at her. Small pockets of students had broken off from what they were doing and were looking over to see what was going on. They could see the teacher was saying something but could not hear her. She shifted her gaze to one of these groups, looked straight at them and repeated herself in a voice that most could hear. Nearly everyone put up their hands. The last little group right at the back had stopped messing about and were trying to find out what they were missing. All this took place in less than a minute. Janice put her finger to her lips and made a sign for silence. When everyone was quiet, she told them to put their hands down as she had something important to say. She had gained control and kept calm in the process. Furthermore, her anxiety level had remained low.

Teachers have to keep order but when an unexpected incident occurs, they respond to it. For example, a class are working through some problems you have set when something flies across the room. Your anxiety level rises as adrenalin is pumped into your bloodstream. The conflict begins and the chase is on. You need to respond because you know you have to. Your body dislikes stress and is equipping you to deal with the problem. It is a fight-or-flight situation and the adrenalin is preparing you for one or the other so that normality can resume.

When things are going well and the class are all working quietly, you have no need to get worried. Your anxiety level is poised in case something may happen but you are fairly relaxed. There are no incidents to respond to, so you do nothing. This should not be the case; there are things you can do during quiet periods to keep your students on task (Case Study 5.4).

Case Study 5.4

John was very keen on positive recognition of achievement. He had been teaching the class for three weeks and had set up his behaviour code during that time. There was still a considerable amount of work to do but he was determined to succeed. The students were working from the textbook in pairs and had been told to do it quietly. John did not sit at the desk and watch, he moved around the room stopping to give a word of encouragement or praise every so often. 'You are getting on well, Kim. Keep it up.' Kim beamed with pride. 'That's a good answer, Brian. I wondered whether anyone would discover that. Well done. Good work, girls. Keep it up and you'll both get merit points at the end of the lesson.'

In Case Study 5.4 the students were obviously pleased when John praised them and they seemed to swell with pride. The behaviour remained good throughout the lesson and the level of concentration and motivation increased rather than decreased. John is an example of a teacher who works on maintaining good behaviour even when things are going well. Focusing on the positive behaviour and anticipating problems before they arise are the keys to keeping stress levels down and avoiding irrational and unfair responses to undesirable behaviour.

WHAT REWARDS CAN I GIVE?

There are two ways of giving rewards. You can give them to individual students or to the whole class. Rewards should always be in proportion to the achievement. Valuable rewards should not be given away easily. For example, you would expect students to behave consistently well over a period of time to earn an early lunch pass. Tailoring your rewards to the age of the students is essential. Year 10 students would probably appreciate some free time on the computers whereas Year 7 students may prefer to go to lunch early. Rewards need to be given consistently and fairly. Students will compare and question the distribution of rewards, so have clear criteria. Do not use your rewards as sanctions. Avoid giving them out then taking them away later in the day if a student does not behave properly. Try to use alternative consequences; after all, they earned the rewards fairly. There are many rewards you can give. Here are some examples.

Praise

Praise is easily given and greatly appreciated. Make a point of praising as many students during the day as you can. It is very easy to fall into the trap of expecting good behaviour as a matter of course. The student might need to make a great effort to do something that you regard as normal. Praise costs nothing to give and needs no organisation to deliver.

House points or merit points

Your school may already be using house points or merit points to encourage the students. Points are given on an individual basis but are included in a team challenge.

Merit points differ as they may count towards special awards such as certificates and privileges.

Free time

Free time can be given to students of all ages. You allocate a set time at the end of the lesson, day or week for the students to choose from a range of activities you provide. They earn free time either individually or as a whole class through good behaviour and effort.

First in a queue

First in line for break, lunch or end of school can be extremely effective as it links up with other pleasures. For example, the student who gets out of class first will be nearer the front of the queue for the tuck shop, dinner or the school bus. They will have a longer break and more time. They will be able to meet friends from other classes earlier and they will have a free feeling by getting out first. It is amazing how responsive students can be when getting out first is used as an incentive to behave.

Letters, postcards and telephone calls home

Letters, postcards and phoning home are powerful motivators for students of all ages. Parents like to hear good news about their children and it helps you to establish good links between the school and the home. Writing letters and making calls does consume valuable time and it would be easier not to bother, given all the demands made on a teacher. However, it is a good investment and the students will soon come to value your calls highly. Letters and telephone calls take up more of your time, so you should want more in return. One way they can be used is within a hierarchical reward system that positively recognises good behaviour (Table 5.1).

Table 5.1 *A hierarchical reward system that positively recognises good behaviour*

Action	Reward
First sign of good behaviour	1 stamp* or point
Further good behaviour	1 stamp each time
10 stamps	1 postcard home
20 stamps	1 personalised letter home
30 stamps	1 telephone call home
Stamps are ready-inked with motifs like a star or the words 'Well done'.	

This cycle can be repeated throughout the year. You can keep a record of what each student has received, which may be useful when writing annual reports to parents. Figure 5.1 (overleaf) is an example of a postcard home to a parent.

A personalised letter goes a step further. You have more space to describe how well the student has been doing. You can word-process it and use the 'replace' facility to change the name and the gender words, e.g. his and hers, she and he. Figure 5.2 shows an example. You should aim to send positive letters home by mid-year to most of the parents of the students you teach.

---

12 October 200X

Dear Mr and Mrs Brown

I am writing to let you know how hard .... has been working recently. He has made a real effort to behave well in my lessons. You should be very proud of him.

Yours sincerely

Mr David Wright
Class teacher

Figure 5.1   *Postcard home to a parent*

---

12 October 200X

Dear Mrs Brown

I am writing to let you know how pleased I am with Sally's attitude and commitment to her studies in art.

I run a scheme to reward children who exhibit the right behaviour and enthusiasm needed to do well. Sally has excelled in these requirements, which has prompted me to inform you because I know how much pleasure it can bring to hear that one's child is doing well at school. I am extremely pleased with Sally's approach and if she continues in this way, she will be developing valuable study skills.

Sally is showing a very conscientious attitude doing her homework. She is working well and I was particularly impressed by the way that she organised her time to get her homework in ahead of deadlines. I hope that reading this letter gives you as much pleasure as it gave me to send. You should be extremely proud of Sally and I look forward to reporting further successes to you.

Best wishes

David Wright
Sally's teacher for art

Figure 5.2   *Letter home to a parent*

The most prized reward will be the telephone call to parents. Other authors of books on behaviour tend to suggest that the telephone call comes before postcards and letters. This can be problematic and time-consuming because parents are not always easy to contact. You may have to wait until later in the evening, which is an inconvenience. But if you telephone after sending a letter, the parents will be used to hearing good things from the school and the conversation will go smoothly. Case Study 5.5 is a suggestion for a call home to a parent.

Case Study 5.5

I really wanted to tell you how well Neela has been doing in my class. She has been putting a great deal of effort into her work and has produced some very interesting essays recently. She has set a wonderful example to the other students and her efforts have motivated them to try harder as well. I am really pleased with her progress and know that she will go on to do extremely well if she keeps this up. You must be very proud of her. Please tell her I rang.

Privilege pass

Students earn passes giving them special privileges not available to everybody. Here are some examples:

- First in line for lunch
- First choice of games in the IT room
- Seconds at lunch time
- First in line at the tuck shop.

They should be used sparingly by teachers and valued highly by the students. Lunch is a great motivator as the choice becomes limited towards the end. Going into the dinner hall first enables the student to choose their favourite meal. The pass can be used whenever the student likes. Here are some other rewards that you could give:

- Certificates
- Extra computer time
- Sitting by a friend for one lesson
- Earning free time
- A special note in the end-of-year report
- Home visits
- Captaincy of a table, team or class
- Mentoring younger students
- Vouchers for local stores
- End-of-term, out-of-school trips
- Afternoon tea with the head teacher.

CAN I GIVE REWARDS TO THE WHOLE CLASS?

It is useful to have rewards that the whole class can work towards. This encourages the students to work together cooperatively and uses peer pressure in helping them to learn new behaviour. It is a good way of dealing with a particular problem in the class and therefore it is best done as and when needed rather than all year long.

The sorts of rewards that the whole class can earn include free time, no homework one evening, a video (best done at the end of term) or a trip out of school. It is useful to ask the students what they would like to ensure they all buy into it. Once established, make sure the reward can be earned within a suitable time period. Usually the younger students will need to earn it in a shorter time than the older students. Award points and record them on the board or a noticeboard where the whole class can see them.

Rewarding desirable behaviour helps you to shift the emphasis away from the negative response towards the positive. Reinforcing the behaviour you want will turn your classroom into a place where students will want to be. They will learn the appropriate behaviour through being motivated by the rewards. By acknowledging their efforts, you are also helping students to improve their own self-esteem. Confident students with good self-images are more likely to learn well.

WHY DO I NEED CONSEQUENCES?

If rewards work and students are motivated by them, why introduce consequences? What is the point? Why punish undesirable behaviour? Case Study 5.6 may help to explain.

Case Study 5.6

Wayne was very interested in the positive approach to behaviour. He could see how it would help him manage his own classes. He had two Year 9 English groups that were particularly difficult and he felt he was failing with them. They were getting worse and by half-term he was feeling fed up. He decided to use a reward system to get them back. He explained what they had to do to earn points and offered them a range of tangible rewards. The students seemed excited about the rewards.

It went well in the first few weeks. Everyone started earning points and the behaviour improved. Then things began to go wrong, Several boys were talking during a period of silent writing. Wayne noticed and went over to them. 'Come on, boys, this is silent work. You know that you can only earn points if you follow directions. I won't be able to give you a point this session, because you are talking.'

'Oh that's not fair!' they remonstrated, 'We were only talking a little bit.'

'Sorry, boys, but that's the way it is. You chose to break the rules.' Wayne did not get angry or drawn into their conversation. He focused on the broken rule and reinforced the fact that they had chosen to talk. He redirected them to the task and started to walk away.

'I don't want your stupid points anyway,' called out one of the boys in an aggressive way.

Wayne turned round and came back. 'Right, Paul, I will deduct some of your points for that outburst.'

'Hey, why? You said we could earn points and I earned them. Now you're taking them away. Well stuff it!' Paul slammed his book shut and stared angrily out of the window.

Wayne had done his best. He had introduced a very sound reward system. It was carefully organised, the points were awarded accurately and everyone in the class knew what they had to do to earn them. The weakness with the system was the lack of consequences. When something went wrong, Wayne had to invent consequences. Detention and removal from the room were too hard for something like talking during quiet work. Wayne had no option but to redirect and let it go. However, the insolence that resulted led to Wayne feeling he should not only withhold points, but also deduct them. The minor incident flared into a more serious one, leaving Wayne feeling that he had failed.

Consequences are choices not punishments. When you construct your behaviour code, your aim will be to help your students choose the responsible behaviour. The rules establish the boundaries and any students who step over the line choose the consequence instead of the reward. In Case Study 5.6 Wayne was not offering his class a choice that could lead towards good behaviour. Effective consequences need to have three characteristics:

- *They are something the student chooses*: students know that when they misbehave they are choosing the consequence over the reward.
- *They are dislikable*: the consequence is not a punishment but it is something that students will not want again.
- *They are appropriate to the incident*: the consequence does not need to be really severe for it to work.

IF YOU DO THAT THEN THIS WILL HAPPEN

There are logical consequences that occur when the adult intervenes by making a connection between the behaviour and the outcome:

'If you don't do up your shoelaces, you will trip over them.'

'If you put your hand in the fire, you will burn it.'

There is a connection between the cause and the effect. Parents need to teach their children these basic relationships to keep them healthy and safe. The children learn that if they do something, then something else will happen. We can build on this and once the rules are established, there can be an obvious progression (Figure 5.3).

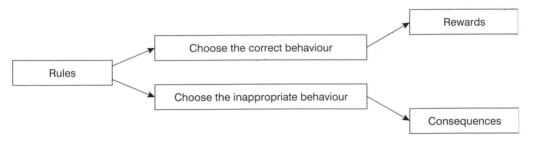

Figure 5.3 *The connection between behaviour and outcome*

As long as you stick to your approach by consistently rewarding the right behaviour and giving consequences for inappropriate behaviour, the students will learn how to act and behave in school. They will learn the link between their behaviour and the outcome and they will be in control of the choices between rewards and consequences.

LINK THE INCIDENT TO THE CONSEQUENCE

When a student breaks a rule or fails to follow a direction, the logical outcome must be a consequence. In a climate of taking responsibility for behaviour, choice becomes paramount. The emphasis must always be on the students making the choices. It is not you telling them to misbehave, they are choosing to. First you make every student in the class aware that you are helping them to behave properly by giving choices. You are offering them the choice between the reward and the consequence and then it is up to them. Therefore the consequence must be linked to the behaviour. For example, a student who drops litter picks up litter during break. Using equipment in an unsafe way will result in working without it or doing a different activity. The students will understand these consequences and grow to learn that the consequence is something they choose. Unrelated consequences such as lines in detention or staying back after school in silence in a room will make them feel that you are punishing them, because there is no direct connection.

The most effective consequences are directly linked to the incidents. So if a student is kept back in detention, they should spend the time writing about the incident. They should describe what happened, how they broke the rule and what they will do to fix things. This is a powerful method of putting things right if used sensitively and carefully.

USE PROBLEM SHEETS

It is not always clear who is responsible when an incident happens. While you were working with a group, something may have happened over the other side of the room. An incident may have occurred out in the playground and you find yourself having to deal with it. A problem sheet (Figure 5.4) is a very good way of defusing the situation. It enables you to split up those involved and get at the truth through their accounts.

I am upset because	Other people involved	This is what I said
This is what they said	**This is how it happened**	**This is what I will do to fix things**

Figure 5.4   *A problem sheet*

Each student is given a problem sheet. They describe how they were upset, who else was involved, what was said and how it happened. They have to consider what they will do to try to fix things and prevent it happening again. This places the responsibility back with the students and enables them to repair the situation by adopting a more sensible approach next time. You can also use problem sheets to compare the accounts and weigh up who was the perpetrator. There is a direct link between the behaviour and the consequence as the students complete the forms in isolation or detention.

How do i present consequences as choices?

Your skill as a teacher will help you present consequences as choices. Your students must see consequences as their choice. They will learn how to behave in your room if they feel they are in control and that is what you want. You are teaching your students to behave responsibly, not just to comply with your rules. Compliant behaviour lacks responsibility. You want your students to behave in the same way for other teachers as they do for you, so it is important that they understand what is required of them. Your behaviour plan should be in operation whether you are in front of the class or not. Teaching them how to behave will also help if you are away, because the rewards and consequences can be applied by whoever is covering for you. Your aim is to get the students to follow rules and directions in an organised and efficient way. The key is to make sure they know that consequences are inevitable if they do not behave appropriately (Case Study 5.7).

Case Study 5.7

Jane has been talking and disrupting the other students around her. The teacher cannot let her continue. Action is needed. 'Jane, this is silent work. Either you work in silence or you will have to move to a desk on your own.' The teacher is placing the decision with Jane and it is up to her to decide. She stops for a few minutes then starts talking again. 'Jane, I expected your cooperation but you have chosen to talk, so you will have to move. Stand up and bring your things over here.' The teacher re-emphasises that Jane chose to talk and has therefore chosen the consequence.

Giving the students a choice shifts the action from you to them. You will no longer be the ogre who deals out punishments and the students will cease to be victims. They cannot complain that things are unfair, because they were fully aware of the consequences of their actions. Jane had to sit at the desk on her own because she chose to talk rather than work in silence. Students who are in control are able to develop and become confident. This improves their self-image. When they make a mistake, they know it is something temporary and can be put right. The focus shifts from the student to the behaviour itself.

When should i give a consequence?

Consequences may be given immediately or postponed until later depending on the circumstances (Case Study 5.8). There will be times when the consequence needs to be applied during the lesson. Breaking the rules of no swearing or fighting, or using up a number of warnings in the discipline hierarchy should result in an immediate consequence. In Case Study 5.8 the student had the choice and decided to break the rule knowing that the consequence would follow immediately.

Case Study 5.8

Steve had been teaching the Year 8 geography group for a term. He had a behaviour code and the students knew what to expect when they did **not** behave appropriately. Craig came into the room and slumped down, giving off very negative vibes. Steve noted his behaviour but ignored it while he got the rest of the group started on the work. Then he went over to him.

'You haven't written anything yet, Craig. Do you need some help?'

'This is boring.' Craig slouched, pouted and fiddled with his pen. 'I can do this stuff, it's too easy. Can't we do something more interesting?'

Steve ignored the secondary behaviour. 'You may think it is boring but it is the work we are doing today. Would you like some help?' He refocused Craig on the work by cleverly agreeing with him.

'I'm not doing it, it's stupid.' He slouched further into the chair.

'Well, Craig, I'm here to help you do it. If you choose not to do it now, you will have to do it later. You know our rule, all class work must be completed even if you don't finish it in the lesson. Now let's see you begin.' Steve does not offer any further help but turns away expecting Craig to start work. Craig can choose to do the work in the lesson or later on, either in detention or at home.

SHOULD I EXPECT THE STUDENT TO COMPLY IMMEDIATELY?

Students react to situations differently and respond to directions at different rates. You will need to exercise patience and give them a little time if you want to avoid getting into conflict. Choices need to be considered and students do not always know what to choose straightaway:

'Michael, put the mobile away or on my desk.'

The choice is offered. Michael starts to think about his choice. You turn away and continue with what you were doing, expecting Michael to decide. Here are some other examples of waiting:

'Stop talking or come and sit at my desk.'

'Sit down or come and stand at the front.'

'Use the ruler properly or give it to me.'

'Turn round and continue your work or stay back at break to do it.'

Figure 5.5 explains what is happening in all these examples.

Figure 5.5 *Students need take-up time to consider their choices*

You continue to keep an eye on the student, scanning the whole class and checking progress while you are teaching. These examples contain a consequence as a choice. You allow time for the student to decide then act if necessary. Note there are no warnings. You want the disruption to stop and the students to learn that they are making the decision not you.

How do I prevent consequences from becoming punishments?

Consequences follow from poor choices. The students bring the consequences on themselves. Therefore the consequences need to be suitably distasteful so the students will remember them next time a similar situation arises. Furthermore, you need to guard against getting angry and giving out consequences when you are not in control of yourself, for example:

'That's it! You can sit on your own for the rest of the lesson!'

'Right, you're in detention. That'll teach you!'

'I'm fed up with you. You're going to regret it!'

The students will learn to hate you rather than realising what they did wrong. Your aim is to use the consequence to help them realise they have made the wrong choice. Consequences should be in proportion to the behaviour. Using a consequence that is too severe will lead to bad feelings:

'You have had your three warnings, Stephen, and you chose to continue talking so you will stay after school and write out . . . two hundred times.'

The teacher is being too harsh. He may want to keep the student back but writing out so many lines will take a considerable time. Stephen will end up feeling bitter. He did not really do anything serious. Very severe consequences are better saved for serious incidents.

Dropping litter should lead to being a member of the litter patrol. Writing graffiti on the walls should lead to cleaning it off. Breaking or damaging school property should be paid for either with the student's own money or by doing jobs. Alternatively, the student could forgo a school trip and the money could be used to pay for the damage. Making a mess in the art, cookery or technology room could result in staying back and cleaning up. Fighting or hurting others in the playground should result in losing the right to spend break at the same time as the rest of the school. In very serious cases the school may suspend the student.

You may wish to obtain their account in writing (Figure 5.4, page 85) so you can help them see where they went wrong. Letters of apology are also a good way of making the point. The letter could be sent home for the parent to sign before it is given back to the teacher.

Do my consequences need to be harsh?

The most effective consequences are not necessarily the most severe. The students need to see the consequences happen every time, so they should be easy to apply. Remember that if you give a detention, it is your own time you are giving up, so make sure you are prepared to do that. Once you have gone beyond warnings, the consequences should happen and they need to be uncomfortable but not necessarily harsh. Most of the class will behave well once you begin your plan, so do not set things up that target the few poorly behaved students, because the consequence will need to be applied to everyone.

A consequence should be uncomfortable enough to remind the student that they made the wrong choice. In less serious cases, such as failing to follow directions, use warnings first. Once a student has received all the warnings you can give, the consequence should be administered within the room. For example, they may have to move to a different desk or work away from the rest of the group for five or ten minutes. Continual disruption after this consequence could lead to a deferred consequence after the lesson or at the end of school. When possible, holding the student back for one minute is a very powerful consequence. It does not cause any disruption to your own routine and makes the student feel isolated because everybody else has left and the new class are waiting to come in. It is quick and effective. This consequence will generally work for 90% of the daily disruptions within the room. There may be some harder cases to deal with. Students who continue to behave in an unacceptable way will move on to the next set of consequences within your staged response. These consequences will be progressively more severe and need to involve more people such as the head of year, special educational needs coordinator (SENCO) or parents.

STRATEGIES WITHIN THE CLASS

Let's see how this staged response works in practice (Case Study 5.9). The class is a Year 9 English set. The teacher has just taken them on mid-year and is beginning to coach the students in how he wants them to behave. He has a number of quite difficult kids. The class are predominantly working-class, coming from an area with considerable unemployment, ethnic diversity and one-parent families. They could not be described as easy.

Case Study 5.9

Des was introducing *Romeo and Juliet* to the class. He began by reminding the students of the behaviour he was expecting and how the rewards and consequences would work. He introduced the topic and explained the directions for the activities. The students were working in small groups on a script for a meeting between Romeo and Juliet. They had to imagine it was set in a club in modern times. Des noticed that one group was rather loud – a boy was out of his seat and acting the fool.

'It's good to see you so enthusiastic, Tom, but you should be sitting down.'

'I was just getting into the part!'

'Good, now quieten down and let's see you get your script started.' Des smiled and turned away expecting the group to do as they were asked. However, Tom was not that easily calmed and he continued to distract. Des returned a few minutes later and spoke directly to Tom.

'I asked you to work quietly in your seat. You have chosen to ignore me and continue to wander, so that's a warning.' Des had a clipboard with a behaviour log (see Appendices). He wrote Tom's name on it and put a mark in the first response column.

Tom went back to his seat and rejoined his group. Des watched him out the corner of his eye and noticed that he seemed very unsettled. He resumed his rounds monitoring and supporting the groups. A few minutes later the disturbance began again; this time Tom was fooling around and showing off to the girls in the group. Des returned and spoke to Tom.

'You are still standing up and making excessive noise, Tom. I've had to speak to you twice already. I want you to move to the seat by the window and work on your own for the rest of this activity.'

Tom might have realised he had gone too far and calmed down. Often the student realises they have used up all their warnings, and the first consequence is sufficient. However, Tom was obviously acting differently on this occasion. Des would have liked to discuss his behaviour with him but he did not have the time during the lesson, so he kept to the staged response and hoped that Tom calmed down once he was away from his group.

Things did not improve and Tom continued to be very disruptive, so Des had to intervene again. 'Tom, you are choosing to disturb the rest of the class rather than get on with your work, so the next consequence will be to stay back after the lesson for two minutes unless you stop now and work quietly.'

Tom ignored Des. The demands of the class mean that sometimes there is little you can do with a student behaving like Tom, and this is where many teachers become frustrated. Things do not seem to be working and it looks like the situation is deteriorating. In reality things are not getting worse. Tom continued to make poor choices but Des stuck to his behaviour code and didn't get sucked in. He could have lost his patience and got into a full-blown conflict with shouting and frayed tempers, but that would have been harmful to the rest of the class. The solution was to have Tom removed from the room so he could do no more harm to himself or the other students.

EXITING A STUDENT FROM THE ROOM

A time will come when a student's behaviour is unacceptable. They can no longer engage with the work and need some time to cool off and calm down. A student who is failing to respond after a period of time is obstructing the other students' right to learn and feel safe and should be exited from the room.

It is common practice in secondary schools to make a student stand outside the room. If you are going to do this, check that this is in line with school practice. The student should use the time to cool off and be expected to sit quietly. You should limit it to five to ten minutes and make it obvious that you expect them to return to work after that time. The drawbacks are that they may try to distract others or they may wander off and then you have a bigger problem to deal with. Other teachers passing by may ask the student questions and this gives them attention they should not be getting. Instead they should ignore them or just say a quick hello and walk on.

When you have no choice but to exit a student from your room, do it as unobtrusively as possible. You should explain to the whole class when you first set up your behaviour plan that being sent out is a consequence you will use. Make sure you have agreed the procedure with the other teachers. Some schools may have a designated place where the student should be sent. If this is not the practice in your school but you feel you will want to exit students when necessary, it is worth ensuring that:

- You have an arrangement with another teacher so they can go and sit in their room.
- You send work with a student that they can do without requiring help.
- You keep a record of the incidents that led to exiting the student.

Excluding a student from class is a serious step and you may find it makes you feel considerably stressed. It is therefore important to plan how you will do it. Aim to warn the student in advance that it could be a consequence you will have to use. Remind them of the rule and ask if there is a problem then redirect them to the task and offer to talk about it as soon as you have time. Here are some basic guidelines to consider when exiting a student:

- *Keep calm*: use an assertive voice and do not shout. Try to control your anger and do not express your feelings at this point.
- *Keep your distance*: do not invade a student's personal space.
- *Avoid making threats*: do not make statements about what may happen. Stick to the procedure for your school.
- *Focus on the behaviour*: focus on the rule that has been broken and the rights of the other students.

Students who are beginning to behave in a way that will cause them to be exited from the room should be warned they are reaching that point:

'Robert. If you continue to . . . I will have to ask you to leave our class.'

This will ensure the student knows that exit will be the next step and you will avoid getting emotionally entangled.

GAINING SUPPORT FROM COLLEAGUES

Make sure you have discussed exit procedures with your colleagues and everyone is aware of what will happen. Always keep notes for use once things have calmed down. Your behaviour log sheets and a short written account of what was said and done will be sufficient. The aim is to exit the student with the minimum disturbance and then rebuild the relationship once the student has had the consequence. You should contact the form teacher, the head of year and the parents because there may be something going on outside school that has a bearing on the student's reason for behaving in this way. Keeping parents informed from an early point fosters good relationships, ensures everyone is working together and if it gets to a fixed-term exclusion, everyone concerned will know why.

WHAT HAPPENS IF THE STUDENT WON'T LEAVE THE ROOM?

Difficult students may refuse when directed and there needs to be a procedure to assist their removal. Generally, a student will dig themselves into a situation that is hard to get out of. They become cornered and will react in the same way as a frightened animal. They will freeze, run and hide, spit and snarl, or belligerently cling to anchorages affording safety or protection. They will say and do things that they will regret later. Once a student has sworn at a teacher, lashed out or done something equally serious, they know they are in a crisis that is hard to redeem.

When a student is directed to leave and they refuse, you are in a win-lose conflict. Either you win and they lose face or they stay put, deadlock occurs and you are the loser in front of the rest of the class. One effective strategy is to allow the student an advocate. This is usually another member of staff and not necessarily someone more senior, because the student will see them as an authority figure representing the school and will lose face if they give in to them.

Many secondary schools have behaviour mentors. They are often drawn from the learning support assistants and have special responsibilities for students with behavioural and emotional difficulties. Their different status enables them to form relationships with students as advocates that can be useful during times of crisis. Leave the student alone and do not attempt any further contact with them until the advocate arrives. They should then call the student from the room. This is done calmly, quietly and assertively:

'Robert, come with me please.'

The student now has a way out with a neutral third party that prevents loss of face. The advocate should follow an agreed procedure that will help the student to calm down, consider their choices and begin the rebuilding process with the teacher.

Alternatively, tell the class they are going either to the hall or outside to do a short activity that they will really enjoy. Leave the room but inform a colleague that the student is still in the room and needs to be monitored. Once you are gone the student will probably go with the other adult without any further problems.

CHECKLIST FOR A CLASSROOM EXIT PROCEDURE

- When will you use the exit procedure?
- Did you warn the student? (Not applicable for serious incidents.)
- What will you do if they refuse to leave?
- Have you organised the exit procedure with other staff and do you have advocates if you need them?
- Have you a recording process?
- How will you follow up later?
- Have you involved the parents, form teacher and head of year?
- What will be the consequence for the student?
- How will you rebuild the relationship with the student?

SUMMARY

- Rewards and consequences are needed to motivate the students to choose the right behaviour.
- Refocus your attention and catch the students being good rather than bad.
- Rewards can be given to individuals and to the whole class.
- Consequences should never be given to the whole class, only those who chose to break the rule.
- Consequences must be inevitable and where possible they should match the behaviour.

- Exiting a student from the room is serious and should only be used as a last resort or during a serious incident.
- Always warn the student when they are getting near to being exited from the room.
- Have an arrangement with other staff for sending students to them when they are being exited.
- Send work with a student when they go to another room.
- Organise an advocate for when you have a student who refuses to leave.
- Consequences do not need to be harsh, just dislikable.
- Always repair and rebuild the relationship after the consequence has been completed.
- Aim to replace extrinsic rewards with intrinsic ones so the students know what is acceptable behaviour.

6 EMBEDDING THE BEHAVIOUR CODE IN YOUR TEACHING

Learning is a journey of discovery. It begins in the early stages of a child's life when he starts to make the connections between his actions and the effects. As self-awareness develops, the child starts to identify himself as an individual person with his own needs and desires. The world becomes a fascinating place with so many mysteries waiting to be explored. Anyone who has had children of their own or worked with young infants will know that they seem to be so full of questions about everything they experience.

Children come to school with this thirst for knowledge about the world. So what happens during those eleven years? Why do some children get switched off whereas others take off and pursue their chosen careers? As teachers, we have expectations. We know we must teach our students what they need to know so they stand a chance of passing their certificate examinations. They do not come to school knowing everything already but some do have a greater disposition to learn than others. The same goes for their behaviour. Some students will be better equipped before they come to school than others and this is due to the nurturing and parental bonding they have received at home:

- Some will pick things up more quickly than others.
- Some will have difficulties learning and need alternative strategies.
- Some will regard you as a leader in their journey of discovery.
- Some will find it so difficult to learn certain things that even your attempts to help may not work.
- Some will need the support of their parents more than others.

Teachers who expect students to behave but do not make their expectations clear will find them trying to guess and not always getting it right. This leads to misunderstandings as the teacher interprets their errors as poor behaviour. It can easily be avoided by teaching new groups the behaviour code. The difficulty many secondary teachers have is the pressure of time. They have to cover the syllabus, prepare the class for the tests and demonstrate success with results. It can seem a hard decision to use precious time at the beginning of the school year on things outside the syllabus content. Many teachers would like to launch straight into the course of study while the students are still keen and fresh. However, investing time getting the routines, rules and methods of studying right at the outset will ensure the whole class know what you want. Furthermore, you will be reinforcing your position as the teacher and adult in the room. It is not just the younger groups that will need this. All students will benefit from reminders at the start of a new school year or term.

Streaming and setting can result in certain kinds of students being together in the same class. Groups of students with below-average ability may include some who are having difficulty with their behaviour. Most teachers will be aware of this and plan accordingly. The danger comes when a teacher who is less confident managing behaviour finds himself with an above-average ability group and assumes they will behave well.

Students do not necessarily behave well because they are bright. There will always be some who will want to test the teacher, some who are not challenged intellectually and some who are good at school work but are less mature and act in silly ways.

Investing the time establishing the correct classroom climate is worthwhile. The higher ability students are likely to adapt more rapidly, so you may need less time to establish the system. The less able will need more time to process and practise the rules and routines. They will also need to revisit what they have been learning to make absolutely sure they know what you are asking them to do. Therefore you need to build in time to teach the code in the same way as you would include things like fire drills and health and safety procedures.

WHAT ANY LEARNING PROCESS SHOULD INCLUDE

- *Context*: give the students the big picture. Help them understand why good behaviour is necessary and how it will help them to learn.
- *Anchoring*: begin with the familiar and show how the new knowledge and skills stem from it. Help the students remember new things by anchoring them in their minds to memorable experiences.
- *Organisation and processing*: new things need to be filed in the brain in ways that will make sense when they are retrieved. Break down ideas into small chunks and show how they are connected by using mind maps, lists, groups and categories. This will help the students commit them to their short-term memory in a logical way. For example, you could attach rewards to the notion of choice. When going through sets of directions for different routines, group things like technology and art or PE and assemblies.
- *Consolidation*: get students to explain to each other what they have learned. Telling someone else what you have just learned will help you understand it yourself.
- *Long-term memory*: revisit what you have taught a few days later. Devise activities that enable the class to use what they have learned in a different way. Help them tackle different problems and find solutions, drawing on their new knowledge. Using it in a variety of ways creates a number of links to it in the brain. Making more links will increase the likelihood of remembering it. The more links there are, the greater the opportunity to remember it. In this way, the students will be taking what they have learned and committing it to their long-term memory.
- *Practice*: practising and using new things will strengthen the links and pathways within the brain and make it easier to remember.

WHERE TO BEGIN

What

Teach the following:

- Rights and responsibilities of everyone in the class
- Reasons for having a behaviour code
- What could go into the code
- Your approach, which will be based on choices
- How you will recognise good behaviour
- The consequences of poor choices.

How

Design special lessons that will help your students to contribute to the behaviour code and to learn it. Use discussion and involve everyone. Brainstorm and mind-map ideas on the board. Then practise some of the routines with the whole class to test and refine them.

When

Do not feel you have to spend the whole of the lesson. Short bursts may suit your groups better. Revisit and remind the students of what they have learned at the start of each lesson. Five to ten minutes may be adequate for this.

A commonly held understanding

The basis of a behaviour code is a commonly held understanding of the rights and responsibilities of the individual. Students are able to engage quite effectively with this notion and it can be reinforced in other areas of the curriculum such as citizenship, religious education and history. Many students will have a strong sense of justice and should be actively encouraged to join in and contribute to drawing up a class behaviour code with you. They will not be able to do it without your help. You may have to assist them in making the links between choices and negative consequences. This chapter includes some activities that will help your students engage with the ideas and guide them towards your own objectives.

The experience of drawing up the rules may not be a new one for your groups. Many students may have done it with other teachers. The difference will be in things like the hierarchy of responses, the rewards and consequences, and the subtleties between rules and directions. The beauty of having a code is that it gives you an enormous confidence boost, so the next time a class gets difficult you will feel prepared. Here are two advantages of having a behaviour code:

- Your students will be aware of their choices and know what the consequences will be.
- You will become more consistent in the way you deal with the many different incidents that occur, and this will minimise any chance of shooting from the hip or overreacting.

SAMPLE SPECIAL LESSONS

Boxes 6.1 to 6.7 contain some activities that have proved successful. You may want to use them as they are or adapt them to suit your own purposes. Like any lesson, you will need to gather the resources and prepare the delivery. The suggested sessions that follow can be as long or as short as you choose. Sometimes it is better to keep everything as short and direct as possible, because the students need the system in place to help them immediately. This will probably be the case for teachers taking new groups mid-year or supply teachers who are filling short-term absences. When you have new groups at the start of the year, there will be more time to spend teaching the behaviour code, so these ideas could be used. Times are not specified for individual activities, so you can decide how long to make them for yourself. As a guide, most of the activities should be between five and twenty minutes long.

Box 6.1: What makes a good teacher? _____

Objective: To identify the qualities of a good teacher.

Resources: Whiteboard or flip chart, marker pens, Figure 6.1.

Activity: As a whole class, brainstorm what the students feel makes a good teacher. Write up all the ideas no matter how outrageous they seem. Impress on the students the contractual obligations that teachers have then review the list to remove any suggestions that would be impossible. Show the students how to connect their chains of thought. For example, the suggestion that the teacher 'helps us if we make a mistake' can lead to 'not taking the mickey if we get something wrong'.

Keywords: Respect, sense of humour, interested, flexible, mistakes, protects, fair, consistent, approachable, believes, fun, firm, friendly, knowledgeable, helpful, kind.

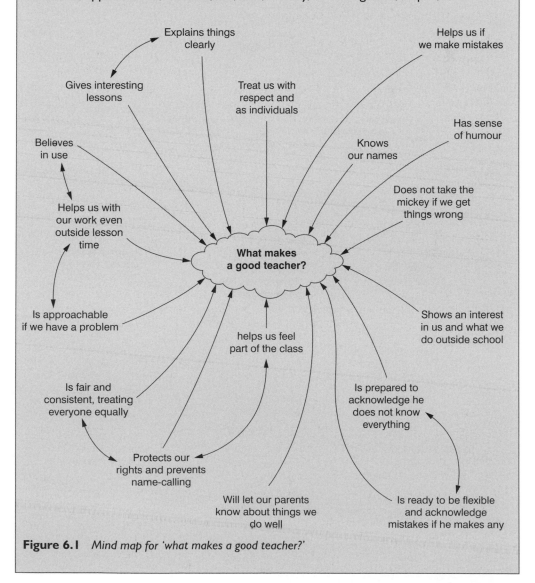

Figure 6.1 *Mind map for 'what makes a good teacher?'*

Box 6.2: What makes a good student?

Objective: To identify the qualities of a good student.
Resources: Whiteboard or flip chart, marker pens, Figure 6.2.
Activity: Begin in pairs and spend two minutes thinking of things that would make a good student. Then each pair share their ideas with the whole class and record them as a mind map. Links could be made with the ideas from Box 6.1. For example, 'listening when someone is speaking' can link back to 'being aware of the feelings of others'.
Keywords: Listens, speaks kindly, mistakes, support, preferred learning styles, boundaries, example, deadlines, homework, helpful, organised, prepared, asks questions, tidy, neat, legible, clever, determined.

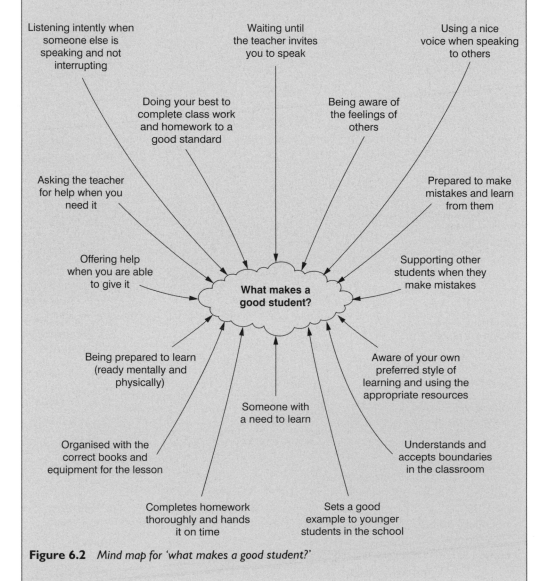

Figure 6.2 *Mind map for 'what makes a good student?'*

Box 6.3: Linking rights and responsibilities _____

Objective: To identify and list some rights and responsibilities of students.

Resources: Whiteboard or flip chart, marker pens, Figures 6.1 and 6.2.

Activity 1: Discuss the rights of the individual in our society. Talk through the links between rights and responsibilities and how everyone in the community has a responsibility to uphold the rights of the individual. List the rights and responsibilities of students and teachers.

Activity 2: Working in pairs or small groups, talk about one right from the list and try to find the role of the teacher and the students in protecting it. What do they each have to do to uphold it?

Keywords: Right, responsibility, uphold, support, protect, safe, secure, laws, opportunities, individual, community, opinions, boundaries, freedom, fair.

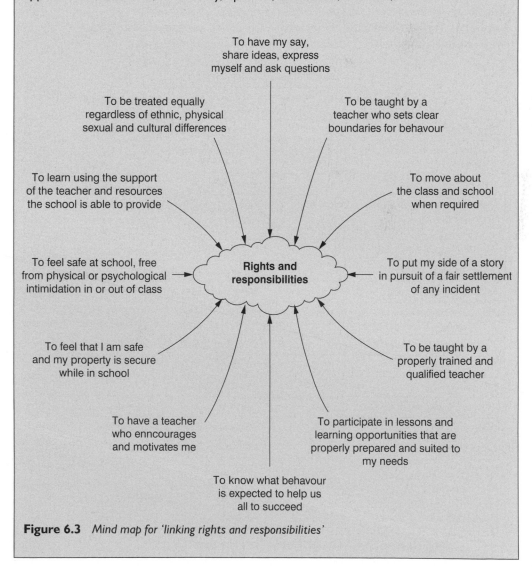

To have my say, share ideas, express myself and ask questions

To be treated equally regardless of ethnic, physical sexual and cultural differences

To be taught by a teacher who sets clear boundaries for behaviour

To learn using the support of the teacher and resources the school is able to provide

To move about the class and school when required

To feel safe at school, free from physical or psychological intimidation in or out of class

Rights and responsibilities

To put my side of a story in pursuit of a fair settlement of any incident

To feel that I am safe and my property is secure while in school

To be taught by a properly trained and qualified teacher

To have a teacher who enncourages and motivates me

To participate in lessons and learning opportunities that are properly prepared and suited to my needs

To know what behaviour is expected to help us all to succeed

Figure 6.3 *Mind map for 'linking rights and responsibilities'*

Box 6.4: *Protecting rights and responsibilities* _____

Objective: To produce some rules for the class.

Resources: Whiteboard or flip chart, marker pens, A1 sheets of paper, Figure 6.3.

Activity 1: Introduce the notion of rules then, working in pairs or as a whole class, think of one rule we have in our country and discuss why we have it. What happens when it is broken? Think of one rule you have at home. Explain why you have it and what happens when it is broken. Think of one rule we should have in the school or our class. Why should we have it?

Share the outcomes of the discussions as a whole class and list the rules on separate, large sheets of paper together with the consequences. This will enable the class to contribute their ideas about the rules that could be used in the school.

Activity 2: Help the class to distinguish rules, which should be in force at all times, from directions, which will apply to specific routines and circumstances.

Keywords: Rules, community, home, school, directions, consequences, rights, responsibilities, stability, laws, codes, conduct, behaviour, crime.

Laws and Rules in Our Society	

LAW	CONSEQUENCE
30 mph speed limit	Three points on your licence and a fine
Travellers must purchase a valid ticket before travelling on the train	£100 penalty fine
No smoking	Asked to leave
Dog owners must not allow their pets to foul the pavement	Fine

SAMPLE RULES AT HOME	CONSEQUENCE
In bed by nine o'clock	No television in the morning
No jumping on the beds	Make own bed
Put your dirty clothes in the linen basket	Wash own clothes

SAMPLE RULES AT SCHOOL	CONSEQUENCE
No toys in class	Toy confiscated
No fighting	Internal isolation
Everyone should wear a tie	Lent a tie by the office for the day
Wear correct PE kit	Lent kit by teacher and a note home
Don't drop litter	Litter patrol at break

SAMPLE RULES IN CLASS	CONSEQUENCE
No swearing	Detention and write an apology
No running in the classroom	Go back and walk

Figure 6.4 *A finished chart for 'rules and laws need to be kept'*

Box 6.5: Rules and laws need to be kept —————

Objective: To link actions to consequences.
Resources: Figures 6.3 and 6.4, whiteboard or flip chart, marker pens.
Activity 1: Using some of the rules from the last activity, work as a whole class to decide the consequence for breaking each rule. Stress the difference between a punishment and a consequence.
Activity 2: As a whole class, decide which rules apply to the classroom. Agree some basic rules including 'follow directions'.
Keywords: Rule, law, direction, consequence, dislikable, uncomfortable, illegal, crime, punishment.

Box 6.6: Rewards —————

Objective: List the rewards that the class would value and want to work towards.
Resources: Whiteboard or flip chart and marker pens.
Activity: Brainstorm with the class what rewards they would value. Begin by reminding them that their suggestions need to be realistic. Asking for things like a day off school would not be possible. During the activity you could begin to separate the rewards into those the individual students would get and those the whole class could work for.
Keywords: Reward, earn, motivate, value.

Box 6.7: Consequences —————

Objective: To make a list of consequences that could be used in the lessons.
Resources: Whiteboard or flip chart and marker pens.
Activity: Remind the students of the connection between their actions and the consequences. Explain that consequences need not be harsh, just dislikable and that they should be linked to the action wherever possible. The whole class then work together on thinking up consequences for their rules.
Keywords: Rule, direction, poor choice, consequence.

Once you have constructed your behaviour code it needs to be circulated to everyone concerned together with an explanatory letter. The students should get a copy of the code to put in the front of their folder or exercise book. You will also want to send copies to the parents to gain their support. Figure 6.5 is a sample letter to help you structure your own. You may want to give copies of your code to some of your colleagues. The code itself should be simple and short. The contents should include the rules, rewards and consequences (Chapters 4 and 5). Put a copy in a prominent position on the classroom wall.

---

12 October 200X

Dear Mr and Mrs ...

I am writing to introduce myself as <student name>'s new teacher. I will be setting high standards and working with <student name> to ensure s/he makes good progress and gets as much out of the course as possible. To achieve this, s/he will need to do three things:

- Always come to the lesson with the correct textbook, exercise book, writing equipment, ... (make your own list as appropriate).
- Complete homework by the deadlines and to the required standard. I will use exemplars so that the students are aware of what this entails.
- Review notes and organise them tidily in the file provided for revision purposes.

I also have high expectations for behaviour. To achieve this, I have a behaviour code that is in line with the school policy. I enclose a copy with this letter for your information. The students have contributed to the code over the previous weeks and have agreed to use it in the lessons.

Our approach is based on the positive reinforcement of appropriate behaviour. We encourage the students to make choices and reward them when they choose to behave well. When they make a poor choice and behave inappropriately, they are sanctioned. In this way, children learn that there are consequences to their actions.

Please talk to your son/daughter about the behaviour code and if you have any questions related to it, feel free to contact me and I will try to help.

Yours sincerely

Subject teacher

Figure 6.5 *Letter introducing the behaviour code*

REINFORCE THE BEHAVIOUR CODE AT EVERY OPPORTUNITY

Introducing a new code (Table 6.1) will not be a simple process. The students probably won't adopt everything and adhere to the rules exactly. They may have seemed very enthusiastic about it while they were drawing it up, but when it becomes a reality it may cause difficulties for some of them. Anything that requires a change in routine obviously needs to be learned. Not everyone learns at the same rate so, undoubtedly, some students will forget or make a mistake and get caught out by the new system. The question teachers often ask when introducing a new code is, 'Should concessions be made?' Concessions can be made but they might confuse the student. They will see you are making a concession that may conflict with what they believe should actually happen. It is better to adhere to your system.

Table 6.1 *A behaviour code containing staged consequences*

Incident	Consequence	Behaviour log
First incident in the lesson	Warning given	Enter a tick
Second incident in the lesson	Five minutes of time-out given	Enter a tick
Third incident in the lesson	Stay back after class for two minutes	Enter a tick
Fourth incident in the lesson	Lunchtime detention	Enter a tick

However, students who have four incidents during a lesson will have been given plenty of chances to learn how to stop themselves. You will be giving the rewards to those who make responsible choices, so it is reasonable to give the consequences to those who do not. It may seem hard at first but with persistence your efforts will pay off (Case Study 6.1).

Case Study 6.1 *Derek*

Derek needed a system because the students were unruly and made it exhausting to teach technology. He found he spent so much time correcting students who could not behave that they hardly ever seemed to finish their projects. Technology was organised in six-week blocks. The groups would move to a new room, a new teacher and a different discipline of technology after the six weeks were up. Derek's projects were good and resulted in some first-class products that were impressive when they were completed. But wasted time held up their completion and some students became disenchanted. If only he could get better control, they would stay on task and the projects would be completed on time.

He went on his half-term break determined to come up with a solution. After reading several books on behaviour management, he felt he could see the way forward. He constructed an emergency plan and returned to work optimistic that things were going to change. The first group arrived for their lesson and he let them into the room. Then he explained the changes and the new seating plan. When all the students were sitting in their new places, he told them that he was now using a new behaviour code he had designed. Many responded to the code positively and the lesson went well. The experience was the same for all of his groups in the first week and Derek started to feel good about the changes.

The following week, the groups returned and he reminded them of the new rules before they entered the room. Many of the students did not follow his directions for going in, so he had to give out a lot of warnings and yellow cards; some even got as far as consequences. But Derek stood firm. The week after, students who got warnings responded well and stopped themselves from going too far. The majority adhered to the directions and worked hard to earn the rewards. Within three weeks, all of his groups were under control and he was able to concentrate on getting the work done to schedule. The projects were completed and the students felt much more positive about technology.

CONSOLIDATE THE CODE BY REVISITING IT

Introducing the plan is the first step but it does not stop there. The students will need reminding until they have accepted it and made it part of their working method. This is done by briefly running through the rules, rewards and consequences at the beginning of each lesson during the first few weeks. The students will see that you are taking it seriously, not simply introducing something and letting it run on its own until it gets forgotten.

In the early days, rewards should be given more generously as incentives to take on the new routines. The class can then be gradually weaned off the rewards. The best time to use the extra rewards is when you need students to follow directions that they may not be used to. For example, lining up outside and entering a room can be noisy and disorderly, so giving a lot of rewards will help the students recognise when they are doing things right for you.

One way of making the start of the lesson a positive, educational experience is by giving the students a task as they enter the room. It should take them about five minutes to complete and can be done individually or in pairs. Boxes 6.8 to 6.11 contain some activities you could try. Reward the students if they come in quietly, follow directions and get on with the task without making a fuss.

Box 6.8: Memory game

Use: This activity is used once the students have begun a unit of study. It challenges them to think quickly and gets their brains into gear at the start of the lesson.
Aims: To enable students to recollect and summarise the two most significant things they can remember from the previous lesson. To produce a mind map of the key points that will then remain on display during the week of study.
Resources: Post-it notes.
Time: 3–5 minutes.
Procedure: When the students arrive they are given two Post-it notes each. They are asked to think about the last lesson. Their task is to think of the two most significant things they learned in the previous lesson and write them on the Post-it notes. They can work alone or discuss things with another person. Then they come out and stick their notes on the whiteboard, return to their seats, take out their books and wait for you to start the lesson. The result is a board covered in key points that the students remembered. This can be very useful as a starting point for the lesson, a revision aid and a very good way of checking the effects of your teaching.

Box 6.9: Spaghetti words _____

Use: This activity is used to help the students remember the keywords from the last lesson.

Aim: To enable the students to link the keywords to their meanings or uses.

Resources: Activity sheet.

Time: 3–5 minutes.

Procedure: The students are given a sheet with five to ten keywords that have been jumbled up. They work in pairs to solve the anagrams (Figure 6.6). Then they have to decide where they go on a diagram that is also on the sheet. Once they have completed the task, they should agree between themselves what is going on at each stage. This is a very good activity involving a process or life cycle. In this example, the keywords used are 1: evaporation, 2: freezing, 3: precipitation, 4: melting.

- Solve these anagrams

  zeerfgni _____   ventipraooa _____

  ginmtel _____   cprtatniopie _____

- Use them to label this diagram

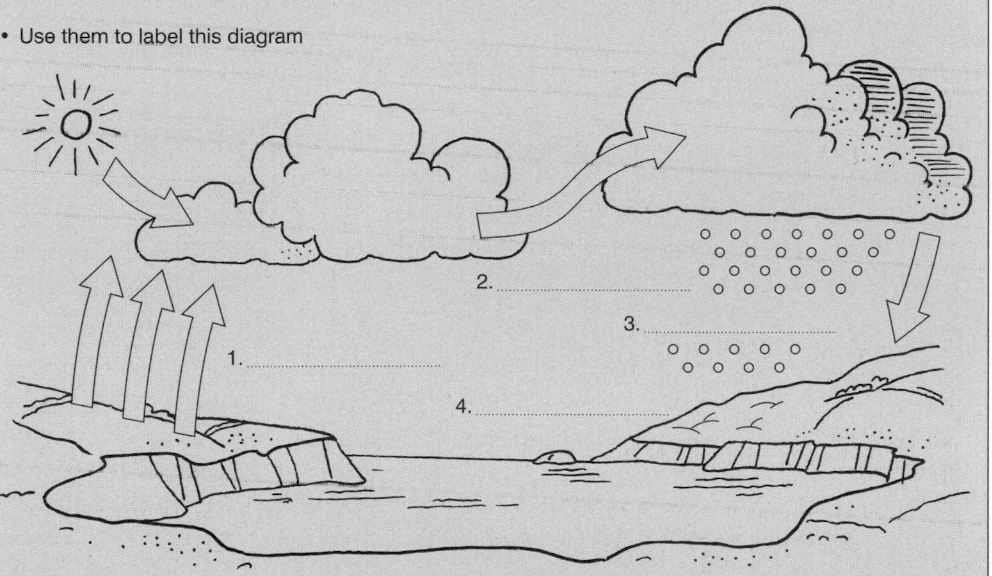

- Be ready to describe what is happening at each stage

Figure 6.6 *The rainfall cycle*

Box 6.10: Keyword grid

Use: This is used near the end of a topic or unit and helps the students bring together their knowledge of the terms used.

Aims: To enable the students to work together in building a list of keywords and to see their relationships.

Resources: A4 paper.

Time: 3–5 minutes.

Procedure: Each student is asked to come up with one pair of keywords. They write them in the alphabet grid on the whiteboard.

A	B	C	D	E	F
G	H	I	J	K	L
M	N	O	P	Q	R
S	T	U	V	W	X
Y	Z				

The students then discuss the words with a partner and make connections between them in the form of a mind map (Figure 6.7). The teacher calls the class together and asks some of the students to give their keywords and describe the connections for example: The Battle of Britain and Radar.

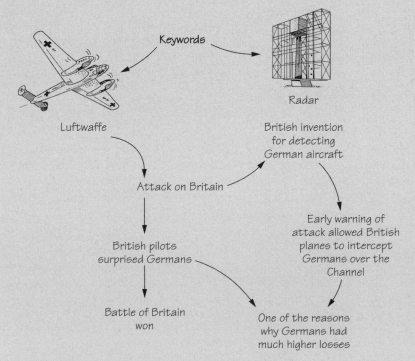

Keywords

Radar

Luftwaffe

British invention for detecting German aircraft

Attack on Britain

Early warning of attack allowed British planes to intercept Germans over the Channel

British pilots surprised Germans

Battle of Britain won

One of the reasons why Germans had much higher losses

Figure 6.7 *Luftwaffe and radar are the keywords for this mind map*

Box 6.11: Cross challenge ————————————————————

Use: This activity is an ideal one to bring together knowledge gained in a mathematics or science topic. The puzzle is a cross where all the numbers are obtained by finding the solutions to clues.
Aim: To use the knowledge gained during a topic to solve a related puzzle.
Resource: Activity sheet.
Time: 3–5 minutes.
Procedure: The clues are given on the same sheet and the challenge is to build up the algorithm using the solutions. There is a missing number in the middle that also needs to be solved once the students have worked out the other clues (Figure 6.8). The students need to add the signs to make the puzzle work.
- a. Twice the number of degrees in a circle
- b. ?
- c. Seven right angles
- d. The number of hemispheres in a sphere.
- e. The number of degrees in a straight line.

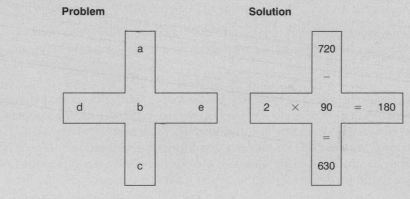

Figure 6.8 *Cross challenge: problem and solution*

CONSISTENT CONSEQUENCES

The purpose of the behaviour code is to help the students make sensible choices about their behaviour so they will eventually be able to take their places as well-adjusted members of the community. The cooperation of the students is secured by an agreement that depends on fairness. The majority will accept the consequences if they feel the judgements are fair. You must demonstrate this by tackling every incident where a rule is broken or a direction is not followed. There will be students who will be watching to see whether you deal with everyone in the same way. If they feel that you have let a student off or treated them in a different way, they will react. They may complain to you that it does not seem fair. You will have to deal with their grievances, which can be time-consuming and pull you away from your teaching. During this time another incident may occur that will also need your attention. The result will be a very stressful situation for you that could have been avoided with forethought. In extreme cases the student may take his grievance away with him and it could surface later, causing quite serious and perhaps unexpected repercussions (Case Study 6.2).

Case Study 6.2

Dave was taking a small group of students for art in the learning support unit of a large comprehensive school. All the students had some difficulties with their behaviour and some were close to exclusion. The unit was the dedicated resource for helping them. The lesson was about figure drawing and they had already done some photography on the theme.

Charlie had many of the characteristics of attention deficit hyperactivity disorder (ADHD). He had not been diagnosed because his parents were in denial and refused to accept that he was different. They felt he was like any other youngster, energetic and interested in lots of things. Part-way through the lesson, Charlie decided he could not be bothered to do the work anymore. He put his pencil down, helped himself to some paper and rolled it up into very tight tubes. He joined them together to make a spear and added some flights to the end.

Dave could see he had stopped work and tried to challenge him. 'Charlie, you need to complete the work this lesson because we are moving on to a new project next week.'

'I don't care. It's boring, so I'm not doing it anymore.'

Dave could see Charlie was going to be difficult but he did not follow the agreed behaviour code of redirection then a warning. He was wary of him and just let him carry on playing with the paper. He was not aware that the other students were watching. They were unhappy with Dave's response and felt he was giving Charlie special treatment. After school, Dave was chatting to a colleague in the staffroom and overheard someone saying that Chris in Dave's art group had got into a slanging match with Charlie and it had ended in a fight. However, Dave did not really register what it was about and what caused the problem.

The next day he got a message from the head of year to meet him at break. He told Dave that Chris and Charlie had been involved in a terrible fight after school and three members of staff were needed to split them up. Chris had gone home and trashed his room then stolen a car with some other kids and smashed it into some roadworks. He'd spent the night at the police station and told the duty sergeant that he was really angry because of what happened at school. He said he felt that another kid had got away with stuff and he didn't feel it was fair.

Dave hadn't realised that Chris was that upset by it all. He learned a lot from the incident and made sure he did not let things go that should be challenged. The purpose of the behaviour code is to help every student improve their own behaviour, not just the poorly behaved ones. Even the normally well-behaved students should be able to make improvements.

RULE REMINDERS

Before any action, consider what reminders could be given. It will enable you and the student to refocus on the direction that was given. Prefacing a warning with a rule reminder enables the student to see where they went wrong, which will prevent disputes that accompany secondary behaviour. The behaviour code will only be successful if you keep up the reminders and continue to coach the students for as long as needed. After long holidays, you will probably find that refresher sessions are needed to prevent the students making poor choices because they have forgotten what to do.

SUMMARY

- Involve the parents in formulating the behaviour code so they will feel they have some ownership of it and will support you in implementing it.
- Create special lessons to teach the class the behaviour code in the same way you would teach a subject.
- Underpin your behaviour code by discussing the rights and responsibilities of everyone in the class.
- Put up visual displays that summarise the rules, rewards and consequences.
- Circulate the behaviour code to parents and staff in the school.
- Give students a copy of the code to put in the front of their exercise book or folder.
- Revisit the behaviour code to refresh it with the class when necessary.

7 DEVELOPING A POSITIVE ATMOSPHERE

Behaviour and learning are inextricably linked. Students who find the lessons interesting and engage with the work are less likely to misbehave. The challenge for any teacher is in planning lessons and designing activities that suit the needs and interests of all the students in a group. This is a tall order when you consider the widely differing intellects, interests, backgrounds and experiences that each student brings to the lessons. Classes of students can no longer be considered as homogeneous groups and given the same things to do. Each student has their own needs and expectations and the teacher is charged with meeting them. Unacceptable behaviour can occur when students find the work too easy, too hard, uninteresting or irrelevant.

WHERE TO START

The aim throughout this book has been to describe a method of managing behaviour that places the choice with the student. The goal is to use the behaviour code to aid the learning and teaching processes, not to control the students. For this reason, it is worth spending time examining the way people learn and the learning process.

The primary needs of the body must be satisfied before a person can begin to learn effectively (see Maslow's hierarchy of needs on page 2). We all need nourishment, shelter, warmth and a feeling of security. Without these, our mind becomes distracted in the quest for them. Consider trying to learn about the St Lawrence Seaway in a classroom that is so cold you are shivering and trying to get warm. Or imagine studying the causes of the First World War when you are hungry because you missed breakfast. Maybe you have had a traumatic event in your life. Consider what it might be like for a student going through something similar. For example, a student whose parents are splitting up will find it difficult to concentrate. They will be feeling vulnerable, possibly erratic and ill-tempered during this period of uncertainty and find it hard to give the required attention to their school work.

The human body consists of complex hydrocarbons. The body's life processes are chemical reactions. The brain controls these processes and also relies on the same kinds of chemical reactions, many of which take place in liquid environments. Water is a vital requirement of the body and provides the medium where reactions can occur. It is very easy to underestimate this and ignore the need to maintain a healthy intake of water. There has been a growing awareness of this among the educational community and many schools have begun providing their students with bottles so they can have their own supplies of fresh water to drink whenever they need to, in or out of lessons. When the students are first given their bottles they seem to want to drink all the time and have to go to the toilet, which can become an issue during lessons, but they settle down after a few weeks.

Fresh air is another basic requirement. Hot, stuffy, poorly ventilated rooms result in lethargic, brain-numbed students. A steady flow of fresh air can do wonders for the levels of participation and work output. In the summer term some classrooms can become unbearably hot from the sun shining through the windows, as many schools in the UK are still without air conditioning. There are several solutions to this problem. Sheets of darker-coloured sugar paper or newspaper can be put over the windows to reduce glare, and a portable fan can get the air circulating to make the room more comfortable.

The appearance of the room can also make a difference. You can set the tone by making sure everyone who comes into your room respects the rights of others. Putting positive affirmation signs around the room can help. Slogans like 'You are now entering a no put-down zone' can be useful because they give all the students the same message that verbal abuse and negative comments are not tolerated in your room. The appendices contain examples for you to photocopy.

GETTING THE LESSON RIGHT

Good lessons have structure, challenge, interest and opportunities to practise what has been learned. Lessons should include the following features.

The big picture

Students will switch off for many different reasons but a common reason is not knowing why something needs to be learned. They need to know how it fits into the big picture. The lesson is part of the learning journey. The big picture is an overview of that journey. It is like the picture on a jigsaw-puzzle box. The whole thing will be clearer and make more sense if the student can see where the piece, the lesson, fits into the whole jigsaw of a subject. Here are three ways to draw the big picture:

- A new topic or unit should be introduced together with a brief description of the steps the class will take to reach the end.
- At the start of each lesson, the students should be reminded of what they did previously.
- Describe what the students need to do next and set the objectives and learning outcomes for the activities they will engage in.

In this way, the students will have a good idea of where they have come from, where they are now and where they are going. It is like giving a road map with directions and it will minimise the chance of students getting lost.

Whole-class teaching

Whole-class teaching is the time when you introduce the students to new ideas, concepts and material. The students can ask questions and you move forward together in the search for answers, acquiring new knowledge and skills. The teaching takes place during this part of the lesson. It is where you will use your own particular strategies to introduce and explain what the students need to know to complete the activities that come next. Words alone will not be enough, because not every student will learn by linguistic methods. The challenge for the teacher is to find alternative ways of getting over what they want the students to learn. At the end of the lesson, the students are reminded of how the work they have been doing fits into the whole unit and what they will be doing in the next lesson.

Small group and individual work

Once the whole class have been introduced to the new material and the teacher feels they are ready to venture forth, they can get started on the tasks that will enable them to apply it to a range of problems. Activities need adapting so they are differentiated or open-ended to enable students of all abilities to access them. This is often the hardest part of planning lessons. You need to know the abilities of your students then you can devise the tasks so they will gain success.

The plenary

An important part of the lesson is the ending – bringing the students back together as a group and getting them to discuss what they have learned. It enables individuals to test their own learning and you can assess whether your teaching has been effective. This part of the lesson also allows you to recap the main points, put them back into the context of the big picture and tell the students where they will be going next. Good lessons will contain many of these features and address the needs of the class as a whole as well as the individual students. Getting the interest level, pace and challenge of a lesson right will minimise problems with behaviour that arise through the boredom and difficulty of the work.

ENCOURAGE AND PRAISE

Imagine you are the coach of a football team and your students are the players. You give them the tactics to succeed in the form of the behaviour code plus the new subject knowledge and skills. When they go out and play, they will try to give you their best but sometimes things will not go as well as everyone would like. In sport the support of the fans plus the extra push from the coach can lift the team and raise their game to new heights. There is nothing like the buzz you get when you know someone is rooting for you and willing you on. The best kind of support a teacher can give is encouragement, especially when things are going wrong. Knowing you are there will prevent them from giving up.

A team that starts to lose will grow despondent. Individual players will have varying views on the value of the game and their chances of turning it around. Some will continue to persevere whereas others will feel there is no way back. Any attempt to win seems futile to them. They will begin to feel that they might as well give up, except that would be embarrassing. Footballers do not walk off the pitch in the last ten minutes when they are obviously not going to win. Something keeps them playing. They will have lost the fire they had at the start and may feel there is nothing worth playing for. The team with its loyal fans will be spurred on by their support and will keep trying even when there seems no chance of winning. Strange things do happen and surprises can occur. Teams do get lucky breaks and score goals in the dying minutes. When this happens their supporters suddenly explode into life, supplying a barrage of sound to raise their team's morale.

Students go through similar trials. They may keep making the same mistakes and just cannot seem to see why. They will look like giving up and they will give up, unless someone can show they believe in them. We need to be alert and spot the changes in mood that occur with students when failure looms. Stepping in with a few well-placed words of encouragement or praise and some advice can be all that's needed. However, some students are very needy and will require considerable support to get them out of the failure zone. It is then that their behaviour can break down. The student who is struggling and feeling success is nowhere in sight may give up and vent their feelings through aggression, abuse or distracting behaviour. They may slam doors, kick over chairs throw books and bags, tear down displays and spew out a tirade of foul language at the teacher or other students. This can be avoided with the right response.

MOTIVATE

Lift the students by finding good in things they do. It may be their work or their behaviour. The knack is to identify something that you know they have been working on and praise them promptly. Make the praise specific. Avoid non-specific comments like these:

'You are doing well.'

'You are working hard.'

Praise like this will probably be well received but it will not be as effective as praise for a specific effort made by the student. Here are some examples:

'I can see a real improvement in your playing now you are thinking about the dynamics of the piece.'

'I noticed you double-checking your calculations and it has paid off because you have got it right.'

'Your diagrams are really neat and clear since you started using a fine pen.'

'I really liked the way you described the change in the pigs' behaviour in *Animal Farm*. It shows you have a real insight into what Orwell was trying to do.'

'You have made big efforts to take turns in your group recently. Well done!'

'You have really been trying to ignore Leon when he makes personal comments.'

Direct praise like this shows that you have noticed some improvement the student has made.

Praise should be made personal so the recipient knows you are addressing them. General comments to the whole class have some use but the individual students will not feel the same sense of pride as if they had been addressed by name. It is not possible to give praise to every student in a lesson, because there is simply not enough time. The solution is to use personal and collective praise. In that way, a positive atmosphere will start to pervade your lessons. Personalise the praise by saying the student's name first:

'Clarissa, that was very well read.'

When there seems to be nothing worth praising in a student's work, look for aspects of their behaviour to comment on.

Shy students

Not everyone wants to be singled out from the crowd, even for something they have done well. There will be students who are shy or modest and prefer to remain anonymous. They will still need to be encouraged and motivated but a different approach is required. Use private signs or comments made when the rest of the group are busy on the task. Alternatively, well-composed comments at the end of written work or on reports will ensure that only the student can read them. Telephone calls and letters home may be an option but it is worth checking with the student first. They may not want you talking to their parents and they may prefer written comments.

Street credibility

Some students view praise coming from a teacher as damaging to their personal image. In a culture of independence where young people strive to define themselves apart from adults, any public praise or comment that appears to condone their behaviour or make them acceptable will harm their status among their peers. The irony is that they may like the praise but do not want to be seen to like it when they are with their friends.

The culture of the teenager can vary in its defining criteria. Some groups will value the 'sporting jock' image of boys who are fit, attractive and good at physical activity. Others may go for the 'tough guy' image of boys who seems to dominate, overwhelm challengers and use aggression to maintain their position. The culture of academic achievement is a difficult one because it has traditionally been portrayed in the media by the 'nerd' image of someone wearing anorak and glasses and who is socially inept. But there can be alternatives and some groups of teenagers manage to be sporty and academic. There are the female equivalents to these types but the defining criteria will be different.

When praising these apparently anti-adult individuals, care must be taken to do it in a way that will not harm their social status. For example, giving out test results is best done quietly and privately so the student does not have to reveal their score unless they want to. Those who decide to tell others will often use a variety of interesting tactics to preserve their image. For example, the boy who does well in a test may tell his friends his mark but play down his effort. He will make a big deal about not having done any revision because he had a new Play Station game he wanted to finish or he was out with his girlfriend and did not get time.

Use 'do' instead of 'don't'

When a student gets it wrong, we can either turn it around in a positive way or tell them off in the hope that they will learn from the experience. Here is a 'don't' comment:

'Don't stuff your notes in the folder like that, Michael!'

This comment does very little except tell the student what not to do. It does not direct them back to the right behaviour and does not put the responsibility for action with them. Changing it into a 'do' comment makes it more positive and useful:

'Michael, you need to file those notes in the section of your folder headed "Causes of World War II".'

This statement gives the student something to do and corrects in a positive way.

TURN ASSESSMENT INTO A TOOL FOR LEARNING

Assessment begins in the lesson immediately a new piece of knowledge or skill is learned. Showing your students that you are actively involved in the learning will help to build a relationship and a partnership with them. Offering constructive comments instead of critical ones will motivate and encourage the students to search for their own answers and improve on their performance. When you do use questions, make them open questions to help the students explore an idea. Open questions usually begin like these:

'Can you explain . . .?'

'What kind of . . .?'

'How could you . . .?'

'Describe . . .'

The responses you can expect from the students will draw on their experiences and opinions and be more detailed than if you had asked closed questions:

'When did Columbus discover America?'

'What is the area of a rectangle?'

'Do you think Northern Ireland should be part of the British Isles?'

Questions like these reveal which students know the answer but not whether they understand the circumstances or processes that led to it.

There are several useful ways of finding out how much students understand about a subject without resorting to a series of questions. Here are some examples:

- *Talk partners*: one student explains the concept or idea to another student.
- *Key points*: students summarise a piece work.
- *Construct questions*: students construct questions that could be asked or they make up a quick test paper.

Self-assessment

Checking for learning on a regular basis is a sure-fire way of gauging the effect of your teaching and empowering the students to judge for themselves how well they are doing. A good practice is to set objectives, targets or learning outcomes that are specific, distinct and achievable within five to ten minutes. When the student completes the task, they should be able to tell whether they have been successful and decide if they

- Understand the work
- Grasp most of it but need a bit more help
- Are having a great deal of difficulty and really need significant support, further explanations and practice.

The students will need some way of indicating how they feel at the end of each lesson. Younger students can be quite happy with the smileys (Figure 7.1). Older students may not want to put smileys on their work, so a numerical score could be used (Figure 7.2).

Figure 7.1 *Younger students like smileys*

9	6	3
10 – 8	7 – 5	4 – 1
Got it	Nearly	Help needed

Figure 7.2 *Older students like scores in a circle*

Critical signposts

Many teachers write brief qualitative comments like 'excellent', 'good', 'more effort required'. Some teachers prefer to write more copious notes about a point or idea together with ways to improve it. Do the students read anything you write or are they satisfied with the grades? Marking a piece of work and giving it a grade may just encourage the students to compare themselves with others, whereas questions like this will invite a response:

'You have made some good points but several technical words are spelled wrongly. Can you find and correct them?'

Then, when you give back the books, you can allow five minutes for the students to read your comments and do the corrections. In this way, the students engage with your comments and will learn by making the changes.

GIVE YOUR STUDENTS THE RESPONSIBILITY FOR BEHAVING

Use the language of discipline to help the students learn. Place the responsibility with them and use words and phrases such as you, yours, choice, choose, your action, you decide. Emphasise the choice they have; give examples of behaviour and how they can either lead to a reward or a consequence. Stress that if the student chooses unwisely, they will end up with the consequence because they are responsible for their own actions. You do not need to get involved with their choice. That is something that the students have the freedom to decide for themselves. But advise them when necessary.

SELF-ESTEEM: THE ROUTE TO GOOD BEHAVIOUR

Students who feel good about themselves will have less difficulty learning how to behave. Students who have issues in their life that affect their self-esteem will communicate their feelings through excessive or undesirable behaviour. This can be addressed by treating the students as individuals. Learn their names and get to know more about them such as their birthdays, their likes and dislikes, and what makes them tick. When students do something well or achieve something in or out of school, note it down so you can use the information to boost their confidence at appropriate times.

Greet the students at the door. Show them you value their presence. Share your own experiences with them and show you regard them as worthy of attention. Try to avoid demeaning experiences that will have a negative effect on their view of you and the school. Be wary of using draconian methods by setting up routines in the room to avoid problems arising.

Young people with low self-esteem will often avoid taking risks because they fear failure. They may make up quite elaborate and creative reasons why they should not do something. Alternatively, they will simply say they can't do it. Reinforcing a 'can do' culture requires you to reply positively. Scenarios 7.1 to 7.3 show how this can be achieved.

Scenario 7.1

'Now, Hannah, we are going to start designing a desk-tidy.'

'I can't do it!'

'Hannah, you mean you can't do it *yet*, but by the time we finish this activity I have got here, you will be able to design the desk-tidy.'

Scenario 7.2

'We are going to learn how to bounce the ball while we are moving towards the basket.'

'I can't do that, I'm no good at basketball.'

'You can't do it *yet*, Mohammed, because I haven't shown you how to. But once I have and you've practised it a few times you will be able to do it.'

Scenario 7.3

'The next activity involves finding the area of the room so we can calculate how much lino we will need.'

'I don't know how to do that, so I'm not bothering.'

'Of course you don't know how to do it *yet*, because I haven't shown you. But I bet that in five minutes, after I've taught you how to work it out, you will be able to do it.'

The emphasis is on being able to do something eventually. Nurture the 'can do' culture in your class. It depends on putting down the right foundation. Students in your class must feel safe if they are to start taking risks. They must trust you and feel that they will not be ridiculed when they make a mistake. You need to help them see mistakes as learning opportunities not failures.

One way of doing this is to teach them something that usually begins with making lots of mistakes such as learning to juggle or playing a game where they have to throw something into a bucket. Make it difficult to begin with but possible to do once they have practised and made judgements that lead to success. At the end of the game you can discuss it and show them how the errors were necessary so they could adjust their aim or improve their coordination.

KEEP THE LESSON MOVING

Lessons with the wrong pace will become nurturing grounds for poor behaviour. Go too quickly and you will leave some students behind; they will give up, go off task and cause trouble. Go too slowly and some students will not be challenged; they will get bored and eventually misbehave. They become lethal because they are quicker-witted than those who get left behind. They end up using their intelligence to wind up other students and bait the teacher.

Gauging the pace correctly comes with experience but a new teacher can minimise the risk by finding out about their students. Knowing their strengths and weaknesses and pinpointing any barriers to learning will help you judge how they will engage with the work and complete the tasks. Once you have matched your normal ability group against the task and feel you are addressing the needs of the majority, you can start to consider how the work can be made more or less challenging to cater for needs outside this norm.

HOW POSITIVE IS THE CLASSROOM?

A positive classroom is a happy place where interesting things happen and individual success is celebrated. It is useful to review your own classroom from time to time to check how positive the atmosphere is and how the physical environment supports this aim. The following questions will help you do this. Not all questions will apply but they will help in striving for a well-organised, positive environment conducive to learning.

- Do you know the first names of the students?
- Do you welcome the students individually?
- Is the room easy to move around in when it is full of students?

- Do you adjust the heating and ventilation when necessary?
- Do you use the walls for notices and displaying the students' work?
- How do you plan activities to cater for the different learning styles of the students?
- Do you praise and encourage more than you criticise and reprimand?
- Do you link criticisms and praise to specific things the students have done?
- Do you phrase your directions using 'do' or 'don't'?
- Do you use open questions that help the students explore a concept?
- Do you praise and acknowledge effort?
- How do you offer the students choices?
- How do you encourage the students to try to resolve conflicts?
- Do you tactically ignore low-level disruptions when they first occur?
- Do you defer consequences to prevent the lesson from being interrupted?
- Do you try to treat all the students in the same way, even the ones you consider disruptive, uninterested or showing some characteristics you don't like?
- Do you model the behaviour you want?
- How do you challenge students who are abusive to others?
- Do you tolerate negative peer pressure?
- How do you deal with bullying?
- Ho do you deal with a student who attempts to wind up other students?
- Do you challenge racist or sexist comments?
- How do you try to broaden the horizons of your students?
- How do you promote equal opportunities in your room, your lessons and your resources?

WORKING WITH PARENTS

The most effective approaches to behaviour management are based on good partnerships between the school and the home. These partnerships need to be developed. They do not exist at the start and do not happen by chance. It is worth writing a letter of introduction to the parents when you take a new group at the start of the year. Introduce yourself by name, briefly outline your personal ethos and signpost important events coming up during the forthcoming term. This letter should be sent home in a sealed envelope with the student. Figures 7.3 and 7.4 (overleaf) show two model letters.

EMERGING PROBLEMS WITH BEHAVIOUR

The first signs of inappropriate behaviour do not necessarily warrant seeking SENCO support for the student. You need to try out your own strategies for a reasonable period before you call on other professionals for help. In the interim, things may become quite difficult for you in the lessons if the student is causing low-level disruption and not responding to your attempts to manage him. It sometimes feels like there is no one to help because the incidents are not that serious, just sufficiently time-consuming that you feel drained by the end of the lesson. Seeking the assistance of colleagues is the most obvious course of action but if you want to avoid feeling a failure and a victim, you need to take control. One way is to begin your own research project on the student. Observe and make notes of

Dear parent/carer

My name is .... and I will be teaching <student name> this year. I believe that learning is a journey. When students first set out, they need a great deal of help by teaching, explaining and coaching. As they get older, they become more confident and can take on more responsibility for their own learning.

I believe that the best way to support your child is for us to work together in partnership. I will keep you informed of your child's progress via reports, parents' evenings and a home/school diary. Please do not hesitate to contact me if you feel it is necessary.

Behaviour is an important foundation for effective learning. Every student will have a copy of our behaviour code. Please take the time to read and discuss it with them.

Here are some important dates for your diary: <important dates>.

I look forward to meeting you in person in the future and I'm sure that together we will be able to support your child on the next step of his/her educational journey.

Yours sincerely

Teacher of <subject>

Figure 7.3 *Letter introducing yourself to a parent or carer at Key Stage 3*

Dear parent/carer

My name is .... and I will be teaching <student name> this year. Years 10 and 11 are very important, so it is essential that we work together to ensure the time is used productively. I will be giving every student a timetable of important dates for the year to help them organise their time and meet the coursework deadlines.

The younger students look up to those at the top of the school, so it is important for them to act in an appropriate way. As role models, they can set an example and give the rest of the students a lead on how to behave. A smart appearance and mature behaviour are essential preparation for adult life, so we actively encourage our Year 10 and 11 students to pay attention to their image.

I believe the best way to help your son/daughter is for us to work together in ensuring they feel supported, able to act sensibly and ready to get the most from their studies.

I will keep you informed of your son/daughter's progress via reports, parents' evenings and the coursework planner. Please do not hesitate to contact me if you feel it is necessary.

Here are some important dates for your diary: <important dates>

Yours faithfully,

Teacher of <subject>

Figure 7.4 *Letter introducing yourself to a parent or carer at Key Stage 4*

- When they misbehave
- What the common features are between the incidents
- The frequency and scale of the behaviour
- Where it occurs most in the school.

Consider the behaviour in the context of what you know about them. You are searching for possible triggers, so try to connect behaviours to events. The home environment and the family dynamic may be contributing, so they are also worth investigating. You may decide to arrange a meeting with the parents or carers to discuss the downward trend in the student's behaviour. This is also an ideal opportunity to get more background information. The questions in the home profile (see appendices) may be useful in helping to structure the meeting. They will also help you in recording the parents' comments. The sample questionnaire is designed to get at the parental experience and parental perceptions of how the student is behaving. The meeting will enable you to discover more about the family routines such as mealtimes, leisure activities and their attempts to manage behaviour. The appendices also contain a set of questions to ask the student. These questions will help you find out more about what the student does at home and how they feel about their family.

Digesting, analysing and evaluating this information together with your own observations of the student will help lead to a clearer understanding of why the student has started to behave differently. Embarking on this will give you a positive feeling of empowerment because you will be doing something that will eventually lead to a solution. It will also alert the parents at an early stage that their child is in difficulty and the meeting will begin the process of sharing experiences and searching for solutions. The next step is to call a meeting of colleagues and consider which other professionals could provide support or guidance in helping the child. Cracking hard cases usually requires more than a behaviour code. Different solutions will be needed. The next chapter describes the characteristics of students exhibiting extreme behaviour and uses case studies to illustrate how they might be addressed.

SUMMARY

- Classes are not homogeneous groups. Students have very different needs and learn in different ways at different rates. Teachers need to consider the varying needs of the students when planning lessons.
- The brain is a site of chemical reactions and to function properly it needs water, the correct temperature and other requirements. People will learn best when their brain's requirements are satisfied.
- Good lessons have structure, pace, challenge, interest and opportunities.
- People respond positively to praise and encouragement. The most effective praise is specific and directed at achievements the student can identify.
- Some students will not want to be praised publicly. This may be because they are shy or because they do not want their peers to see them being acknowledged by the teacher. Praise should be given sensitively with these reasons in mind.
- Positive directions and corrections should be framed as 'dos' rather than 'don'ts'.

- Assessment is a powerful tool for learning. Giving students the opportunity to talk in more depth about a subject will enable them to refine and develop their own ideas.
- Focus your comments on the work to help the students understand what they have done well and what they could do to improve.
- Students who are confident and feel good about themselves will be less likely to have behavioural problems. Boosting the confidence of students with low self-esteem is vital to ensure they become better learners.
- Building partnerships with parents is important in ensuring that the students get the best support available.

8 THE CHALLENGING STUDENTS

The most wearing students are the challenging students. Every school has them from time to time. Some schools seem to get more than their fair share. They are demanding, time-consuming and sometimes frightening. Their behaviour will go beyond the limits of your behaviour code as they stretch the boundaries and test the rules. Dealing with a tough student requires a great deal more than the form teacher can be expected to give. The most effective way is through a team effort, drawing from the experience and knowledge of a wider group that may include members of the leadership team, heads of year, the special educational needs coordinator (SENCO), parents, educational psychologists, social workers, police, young offenders case workers, access and attendance officers, and medical representatives such as mental health specialists and doctors. These students first become noticeable by their continual flouting of the rules with low-level disruption.

GATHERING INFORMATION

The first thing to do when you realise you have a difficult student in your class is to find out more. You will want to know whether other teachers are having problems with the student and if so, what they did about it. You will also want to know whether the SENCO has any knowledge of the student and whether there has been any action. The student may have a history of incidents unknown to anyone in the school, so you should also read through the file.

The SENCO will make the decision to involve other professionals. An educational psychologist could be asked to observe the student and carry out an assessment. Their report is essential if the SENCO is considering applying for a statement. The social services may already be involved. They will work with the child and the family and can provide a valuable insight into the domestic situation. The family doctor and other related practitioners, including mental health practitioners, will work closely with a school when the child is at risk of exclusion. Their knowledge of the child's medical history can be illuminating. The police youth offending teams will know the child if they have been involved in any incidents outside school.

A meeting of these professionals provides a unique forum to share information in a quick and efficient way. A lot of what is known about a child does not always get written down, so it will not get passed on. The meeting enables everyone concerned to get access to that information and to discuss strategies and support that have worked in the past. Parents and carers are a vital part of the jigsaw but sometimes they may be unwilling to engage. Their support will be needed to help the student address their behaviour and redefine boundaries in school and at home so conditions will be right for learning.

THE CRITICAL INCIDENT

Behaviour is context based and children learn how to behave from the others around them. Behaviour can also be a means of communicating emotion. When a child has a traumatic experience the damage can be deep and the effects can surface in ways that seem unconnected to what has happened. If you believe that undesirable behaviour has its triggers then it is possible to move away from a culture of blame to one of understanding. To illustrate this point, you may have gone to work one day with a splitting headache and felt you didn't have the strength to be as patient as usual. When a student misbehaved, you snapped at them. Normally you are calm and rational but on that occasion your head was banging and you just couldn't be bothered. Your change in behaviour was due to how you felt that day.

Challenging students will invariably have a range of common factors that contribute directly or indirectly to their behaviour. One of the factors will be some kind of critical incident that has occurred in their past. Here are some examples:

- Parents divorcing
- Witnessing parents arguing or fighting
- A parent addicted to alcohol or drugs
- Parental depression
- Disowned or neglected by a parent
- Redundancy or long-term unemployment of a parent
- Witnessing abuse or being abused
- A family member going through a serious illness
- Bullied at home or in school
- Involvement in crime or drugs
- A family member convicted of a crime or in prison
- Refugee from a war zone.

The Framework for the Assessment of Children in Need and Their Families (Department of Health, 2000) provides a useful starting point for considering triggers of challenging behaviour. Figure 8.1 (overleaf) shows an assessment framework.

LOOKING FOR THE FIRST SIGNS

How can you tell from the first signs whether a student is going to be really challenging or just having a bad day? With difficulty, because both may fail to respond to your behaviour management methods during the lesson but challenging students will persist and continue to behave inappropriately over time. They will fail to respond to interventions used by teachers and the result will be a referral to a more senior member of staff. Here are some signs that point towards specific problems:

- Arguing with others in the class, especially between students who you would have regarded as friends.
- Work will suffer. The presentation will become untidy and the condition of books will deteriorate. The quality and quantity of what is produced will go down below your expectations for the student as they begin to underperform.
- Things will be forgotten. The student will miss homework deadlines they would not previously have missed and books and equipment will not be brought to lessons.

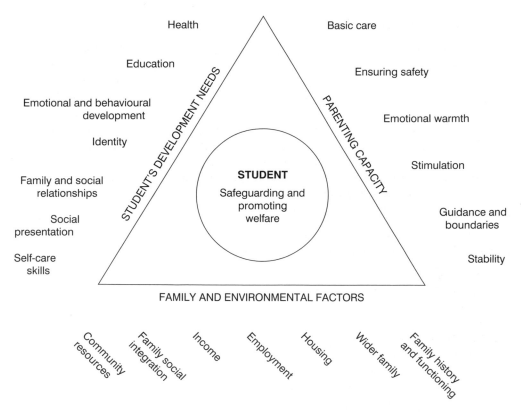

Figure 8.1 *Assessment framework (Department of Health, 2000) The Framework for the Assessment of Children in Need and Their Families*

- Irrational outbursts and a lack of patience and tolerance in coping with daily life.
- Physical appearance may change. This may happen in a number of ways. Weight loss may be due to worry, forced dieting and undernourishment, all with their associated causes. These could include relationship problems, poor self-image, illness or lack of parental care. Bruises and injuries may arise from accidents, sports injuries or deliberate violence. Vacant expressions coupled with glazed or heavy-lidded eyes can be attributed to a lack of sleep, illness or substance abuse. Take care over reaching a conclusion about the cause but any of these changes combined with a sudden swing in temperament could be early indicators of something going wrong.

Persistent inability to conform to class directions may be another indicator:

- Calling out
- Queue jumping
- Being frequently off task
- Leaving their seat and wandering around
- Continual chattering
- Winding up other students
- Continually interrupting
- Overly fidgety
- Easily distracted

- Poor attention when instructions are being given
- Noisy play
- Dangerous activity.

There may also be repeated incidents of unsocial behaviour outside of the lessons:

- Theft
- Bullying
- Fighting
- Being alone for long periods of time.

Note that the signs described are not always direct indicators of a critical incident but when viewed alongside other information they may help to construct a picture of what is going on in a student's life at that moment.

DEVELOPING THE STRATEGY

The aim is to identify potentially challenging students and help them before a serious incident occurs. When this is possible, the strategy will have several strands:

- Analysing any incidents that have occurred so far
- Working with the student to identify areas of behaviour that can be improved
- Providing ways for the student to manage their behaviour when similar incidents occur
- Putting together a personal support plan (PSP).

There are numerous tools for profiling a student's emotional and behavioural development. Primary teachers may use the Boxall profile (Bennathan and Boxall, 1984). Two members of staff who know the student well, such as the class teacher and the learning support assistant, usually complete it. Secondary teachers may find it difficult to complete because they do not have the knowledge of a student that primary teachers acquire during their daily contact. Secondary students are more able to participate in assessing their own needs, so a tool that helps them focus on their behaviour can be more productive. A development wheel is one example. The wheel yields a visual picture of aspects of the student's emotional and social profile that could then be used to plan where support should be given and how.

Many incidents in secondary schools can be efficiently dealt with through the normal methods used by teachers on a daily basis. The serious incidents require more attention and time to be spent on them to make sure that everyone concerned receives fair treatment. The standard procedure in many schools is to separate those involved and get them to write their accounts of what happened. These are then compared to ascertain who was the perpetrator and who was the victim. Separating the students prevents them from discussing what they will write. The accounts can also be used in subsequent meetings with parents, who sometimes find it hard to come to terms with the fact that their child has done something wrong.

A useful tool to use alongside the written account is a behaviour sheet (Ayers *et al.*, 1993). Figure 8.2 shows an example. The interview should be carried out quickly while the details of the incident are still fresh in the student's mind. It requires a member of staff to work with the student because they sometimes conveniently leave things out

Date/time	Antecedents	Behaviour	Consequences
	The trigger	The student's response	The outcome to the student

Figure 8.2 *A behaviour sheet*

and need reminding. This could be the teacher but if the student's anger is directed at the teacher, it may be difficult getting the student to cooperate.

There are three steps in the process. The first step is about the triggers that prompted the behaviour. The interviewer aims to engage the student in when the incident happened, where it happened, who was involved and what they did. The second step is concerned with the student's own response to the triggers. They are asked to imagine that a camera is filming them as they respond to the trigger and then to describe what it would see. Wherever possible, the student should reflect on the action and say what the consequence might be for what they did. In the third step, the student lists all the consequences of their actions. Some may be positive pay-offs and some negative. The interviewer places a plus or minus sign against each one. Ideally, there should not be any pay-offs. The third section is then used as a prompt for discussion and development to help the student track each consequence back to its trigger.

HELPING STUDENTS ACQUIRE SKILLS TO MANAGE THEIR BEHAVIOUR

The student will need help to enable them to control their response when provoked. Schools can have very varied approaches:

- *Whole-class meetings* to discuss areas of difficulty that are common to a number of students.
- *Small group coaching* led by behaviour mentors whose role is to help students redirect anger, control outbursts, ignore distractions and seek support during stressful times. Successful approaches include role-playing to practise how to respond, empathy to enable students to appreciate how a 'victim' feels, and simulations to test out strategies they have learned.
- *One-to-one counselling* to help the student work through their own feelings. Various therapeutic methods can be used by staff trained in them or by professionals from outside the school.

The emphasis should be on teaching the student new ways to behave. Dreikurs *et al.* (1982) devised a method for use when there are no obvious reasons behind the student's behaviour. The student is helped to examine his own behaviour and suggest reasons for it. This requires a great deal of skill from the adult working with the student, because h will probably be very reluctant to talk and visual cues will need to be used:

'I can see you are angry . . .'

'It is clear you are not happy at the moment . . .'

This enables a dialogue to open between you. You can then start to discuss his behaviour and make an offer of help:

'. . . and I would like to help you out. You know you keep interrupting me at the start of the lesson.'

The student will probably not seem as though he is paying attention. He may turn away or preoccupy himself by fiddling with something, but you ignore his silence and carry on:

'Do you know why you do it?'

This directs the student to the problem but do not expect an answer. A response such as '**** off!' or getting up and walking away will be a prompt to suspending this approach until another time. You will know you are getting somewhere if the student remains silent. Tell him what you think the reason is:

'Shall I tell you what I reckon?'

Do not wait for an answer:

'Is it that you want me to notice you?'

'Could you be trying to get me talking about something because you do not want to do the work?'

'Are you trying to show everyone what you know about the subject?'

The aim is not to embarrass the student. You are trying to show that you know what the student is doing. You may get a response, so watch the student very closely for any slight changes in behaviour. He may change position, fidget, look down, turn away, relax his shoulders, etc. Any of these may be an acknowledgement that you have guessed the reason. Alternatively, he may adamantly object, so you will need to reply:

'Well, I thought that was the reason for your interruptions. Tell me what the real reason is then.'

Then he can be encouraged to explain his reasons and you should listen and show you understand:

'You succeeded in what you tried to do and I can't stop you interrupting me but I need you to help me put together a plan that we can use together.'

PUTTING THE PLAN TOGETHER

A personal support plan in a secondary school will require the support of all the staff that teach the student. The plan will provide a means of reorganising the student's experience. Here is what it contains.

    Expectations placed on the student
    Targets for behaviour that are realisic and broken down into steps

- Rewards and how they can be earned
- Consequences
- Exit procedures
- An individual timetable (which may be less than the full timetable)
- Arrangements for before school, breaks, lunchtimes and home time
- Review dates.

Some staff may express concern about having the student in their class and need training, such as training in the use of positive assertive methods, restraint procedures, devising non-age-related teaching materials and baseline assessment methods. The student, parents, teachers and the SENCO should agree the contents of the plan and the first review date to ensure it is properly supported. Figure 8.3 shows how to establish the personal support plan.

The team begins by agreeing they will support each other so the teacher in difficulty gets help, learns from the experience and does not feel isolated. Commence tracking the behaviour

Contact the parents, invite them to a meeting to find out more about how the student behaves at home. Then involve them by asking them to share in drafting a behaviour plan

The aims will be to share information, solve problems and devise a plan of action

Implement a behaviour plan suited to the student's needs and teach them new ways of modifying their behaviour

Set up a school-wide emergency response plan in line with the school's behaviour policy for when the student fails to respond to the teacher's efforts

Figure 8.3 *How to establish a personal support plan*

Types of challenging students

Challenging students will exhibit particular kinds of behaviour, described in this chapter's case studies. Individual students will not fit a category exactly as they have complex needs that manifest in many ways. For example, a student fitting the controlling type may also be hyperactive and even end up being diagnosed with attention deficit hyperactivity disorder (ADHD). Finding strategies for dealing with tough students will not be easy and the pragmatic approach is to identify the type that has the best fit then use it as a starting point. The other facets of the student's behaviour can be dealt with as discrete issues alongside the main strategy.

The controller

In any group there will be some individuals who emerge as leaders but the controller is someone who needs to dominate. Their needs extend beyond the classroom and into the home. They will rule the roost and the parents will be impotent. In the classroom they will attempt to monopolise your time by asking countless questions, trying to engage you in conversation and wanting to do the activity first. They will question everything and try to undermine your decisions whenever an opportunity arises such as an ambiguity around an incident. They will point out things that seem unfair to them and tell you if another student is doing something wrong.

At home they will dominate virtually anything and everything they can, including mealtimes and menus, what is watched on the television, where and when they go out and for how long. They will make life very difficult for their parents and eventually provoke sibling rivalry as others in the household start to resent their selfishness.

The reasons behind their behaviour will vary but stem from a need in the child. It may be that they need attention that was lacking in their past, so they try to secure it for themselves. They may have been deserted by one of the parents and feel they need to fill that space; the other parent may have allowed them the power to do so. Alternatively, it may be poor parenting over a long period, giving them so much freedom that they have lost the boundaries associated with normal adult–child relationships. The result will be a very difficult home life where the parent feels powerless and ultimately bullied by the child. The child in this position will get into difficulties at school because their behaviour will be unacceptable and ultimately create incidents that could lead to exclusion. Outside school, they will have so much freedom that they may eventually get involved in crime or antisocial behaviour because the parent has no control and the child will come and go at will.

Identifying the behaviour is the key and the child will often also exhibit other behavioural traits such as ADHD or poor self-esteem. The strategies for dealing with controlling students are often complex. The student will need to have boundaries redefined and when the boundaries are tested they must be adhered to rigidly. The main aim is for the student to learn that the adult is in charge and has the responsibility for making decisions until they reach the recognised age of adulthood. They also have to learn that things need to be shared and that they cannot always go first. The noticeable sign that your strategies are working will be that the student will appear more relaxed, less prone to outbreaks of temper and easier to be with in general (Case Study 8.1).

Case Study 8.1 *Brad*

When Brad transferred to secondary school, the primary liaison staff warned Kim, his new form teacher, that he would not settle easily. He had a history of incidents in the junior school, nearly all connected with arguments about who should sit with whom, who should go first, who should be in goal, etc. Wherever Brad went, conflict followed.

His parents had separated two years earlier under very difficult circumstances. They had been arguing for months and Brad had endured it. Then his dad started to get aggressive and knocked his mum around. It started with the odd shove, but as time went by the odd shoves changed to punches and then full-blown, uncontrolled violence. His mum put up with it for a while, feeling embarrassed and blaming herself for his terrible temper. She covered up the bruises and made excuses for him but Brad knew what was going on. Finally, everything got out of hand when his dad went too far and pushed his mum down the stairs. She ended up in hospital and Brad knew they would never go back to their home. Luckily, they were offered a place in a refuge for six months. They moved to a new area and Brad went to the local junior school. By then, he was beginning to be affected by the scenes he had witnessed.

His behaviour in Year 6 could be loosely described as controlling. At school he always wanted things his way. He would get quite aggressive with the pupils and teachers if he felt he was not getting what he wanted. Once he got his way, he would share and let the others get involved but would not relinquish control even when pushed to do so. The teachers had realised this and decided they would manage the incidents by letting him be the leader, or be first to try something new in an effort to avoid any conflict. Unfortunately, this strategy was only really damage limitation. The more times Brad got his own way, the more the situation worsened. He became less able to interact with the other pupils. His comments became derogatory until virtually everything he said was a put-down. Whenever a teacher challenged him, he became stubborn and his eyes showed real defiance if they persisted. His mum described his behaviour at home as 'nightmarish'. He would only do some things she asked and then only if she bribed him with a treat.

Kim was very apprehensive about having him in her class as she had never experienced any students with such a disturbing catalogue of events in their past. He didn't have a statement, so she asked the special educational needs coordinator (SENCO) at the junior school why and was told that his behaviour was not that bad as long as he was allowed the freedom to do things his way. Kim knew that he wouldn't get that freedom in her school and questioned whether it was a good idea anyway to give him so much freedom. It would not be in his best interests. How would he come to terms with the feelings he had of needing to control every situation?

Kim requested Brad's file and went through it carefully. She discovered that an educational psychologist had been working with Brad and that a social worker had worked with Brad and his mum. Kim felt she needed a meeting with them so she could find out more about his behaviour and how they had worked with him. She arranged the meeting via the SENCO and the head of year; it was also attended by one of the learning mentors from the school's learning support unit (LSU).

Following the meeting, the school drew up a personal support plan (PSP) with Brad. Kim worked with one of the experienced members of staff in the LSU to develop some strategies that would be shared with the other staff teaching him. One of the key objectives was to help Brad redefine boundaries and accept that he did not always have to control the situation. The educational psychologist was going to do further work with him around why he felt this need. The social worker agreed to continue to meet with Kim and work with the family to extend what the school had put in place.

Kim spent some time thinking about how best to help Brad with his need to control, but without much success. Then one day she was watching a programme about lions and an idea came to her. She discussed it with everyone concerned and they all agreed to try it. When Brad came to the school, Kim explained that everyone would sit where the teachers put them so they could use a seating plan to learn the names of the students in the class. Whenever they needed to line up, it would be in a specific order and Brad was placed at the back. All the staff put Brad last at every opportunity. Whenever he wanted to say or do anything, it would be after everyone else in the class had taken their turn. If he tried to take up staff time with his questions, they would respond with, 'Does this have anything to do with the lesson, Brad? If not, I will discuss it with you after school.'

To further reinforce the pecking order, the staff would always go first. The hierarchy that was being established placed the most important adult at the top, then the other adults, then all the other students, and finally Brad. Whenever Brad made a challenge or complained and said something was not fair, the standard reply would be, 'I am the adult here, Brad, and it's my job to decide what happens.'

September arrived and Brad turned up to find that Kim had organised everything to ensure he would learn his place and quickly appreciate his position in the hierarchy. All the other teachers did the same. The plan was properly supported by a very clear behaviour management system that all the new Year 7 students were taught. Brad spent the first couple of weeks challenging the new boundaries and systems that surrounded him but the staff stood their ground. The culture of having specific places and positions meant that all the students learned where they should be and their place in the order. The educational psychologist and staff working with him reported that Brad had eventually accepted the regime. They had also made good progress with him in the LSU once he had settled.

His mum felt that things had started to improve at home. The social worker and a member of staff from the LSU had coached her on how to tackle things. She used the same approach, putting her dinner on the table first, taking control of things like the television remote control and the newspapers. When he questioned her, she explained her actions in the same way: 'I'm the adult in this house, so I decide what we will watch on the TV when we are all here. If you like, you can choose after I have watched what I want to.' It had been hard for her, but working with the school had given her the confidence to try. He had tried to argue but she had held her ground and eventually Brad started to realise that his mum meant what she was saying.

Brad may have been feeling responsible for his mum and perhaps assumed the role of father figure and head of the family. He may have felt he had to be strong to prevent anyone threatening his mum, as she was the only adult he could trust. Perhaps his mum had been so weakened by the trauma that she was unable to say no when she needed to, and Brad had got used to getting his own way. Whatever the reasons, he started to appear more relaxed as the urge to control was removed. His defiant nature eventually turned to tears when he was challenged and he showed genuine remorse in these situations. It seemed that Brad's child–adult relationships had returned to normal.

In Case Study 8.1 Kim realised that there might be problems and initiated a professionals' meeting to establish what the difficulties might be. Once it becomes obvious that your normal behaviour-management methods might not work, it is time to plan an individualised approach. Early identification of the triggers will enable you to think creatively and plan some strategies for the year team to try. Adopting a multi-agency approach will provide the resources to work with the family. The strategies Kim used were successful because the team were well informed and there was a consistency in approach that prevented the student getting confused or finding a crack to exploit. Sometimes the student will not respond immediately and the team need to review and be prepared to modify their approach if it is not working. Individuals learn at different rates, so be patient and persistent.

THE MANIPULATOR

Manipulators have many similarities with controllers. The differences are in the frequency and subtlety of the things they are is trying to manipulate. For example, a student who is happy with a particular teacher will not try to change anything. They will participate in the lesson and appear to be fine. The problem will occur when they get a teacher they do not like for some reason.

The things that a student will try to manipulate will vary. They may try to change their timetable, the people they work with or how something is done because it may clash with their personal agenda. The reasons for their need to manipulate can vary. They may be seeking attention and have learned that by imposing their will they have got their way and the attention they crave. It may be that they do not like people of a certain gender. This may stem from the treatment they have had, which may include abuse. It may be the parent perceives the child as weak and despises them for it. They may dislike someone because of their position, such as a teacher, or someone who has no power and is therefore an easy target.

Strategies for helping manipulators are very similar to strategies for helping controllers. Identifying the cause will enable you to tailor your response most effectively. Students should not be allowed to dominate, otherwise they will continue to feel that their manipulative approach is working. The teacher should set up an alternative plan for the student that provides them with a choice of either working in a satisfactory way with the person or working away from everyone and the benefits they may have had, such as equipment, computers and the company of other students. Sometimes it may be possible to get the student to work one-to-one with the member of staff over a period of time so they have to come to terms with their dislikes (Case Study 8.2).

Case Study 8.2 *Chris*

Chris was in Year 8 and found school hard. He had a statement for learning and behaviour difficulties because his literacy skills were extremely delayed. Eventually the teachers and his parents felt that a period of time at the pupil referral unit (PRU) would be beneficial because things seemed to be going from bad to worse in school.

George came to the PRU at the beginning of the summer term. He had an enthusiastic teaching style that the students liked. His love of maths was infectious and before long he had most of the class getting into the work. The exception was Chris. He just couldn't settle. He made overtures into the work and then just stopped. When George tried to offer him help, he grew sullen and complained that he was not like Ms Hutton; she always explained things more clearly and she let him do the work his way. George had heard this all before. Students often mourn the loss of a teacher they have grown accustomed to. Nevertheless, he had a job to do and was not going to be put off by Chris's comments.

When Chris downed tools and started sprawling across the table, George was not sure what to do. He tried to get Chris back on task but Chris simply refused. Clearly he was winning and the other students were watching as George struggled to maintain his position. He tried tactically ignoring Chris but eventually the other students started to question why Chris was being allowed to get away with not doing any work. George had to apply the sanctions, so he explained to Chris that he would give him one minute to get back to his place, sit properly and get down to work. Chris made some effort by returning to his place, but he refused to get on with the task set. He broke a pencil and swore at George. George felt that this could not be allowed to pass, so he informed Chris that he was sending for the head of year and he would have to leave the room when he arrived.

Chris didn't wait; he got up, swore again, kicked some furniture and slammed the door back on its hinges. Then he stomped off down the corridor to the main entrance and out of the school. When the head of year arrived, she contacted the secretary, who rang the police. Chris was picked up later and returned to the PRU. George discussed the events leading up to Chris's truancy with the head of year. Further enquiries among other staff revealed that there had been some problems and it appeared that he disliked the male teachers in particular. No one seemed to know why, just that all the problems were with the men. George felt a strategy was needed that would help him to work with Chris in the longer term and that would also show Chris he could not choose who he wanted to work with. George's view was that you have to work with all sorts of people once you leave school, so you might as well start learning now.

After considerable thought, George went to the head of the unit and outlined his plan. He felt he needed to work with Chris on a one-to-one basis that forced Chris to come to terms with the problem. He asked whether his classes could be covered for two days so that he could do the work. This was a very unorthodox request but George was convinced it would work and eliminate a problem that would otherwise be prolonged. There were staff available to cover, so it was agreed.

When Chris returned to the PRU the next day, he found that the head of the unit was taking the class. George took Chris aside and explained that he was going to work with him for the next few days and he needed to explain the rules so Chris knew what to do. Then he went on to explain that Chris could have some rewards if he worked well and kept to the rules, but he would have to earn his breaks. George asked Chris whether he would like to have some time at the end of the morning and afternoon sessions doing something he enjoyed. Chris suggested the multi-gym, which was one of his passions. George agreed and then outlined the consequences. He showed Chris the chart he would use to monitor him. If he did well, he would get a point towards the multi-gym every fifteen minutes. He had to get all the points to earn a full session on the multi-gym. Reduced sessions would be awarded down to 90% of the points. If he got below 90% of the points, he would receive no session.

Things went well until Chris had to do something he didn't like. George followed through and Chris obviously resented being told what to do by this male teacher. George reminded Chris of the rule about following his directions, redirected Chris to the task and gave him one minute of take-up time. Chris sat and watched the sand going through the timer and just before the time was up, he got back to work. George made a point of sitting near him in his space; he controlled the room by changing things in the room like opening the windows, turning off lights and keeping possession of pens, rulers, etc., so that Chris had to ask to borrow and return everything. Whenever they had to go anywhere outside the unit, Chris had to walk beside George. He always had to wait to enter any room until George gave him permission. At lunch he had to collect his food and sit at the table until George joined him before he could start eating.

Chris didn't earn break on the first morning, because he had several episodes of sloppy behaviour, and he did not get enough points for the multi-gym at lunchtime. He had tested the boundaries and found they wouldn't budge, so in the afternoon he behaved perfectly. By the end of the first day, Chris was sick of George being around and in his space, but extremely pleased to have earned the multi-gym. George supervised the reward and helped Chris with some of the exercises by counting for him and providing encouragement when the tasks were hard. He even got Chris showing him how to use the various machines. A few seeds were sown in their relationship.

The next day went quite well. Chris didn't earn his break due to a very poor start in the first forty-five minutes, but with some careful coaching he really turned things around by lunchtime. Chris was getting used to George's presence and had seemed reasonably okay about George telling him what to do. However, he blew it in the afternoon and lost the multi-gym again. Despite this, George felt that overall the experience had worked for Chris. The test would be once he was back in class with the others. As they were leaving the PRU, George told Chris how much he had enjoyed working with him and was sorry he had not earned enough points for the multi-gym that evening. Chris took it well, so George suggested that he might like to earn further time in the multi-gym during his lessons. George offered him some sessions on certain days after school, and Chris agreed. George had very few problems with Chris from that time and the multi-gym was made available as a reward in the future.

THE TOTAL SHUTDOWNER

The total shutdowner is a particularly difficult to manage as they do not do things that are really bad. They do not throw things around, hit or shout at other students or teachers, destroy school property or truant. They use silence and non-compliance as a means of demonstrating their feelings and desires. The more you try to provoke them into doing what you ask, the more resilient they appear to be. It is as if they are using the teacher's emotional energy to fuel their wall of silence. Unlike children with low self-esteem, they do not feel the need to go into a corner, cover their face or run away and hide. They have enough strength to remain where they are and literally shut down.

Their stubbornness has probably been learned as a result of being made to do things that they do not know how to do. They become frozen and cannot take the next step, and the adult has either been unable or unwilling to help them. They may have experienced anger from the adult who perceives their inactivity as insolence. They try to ignore the adult in the hope they will be left alone. They channel their energy into ignoring the adult. They will not seethe then suddenly explode. They will remain rooted to the spot and fixed on something they can see near them until they feel the threat has gone.

Dealing with the shutdowner involves restating the direction, followed by a rule reminder. Assume he has heard you and then give him some take-up time. Return to him at the end of that time and remind him of his choices and the consequences of not following directions. When he fails to respond, inform him that you are giving him his first warning. Restate the direction, offer help and then leave him to it again. Repeat going through your behaviour code, pointing out there will be consequences but do not over-service his behaviour. The rest of the class will know you have been fair and dealt with him in the same way as everyone else. Do not make any emotional investment. Wait until another time to tell him the consequences of his actions (Case Study 8.3).

Case Study 8.3 *Terry*

Terry was a tough Year 9 student. He had steely eyes set deeply into his face. His stocky, overweight build coupled with cropped hair and a rough complexion made him a daunting figure for anyone in his way. He had strong views about himself and what he thought he could do. He believed he was good at information and communication technology (ICT) and often talked about his experiences deejaying. He was reasonably articulate but did not come over as being very bright. Teachers who taught subjects he liked, such as technology, ICT and art, said he usually got on with things but would sometimes kick up a fuss when he had to do something he didn't feel he wanted to, because he already knew it or had done it before. It was in these lessons where the work was not to his liking that things started to go wrong.

Sandra was a history teacher. She had qualified a year ago and completed her probation at the school. Now going into her second year of teaching, she felt she was more confident and getting on top of things, unlike the previous year, where there seemed to be so much to do and no time to do it. She still found the planning and marking were keeping her up late in the evening and she regularly arrived early in the morning to prepare her room for the day ahead, but now there seemed to be some light at the end of the tunnel. Some of her year groups were the same as last year, so she had less planning to do and she was beginning to realise what had to be planned and how much detail was needed. She even found time to go to the pub occasionally at weekends.

In the autumn term, the key topic for Terry's group was the causes of the First World War. Sandra was hoping to investigate why the twentieth century was dominated by conflicts. In the first six weeks she was going to get the class to look in detail at the rise of imperialism, particularly the growth of colonies, the alliance between European powers, and Germany's growing feeling of vulnerability. Terry hated history. It is hard to say exactly why, but one reason was surely his unwillingness to produce pieces of extended writing. He was not very good at English and he also had difficulty writing legibly. As soon as Sandra asked the class to make some notes from their textbooks, Terry's shutters started to come down. Sandra's instructions and information sheets were clear and fairly simple, with good examples of what to look for and what to write down. The students could work in pairs but Terry did not like to share things; he preferred his own company.

Sandra briefed the class, answered their questions and gave out the resources. Then she began walking around to offer help and encouragement. When she came to Terry and found he hadn't started she asked him why.

'This is boring,' he replied, and turned away from her.

'Come on, Terry,' she said encouragingly, 'can I help you?'

He looked at her as if to say, 'Who do you think you are? I don't need you because I have no intention of doing this work.' Sandra decided to leave him for a few minutes and then try again. From the other side of the room, she could see that he was still not making a start. She didn't know what to do. Here was a student in her class who was making no effort to do the work and she had no idea how to handle the situation. Her sense of anxiety began to grow into panic as she realised he was challenging her and winning. She needed to do something.

She went back to him and looked over his shoulder but there was still no work on his pad. 'Terry, you can't sit and do nothing. If you don't get on with the work, you will have to do it after school in detention.'

He looked sideways at her, folded his arms and stared straight at the chair in front of him. By now the other students in the class were beginning to notice. They hadn't seen Terry take it this far before. Normally he tutted and huffed then got down to the work. Sandra knew she couldn't leave it like this. Terry was sitting on the chair and staring at her now.

'Right. If you're not going to do the work now, you will have to do it in detention and I will be calling your parents.' She thought that would get him going and prepared herself for his reply, but he simply turned back, faced the front and stared straight at the chair again. What was going through his mind? Was he thinking, 'Look at me. I've got you going. I'm pushing all the right buttons here. You can threaten me but you can't touch me.' Sandra was getting really wound up by now and the rest of the class were beginning to enjoy the spectacle.

'If you don't start work now, you will not only get a detention tomorrow, you will have to stay in at lunchtime every day next week.' Sandra was shaking as she blurted out the threat, but got no reaction from him, not a flicker. It was as if he was hypnotised and in a trance, so that he could neither hear her nor see her. He was transfixed and unreachable. The tension was unbearable. The only relief was the bell marking the end of the lesson. The students started to pack. Terry stood up without looking around, picked up his books and left the room. A number of the students could see that Sandra was shaken and asked her if she was all right. One of the girls went off and got another teacher to come to her. They discussed Terry's behaviour and helped her find some strategies to use.

No teacher looks forward to this kind of experience, but Sandra's response could have been different and might have produced a better outcome. Terry acted in a similar way in several other lessons and eventually the staff got together and planned what to do. The total shutdowner is trying to cope with a stressful situation in the only way he knows how, to shut out everything. He is sending a message to the teacher that he is not playing ball. He will not do the task, whatever the teacher throws at him. The two features of the behaviour are the cause and the response. Sometimes it is difficult to identify the cause.

In Terry's case it was something to do with the work but he obviously had some more serious difficulties, because he could not resolve problems without resorting to extreme reactions. Your response will either reinforce your position as the adult in charge or, like Sandra, undermine that position and allow the student to call the shots. The end result may not actually be any different. The student may not do the work and may remain unreachable for the lesson. The aim is to demonstrate to the whole class that you have a procedure to deal with incidents like this and that consequences will follow. You also need to stay composed and not invest emotional energy in the student's power-broking. Either they do what you ask or they have to face the consequences. In this way, you will avoid feeling deskilled and be helping the students to take responsibility for their own actions.

Sandra braced herself at the start of the lesson. She felt better knowing that other teachers were also having the same problem with Terry and that she had some strategies to use. Terry probably felt that he was more in control because none of the staff had managed to make him do the work. When it came to individual work, he just folded his arms and switched off. Sandra approached him once she had the rest of the class settled. She could see from his body language that she was in for more of the same.

'I can see you haven't started work yet, Terry. Would you like me to explain it again and give you some help?' There was no response. He was transfixed, staring at the chair. 'I'll come back in a few minutes to give you some time to consider my offer.' Outwardly, Sandra tried to appear composed and calm but inwardly her heart was beating like thunder. She moved around the desks helping students and discussing their progress. Then she returned to Terry, who still hadn't moved. 'I can see that you still haven't started. I am ready to help when you want, but if you don't do the work now, we will have to discuss it later in your time. It's your choice.'

Terry didn't even turn and acknowledge her, but Sandra didn't wait. She just moved away and ignored him. The rest of the class carried on with the work then they put their textbooks away so they could begin the discussion part of the lesson. Sandra didn't go back to Terry any more. She had told him what to do and given him time to choose. During the discussion she noticed him move slightly, then a few minutes later he raised his eyes. He was emerging from his trance. Then right at the end of the lesson she saw him go to say something, but another student cut across him, so he stopped. Sandra took the other boy's point and then asked if anyone who hadn't spoken would like a chance to add anything.

Terry spoke up. 'My great grandad was in the First World War.'

'Eureka,' she thought, 'he is back with us again.' And she wondered why he had broken his silence. 'Thank you, Terry. Perhaps you would like to find out what he did for our next lesson.'

Later in the week, Sandra went to Terry's form room and asked to speak to him outside. She reminded him of the lesson and explained that he had chosen not to do the work, so it needed to be done. He tried to get out of it but she insisted that he did some of it at least. Eventually he agreed when she said that he would have to do it instead of ICT unless he did it at lunchtime. Although she had been successful on this occasion, she and the other teachers had a number of difficult experiences with him until he finally left the school in Year 11. It was always the same and she always followed up later. The problem that Terry had was that he just couldn't pull himself out of the hole he got into during the lesson.

Sandra felt good about the new strategy and felt that she had learned a new skill that was very useful. There were several other total shutdowners in the school and she was not always as successful with them, but that didn't matter because she always felt that it was the student making the choice. It wasn't her fault that they were making the wrong choice. The test was whether the incident was handled well.

THE ATTENTION SEEKER

Attention deficit hyperactivity disorder (ADHD) is one of the most common psychiatric disorders that appear in childhood. It is generally first diagnosed during the primary years. Symptoms are always present before age 7 and can continue well into the teenage years. It is most commonly found in boys and if left untreated could have a significant effect on the well-being of the child and family. Research shows that ADHD tends to run in families, so there are likely to be genetic influences. Students who have ADHD usually have at least one close relative who also has ADHD. Furthermore, at least one-third of all fathers who had ADHD in their youth have children with the disorder.

ADHD is not a learning disability but will affect the child's performance in school. This is because one of the symptoms is acting before thinking, which leads to problems with teachers and other students. Students with ADHD tend to show hyperactive and impulsive behaviour and will have problems paying attention and concentrating on things. They are aware of their condition but have difficulty staying still. As a teacher, you should notice when a student exhibits some of the signs of hyperactive behaviour:

- Excessively fidgets or squirms
- Has difficulty remaining seated
- Is easily distracted
- Has difficulty taking turns in games
- Blurts out answers to questions
- Has difficulty following instructions
- Has difficulty sustaining attention
- Shifts from one activity to another
- Has difficulty playing quietly
- Often talks excessively
- Often interrupts

- Often doesn't listen to what is said
- Often loses things
- Often engages in dangerous activities.

Students with ADHD have higher than average rates of injury. ADHD often occurs alongside problems such as depressive and anxiety disorders, drug abuse, and antisocial behaviour.

The ideal diagnosis will be carried out by a medical practitioner and involve an input from the parents. Medication is available and is best used in conjunction with behavioural therapy to help the students control their activity level and impulsiveness. Stimulants are commonly prescribed and include methylphenidate (Ritalin), dextroamphetamine (Dexedrine) and amphetamine (Adderall). The medication is normally prescribed to help the student at school and is not taken in the home unless the need is great. Once a correct diagnosis has been made and the medication and therapy have begun, significant changes will be noticed. The student will be more settled, more able to participate and more able to learn in the classroom environment, and their behaviour can be improved using the same methods you would use with the rest of the class (Case Study 8.4).

Case Study 8.4 *Craig*

Ralph was in his first year of teaching English at a secondary school in an inner-London borough. He had been given a good induction into the school and felt very supported by his colleagues. They had helped him set up the behaviour code for his classes so that he was able to follow the school policy and knew what to do when a student behaved inappropriately. He was getting very confident handling his classes and did not have any problems until Craig turned up. Craig was in Year 8. He had just moved into the area and started at the school in November. Ralph spent time explaining the classroom rules and associated rewards and consequences. Craig's reaction seemed distant at the time, but Ralph put it down to him being new to the school and maybe a little shy. Ralph took the group for two lessons a week and Craig seemed like he was settling in well. Ralph was a little concerned about the standard of Craig's homework but he thought it could be addressed later once Craig had got over the stresses associated with changing schools and making new friends. Then things started to change.

Craig began arriving late for lessons and, when asked to explain, said he had a got a bit lost. He missed a few homework deadlines and had to make up the work in detention. He attended once then missed further ones. Ralph referred him to the head of year, who got him to attend. He continued to miss deadlines then tried to argue when Ralph gave him more detentions. He also began making comments about one of the other students in the group. At first, Ralph didn't catch what was said, so he couldn't respond. When he did finally hear, Craig denied it. Craig worked half-heartedly in lessons and regularly asked Ralph to go over instructions after he had explained them to the whole class. Ralph tried to give him as much support as he could but he had thirty-two other students in the class who all needed help at some point.

When Craig couldn't get his attention, he would turn and start pulling things off the wall or sweep other students' things onto the floor. It was only a matter of time before the atmosphere in the classroom deteriorated into chaos. Ralph found himself torn away from what he was teaching and unsuccessfully trying to calm irate students who were the victims of Craig's actions. Ralph knew things were not going well and his energy was being sapped. He began to really hate taking the group and even started to dislike Craig quite intensely. His normal calm approach had been displaced by a harassed, short-tempered attitude. He found himself snapping at students with whom he had good relationships. He felt tired but could not sleep properly, he started forgetting to do things, missed deadlines and made mistakes on administrative tasks.

Then one day in December things reached a head. Craig was off task and up to no good. Ralph tried to get him back in his seat but had lost his assertive edge. Craig resented Ralph's attempts to stop him doing what he wanted. He'd had enough and was going to leave. Ralph could see his intention and intercepted him at the door, by standing in his way. Craig wasn't having it, so he turned and made for the other exit. Ralph could see the deputy head at the end of the corridor and called to him to stop Craig. When Craig saw his escape thwarted, he swiped out and punched the deputy on the side of the head. Ralph had left the problem for too long. He should have discussed the student with his colleagues. This incident may have been avoided and something could have been done to help Craig.

The school decided not to exclude Craig. The deputy and the head agreed that his behaviour matched that of other students they had seen and they felt he should undergo some tests to identify the causes. Craig was diagnosed as having a form of attention deficit hyperactivity disorder (ADHD) and was placed on a course of medication. It enabled specialist staff to work with him in the learning support unit (LSU), helping him to develop new strategies to stay on task. Ralph learned a lot from the experience and realised that he was not expected to be able to manage every kind of incident that occurred in his classroom. Sometimes it is better to seek help, and that is not an admission of failure. It is acting professionally. Spotting behaviour that is not normal and seeking advice or assistance is the route to a successful outcome. Craig needed help and didn't know how to ask for it because he probably didn't understand what was happening to him. Judicious intervention at the right time would have contained a lot of the problems and got Craig back on track.

It took a little time for the medication to take effect, because the dose needed to be adjusted to ensure he was on the correct amount. After several weeks, Craig's behaviour did start to change. He became more settled and able to listen to the teachers. His work improved as well. For several years he had been a victim of his overactive brain but now finally he could stay on task. Ralph knew there was lost time to make up, but now it might be possible.

THE STUDENT WITH AUTISM

Students with autism will exhibit a range of behavioural traits. The most common form you will come across is Asperger's syndrome. A person with Asperger's syndrome will have some of the features of autism but not the actual disorder. Some people who have Asperger's syndrome can go through their entire lives without realising they have it. It is hard to diagnose because it varies in severity from person to person.

Many people who have Asperger's syndrome have problems maintaining eye contact with the person they are talking to. You may think they are talking to someone else not you. This is called gaze avoidance. Socially, they may not grasp what is going on and react in a way that is out of keeping with the situation. They may also find it hard to join in with physical activities because they tend to be weak and have poor coordination, often described as clumsiness.

Young people with the syndrome have a tendency to become angry at a change of routine and anxious about doing things they do not normally do. They will cling to routines and outwardly exhibit the signs of being obsessive, although the root cause will be different. They have a tendency to become preoccupied and engulf themselves in one subject which, when turned to positive ends, could result in their making a career of it and becoming very successful.

They do not experience a delay in the development of language but may speak in a different manner or in language that appears odd. They do this because it gratifies them and they feel more comfortable doing it. Some children may be able to read well but are not sure what they are reading. Some also have a problem dealing with facts. A child may have an extensive vocabulary but poor reading or comprehension skills (Case Study 8.5).

Case Study 8.5 *Stevie*

Stevie had just transferred to secondary school and his parents and teachers were concerned for several reasons. Firstly, Stevie had been diagnosed with Asperger's syndrome and had difficulty with change of any kind. He had learned ways of dealing with changes in his life but was still extremely anxious and needed considerable time coming to terms with them. Secondly, his parents had fought hard to get him the support he needed so he could stay in mainstream education. There had been a lot of pressure to move him to the special school in the area.

The primary teachers said they had little experience of autism and didn't know how to help him. The educational psychologist had advised that the teachers in the special school who were skilled in teaching children on the autistic spectrum would best serve his needs. He would be with other children like himself. The special educational needs adviser (SENA) had supported this view and pointed out that it would be better to go to the special school while he was still at Key Stage 2, because he would be able to continue there until he left school at 16. However, his parents felt that he would become institutionalised and find it difficult to manage once he left school for good.

Stevie's parents had visited the special school and found it to be a good place. The teachers were friendly, dedicated and genuinely interested in their students. The children seemed happy and the progress they made was incredible. Ofsted had highlighted this in its recent inspection report. But in the end, they had decided that what they really wanted for Stevie was a mainstream experience because he was slightly above average academically and would possibly do better being taught by teachers with subject specialisms. They researched Asperger's syndrome and pushed the local education authority (LEA) until he was given a statement and the support he needed.

In the end, the primary school took their wishes on board and got support from several specialists. One of the teachers got so interested in Stevie's condition that she signed up for the TEACCH course. TEACCH is treatment and education of autistic and related communication-handicapped children, a special programme specifically for teachers of children with autism. She set up the support for Stevie, trained the staff in the methods designed to help him in the class and also produced an impressive bank of resources to enable him to get the best out of the curriculum. The problem was that there were few, if any, other children like Stevie in their chosen secondary school, so the expertise they developed would need to be shared, and quickly.

The teachers met and developed a joint strategy for the transition. Then the special educational needs coordinator (SENCO) in the secondary school arranged some in-service education and training (INSET) meetings as well as some planning meetings for the Year 7 staff, and by September everyone felt confident they knew how to help Stevie. Over the summer break his parents helped him with the changes and new routines he would need to face. By September he was really looking forward to his new school. The first few weeks went well under the circumstances. He needed to use his exit cards for some of the lessons and there were one or two incidents in the playground at break. Most of the students had been briefed about Asperger's syndrome and how it affected Stevie, so they knew what to expect.

Then a calamity occurred. His form teacher and English teacher – English was one of Stevie's favourite subjects – went off sick and a supply teacher had to be brought in. There was very little time to prepare him or Stevie for the change. From Stevie's point of view, things were going well then suddenly everything was wrong. When he walked into the room, someone different was waiting to take the register and yesterday's visual timetable was still on the noticeboard. Stevie had a set routine for doing things when he came in. The teacher had given him the job of switching on the computers, cleaning the board and then he could have five minutes on the computer doing his football project while the rest of the students were coming in. Stevie stood just inside the door and stared down at the nearest chair leg to his side. His expression was fixed and he clutched his bag to his chest. The supply teacher didn't notice him at first because he was looking through the register. After several minutes he became aware of someone standing by the door, so he looked up.

'Come on in and sit down, I will do the register when the rest of the class get here. What is your name?' Stevie didn't reply, just remained as still as a statue. Dennis Luckock had been a supply teacher for nearly nine months. He had come over from New Zealand soon after he had qualified. He was hoping to get some money together so he could tour Europe. He had worked in a number of schools in and around London but never encountered a student like this. The boy didn't seem to hear what he said so he tried again. 'I said, sit down while we wait for the others,' but Stevie didn't move. He couldn't, it felt like his whole body was locked up. 'You can't stand there, now do as I say and go to your place. You will be in the way and the others are coming now.'

Stevie suddenly felt his body unlock and he shrieked. 'Noooo!' Then he spoke in a very strange way as though through his nose. 'Where is Miss Thompson?' he snapped.

'She is off sick and won't be in for a couple of weeks,' replied Dennis, trying to be friendly.

'She can't be, she should be here. She's my teacher.'

So Dennis explained that he was going to fill in for her, but Stevie had turned his back and was fiddling with one of the posters. Tears had welled up in his eyes. Dennis wasn't sure what happened but the next thing he knew was that a large poster was ripped off the wall. 'What did you do that for?' asked Dennis getting quite angry.

'I'm sorry,' said Stevie quickly. 'It was an accident, It fell down.'

Dennis could see that wasn't the case. 'Posters don't just fall down, you pulled it off and tore it. Now look at it.' He knew he had to discipline the boy but didn't quite know how. 'Right, you're in detention.'

'I didn't do it, you ****er! I'm going to kill you and chop up your body!' Dennis couldn't believe what he'd heard. The student was seriously out of control. He went towards the door to get another teacher to come and assist but as he did so, Stevie turned towards him, threw his bag hard in his direction and turned and ran. As he ran down the corridor, he grabbed at the artwork and ripped it off the walls.

'Leave me alone, leave me alone,' he screamed. The SENCO was called and knew where to find him. He was skulking in the computer annexe next to the learning support base. He was quite distraught and could not be persuaded to leave for over an hour. She explained that his teacher had had an accident and was likely to be off for several weeks. They had been lucky to get Mr Luckock at short notice and she was sorry they had not told him about Stevie. She would make a point of meeting him at lunchtime; meanwhile Stevie would probably be better off staying in the learning support base until the afternoon. Gradually Stevie calmed down. He knew he had done wrong and with some careful talking the school helped him understand that he had wilfully damaged school property and been very rude to a member of staff. He accepted the consequences and agreed to apologise to Mr Luckock after lunch.

The SENCO met the teacher and explained that Stevie had been diagnosed as having Asperger's syndrome. She briefly outlined the characteristics that were applicable to Stevie. These included fear of change, need for routines, odd eating habits and an interest in detail. She also explained that he had a very good memory for detail and a love of words and reading but only non-fiction. She outlined the things already put in place to help him. Stevie had a timetable made up of Makaton signs that he'd been using for many years. The teacher had signs for all the lessons, breaks, etc., and would put them on a Velcro strip on the noticeboard by the door so he could see what his day included. He also had a folder he carried around with him that contained the same signs. He would copy the timetable using his signs so he always knew where he was and what he would be doing.

All the teachers were aware of Stevie's dislike of change. Someone would see him in advance if something was going to change and explain what it was, why it was necessary and when it would happen. Stevie felt secure with this and was able to deal with his own feelings during the change. Stevie's teachers would always try to go through what would happen during the lessons, step by step, which is good practice anyway. They would explain how each step related to the big picture, what they had been doing and what they eventually hoped to achieve. Then, during an activity, the teacher would announce to the class that they would soon be finishing what they were on and tell them what they would do next. This clear signposting of events helped Stevie enormously and allowed him to function at his best. During break and lunchtime one of his classmates would have the responsibility of reminding him in advance that the bell would go soon. What he disliked was the high-pitched sound as loud noises frightened him.

Lunchtimes were a problem. Sometimes he would eat only a dry roll. He had very finicky eating habits and never ate anything sweet. Outside in the playground he would get into arguments because he would try to tell other students how to play a game or correct them if they did anything wrong. He was a stickler for getting things right and would go into a very heavy mood if someone appeared to be cheating. In the end it became easier to let him stay in and use a computer than to let him out and deal with the disputes. However, the SENCO insisted that he went out at least once a day, so she used the exit card system to give him an escape route if things got too difficult. She also began using social stories. This is a treatment strategy developed by Carol Gray to improve social behaviour. It involves giving the student short stories to teach socially appropriate behaviours. The stories are used to help the student get a better understanding of their behaviour and that of other people.

The other students in Stevie's class were very understanding about his condition and were extremely helpful but sometimes he tried their patience and conflicts would occur. The teachers didn't let Stevie get away with clear breaches of school rules or classroom codes but they would be understanding and not impose consequences immediately. They would wait until he had control, because it was senseless trying to reason with him while he felt anxious or angry. Dennis felt much better about Stevie being in his class once he knew all about his condition. He quickly got organised and it was really rewarding seeing the change in Stevie once everything was in place to help him cope. By the time Miss Thompson returned, Dennis had learned a lot about working with students on the autistic spectrum and decided that he would like to specialise in special education when he returned to New Zealand.

THE STUDENT WITH LOW SELF-ESTEEM

The way we view ourselves in relation to others is vital but can vary according to who we are with and how others treat us. Teachers have a great impact in this area and can help students perceive themselves positively or negatively in the things they say and the expectations they have of each student. Self-esteem is the value we have of ourselves as individuals and is the sum total of the interactions we have with other people. However, young people create their self-image from the images others have of them as well as their own perceptions. For example, a child may believe they are very good at drawing because their parents and family members have praised their pictures. This perception can be completely shattered by a few misplaced comments made by a teacher in front of peers. The teacher's authority will work against the opinions of the parents, and comments from their peers will cut deeply into their view of their artistic ability.

When a student's self-esteem is dented in this way, they will become anxious about their ability to do other things and less motivated to try in case a similar negative experience occurs. If the same student moves to a class with a teacher who can motivate and praise effectively to produce a positive climate, the student's perception of their ability may change. They will believe they can do something well and feel secure enough to try to do better. Their feeling of belonging will be strengthened along with their feeling of being secure.

The student with low self-esteem will probably have had negative experiences in the home, community, school or a combination of these. They may have been verbally, physically or sexually abused. The child may have experienced an imbalance between success and failure that has scarred them. They may have actually been successful like a boy who swam in galas at a national level but was constantly criticised by his father because he was not swimming fast enough.

A sense of failure is a common factor and a key variable is the way a teacher, parent or trainer works with the child. The child will experience failure when he cannot live up to his parents' expectations or is told that he is no good at something. The signs of low self-esteem and a poor self-image are visible but need to be interpreted with care. Just because a student presents with one or more of them does not mean they have a poor self-image. There may be more to it. However, it is useful to list them so you can be alerted when you spot them in an individual. Any of the following may be present:

- Destroying work that has been praised
- Destroying personal possessions
- Running away from things
- Standing right in a corner facing the wall
- Pulling a jacket or jumper over their head to hide inside
- Covering their face or lying face down on a desk
- Going under a table or desk
- Attempting to bully or be aggressive to others
- Using diversionary tactics to avoid failure, e.g. work avoidance, complaining about illness, needing the toilet, being the class clown, changing the subject by being chatty
- Saying they are useless at things
- Failing to show enjoyment in relaxed, free, unstructured activities
- Possibly even self-harming, although this will probably be associated with relationship problems within the family.

Changing an individual's perception of themselves is the way forward. Being very positive towards the child can reverse milder cases, and so can developing a classroom climate where there are no limits to learning, everyone feels secure and achievement of all kinds is recognised.

Students with a very poor self-image will need multi-agency help so that experiences and knowledge can be shared and strategies developed in and out of the school. Engaging a learning mentor will provide a useful starting point to monitor the student's behaviour and intervene when they are under stress. Change will not happen quickly, so staff should try to identify any small changes or differences in behaviour that indicate progress. These can then be built on and strategies revised accordingly (Case Study 8.6).

Case Study 8.6 *Joe*

Joe was completely at sea when he was at school. He didn't seem to care about things or what his teachers thought. He lived on the local estate with his mum and younger sister. He never knew his dad. He was a likeable lad but anyone meeting him for the first time might be easily deceived because he could not be trusted. He would nick anything he thought he could sell. He had a reputation on the estate as a crook and had been caught several times breaking and entering. But you couldn't help warming to him; he always had a smile and a greeting for you.

Joe had a speech impediment that he was very self-conscious about. He tended to lisp and mispronounce a lot of words. He wouldn't engage in conversation and stuck to quick comments made in a local accent, which disguised his difficulty. His way was to act a bit of a lad and joke with the teachers he liked.

Lyn knew about his background and tried to ensure he was accepted in the group and that no one made comments about his speech. However, one morning as he was walking through the playground, something happened involving some of the Year 11 girls. He came into the classroom with his head down. Lyn greeted him as she usually did but got no response. He went straight to the back of the room and sat in the corner with his coat pulled right up over his head. She tried to talk to him but the only response she got was '**** off!' so she left him alone. As the other students arrived, she directed them to their seats and told them to ignore him. He stayed in the corner until after registration and when everyone else had left, he got up and followed them. Other teachers reported similar occurrences during the term and they agreed that the best course of action was to ignore him. Lyn felt she was not tackling the cause and that she needed more information about him.

During further meetings, Lyn heard some more of Joe's unusual behaviour. Gerry taught art and had Joe in his class. They had been learning how to do silk-screen printing and Joe had worked really hard on it. Over the double lesson, he had transferred his artwork onto film and made up the screen. He had masked it then produced a two-colour print. Gerry was impressed by the way he had got on with the job. He had mastered the process and begun manipulating the medium quite creatively. At the end of the lesson, Gerry tried to praise Joe's efforts but Joe called his own work rubbish and started finding faults in it. Gerry pointed out the strengths and said he would like to display it on the art room wall, but Joe seemed very negative so he left him to pack up. After the class had gone, he found the print screwed up in the waste bin. It was ruined, which was a shame.

Ken, the English teacher, was starting *Macbeth* and the class were acting some of the scenes as part of their work. He insisted that everyone was involved and gave Joe a very small speaking part. Joe found acting very hard. Ken had watched Joe move around the room and wondered what he was up to, but concluded that he was trying to imagine prowling around the corridors of the castle. Just as his cue came, Joe turned very angry and was gone. Ken rushed to the door but he was too late. Joe was out and running across the playground towards the gate. Ken sent a message to the office and they contacted the police. The deputy and the site supervisor went out to see if they could find him. No one did. He went to ground but returned home later in the evening. This happened several more times and eventually he was excluded for three days.

A few weekends later, a message came to Lyn that Joe had been caught breaking into a small garage. He had to appear in court the following week. Throughout the autumn term, Lyn heard numerous accounts of incidents in and out of school. Joe grew more withdrawn and participated very little in anything, preferring just to sit and stare out of the window. Whenever he was given something to do, he would either look around and act like a toddler, or if the work was too difficult, he would pull his blazer over his head and retreat into himself. The chirpy lad who used to make people smile had changed.

Lyn couldn't work out why and Joe was becoming increasingly difficult to handle. She had the help of the special educational needs coordinator (SENCO) and a member of the behaviour support team (BST) from the local education authority (LEA), but no one was able to find a way in. The educational psychologist carried out some observations and tried to talk to Joe, but with little success. His view was that Joe had a very poor self-image, partly due to his feelings about his speech impediment. He suggested that Joe would benefit from therapy to help him with his negative feelings. This was arranged. The educational psychologist carried out some home visits and reported back that his mum had got a new partner, who was spending a great deal of time in the family home. Lyn decided that it would be useful to arrange a meeting at the school and invite Joe's mum to discuss the changes in his behaviour. She failed to attend and could not be reached because her telephone had been cut off. After writing letters, it was obvious that his mum was not responding.

When a student misbehaves it is usually because something is going wrong in their lives. Sometimes things are wrong at the school and the student expresses their feelings at home, sometimes it is the other way round. Joe's recent behaviour could have been due to the changes at home – a plea for help and attention. A meeting with other professionals to plan a support package recommended another go at speech therapy; this would tackle the root cause of Joe's poor self-image. Unfortunately, the local authority speech therapist was away on long-term sickness and there was a long waiting list.

The SENCO decided to pay for a private assessment, which cost £100–200, so that Joe's problems could be identified quickly and some activities and exercises could be developed to help him. A learning mentor was assigned to Joe for a couple of hours each week to do the therapy with him. An experienced member of the BST offered to do some work with Joe on a weekly basis to help him develop ways of coping that included altering his perception of himself as a victim to someone who can change things by taking action. A social worker endeavoured to work with Joe's mum so that Joe's worries over her new partner could be addressed.

Lyn and his other teachers developed differentiated activities that enabled him to achieve immediate success with the minimum effort. Tasks were split up into much smaller steps then marked immediately to give regular feedback. The tasks were kept to a minimum level of challenge and when Joe did well the teacher would simply give it back and say it was right without making a fuss. Praise was limited at first and usually done privately, either by writing it on the work or offering a few well-chosen words discreetly to avoid embarrassing Joe. The more things he did right, the more he got used to being successful. With this success came a growing confidence, which allowed him to rebuild his relationships with the teachers he used to get on with. Over time Joe's self-esteem grew and made him more able to take on greater challenges, including going for job interviews during Year 11.

THE AGGRESSIVE STUDENT

Some students will be aggressive. There are many ways this may manifest itself. A student may be verbally aggressive and swear and cuss other students and staff. The physically aggressive student will use violent force against other students and adults in a variety of ways. Their threats may be hollow but they should always be taken seriously. Aggressive students may use weapons to threaten or to cause harm, but they will generally try to harm someone by punching, kicking, pinching, biting and scratching.

The student is trying to communicate their feelings. The use of violence will be a learned response that the student has used and found successful in the past. Repeated use will reinforce the success and provide the student with a way of dominating the situation. Alternatively, they may have been subjected to violence in the home, witnessing it or actually being on the receiving end, which has resulted in violent tendencies.

There are many triggers for violent behaviour. A student may lash out for almost any reason if they have violent tendencies and cannot contain their anger. It is very difficult to prevent a violent student from getting involved in an incident by trying to remove the external causes. Identifying when the risk of violence is most likely then containing the student could be an option but does not tackle the internal feelings that cause the student to be aggressive. Focus on the student's anger and lack of self-constraint.

There are many approaches to anger management. They may be based on the association of a pleasurable sensation with a physical object or action. When a stressful situation arises, the student tries to remember that pleasure by using the object or action. This sends pleasurable signals to the brain by releasing endorphins that swamp the negative thoughts. The other method is based on training the student to strengthen their internal self-control. This is done by conditioning. The student role-plays situations where problems occur and is given strategies to ignore the triggers that lead to their aggressive behaviour. They practise the strategies until they have internalised them so they become automatic responses in those situations.

An aggressive student can do harm to other students and staff, so their safety must be paramount when an incident occurs. A serious outburst leading to an assault on a member of staff can lead to permanent exclusion from the school. A head teacher does not take lightly the decision to exclude a student but must also protect the safety of other students and staff. When a head teacher cannot guarantee safety, action must be taken. It can be very stressful dealing with a student who is behaving violently. Staff can train in methods of physical restraint and this is advisable if the school has students who are known to be violent. This must be done by adults that know the proper procedures for restraining, as incorrect practice can lead to accidents and legal action (Case Study 8.7).

Case Study 8.7 *Kirstie*

Last night was not a good night. Kirstie had rung up her boyfriend to see what he was doing but his phone was on voicemail. She tried sending him a text but got no answer. She was bored because there was nothing to do and her mum was on at her to tidy her room instead of lazing around downstairs. Then her mobile rang. It was Ryan, her boyfriend, at long last. She answered the phone, happy to hear his voice and hoping that he could come round later. Unfortunately, his dad had broken down on the way home from work and his mum worked evenings at the off-licence, so he had to stay in and look after his little sister. Kirstie suggested she came round to him but he didn't seem too keen.

Later that night her mum sent her to get some milk and as she passed the park she saw Ryan. He was on his own and she was just about to call out when another girl walked up to him from the other entrance. They literally fell into each other's arms and began kissing. Kirstie couldn't believe what was happening. She had been with him for a year and thought they were so happy together. What was going on? They stopped kissing, walked down the drive and disappeared into the shelter. Kirstie was disgusted and went home with tears in her eyes.

Mel sensed something was wrong with Kirstie when she first came into the classroom. She had taught her in Year 9 and most of the current year and could see she was in a foul mood. When she tried to talk to her, she snapped and turned away. It was very hard getting through, so she left it. Things didn't get better and Mel had to reprimand her several times during the lesson. The touchpaper was lit and the seconds were passing. The explosion occurred at the end of the lesson. Mel didn't know what happened exactly. The class had been dismissed and were leaving the room. Mel was packing up her things because she had to teach a class in another room. Suddenly, there was a lot of shouting and swearing. Mel looked up in time to see Kirstie and another girl in a clinch. Hair was being pulled, there was scratching and kicking plus a lot of shouting.

The other students moved back and joined in the shouting, urging the girls on. Mel was paralysed; she didn't know what to do except to shout 'Stop!' The head of the upper school was passing and came rushing into the room. Within seconds he had parted them and moved the other girl over by the door. Kirstie was uncontrollable. She was shouting and swearing. Then she turned and made her way to the fire exit. The other girl managed to break free and tried to go after her. Kirstie grabbed a chair and threw it. It missed the girl and caught one of the students who had been watching. She collapsed as the chair hit her in the leg. Kirstie turned and was gone. The other girl reached the fire exit and stood laughing and jeering as Kirstie disappeared.

Kirstie had a history of aggressive acts but none had amounted to anything. Minor skirmishes in the playground and the odd loud disagreement with a few punches were the only recorded incidents. On each occasion she had been punished and a letter had gone home to her parents informing them of the incident and the action taken. This time things were different. She was eventually picked up and brought back to the head's office. She was informed that she would be excluded for three days and placed on report when she returned.

After the incident, staff requested training in dealing with students like Kirstie and an in-service education and training (INSET) day was arranged. Procedures for the use of positive handling were agreed and a policy written and circulated. At least four more violent incidents occurred, but they were all handled differently. On one of the occasions Kirstie was on a school trip and had a disagreement while in the coach. She could not control herself and started swearing. Then she threatened a student, so the teacher came and sat near her to try to calm her down. She did not respond and just got more mouthy with the girl behind her. All of a sudden she stood up and tried to reach over and grab the girl's hair.

The teacher intercepted her and managed to hold her in her seat. He calmly explained what he was doing and what he was going to do next. He also asked for another teacher to witness what he was doing. Kirstie was screaming and cussing as she wriggled and tried to escape. The driver stopped the coach and the teacher managed to start calming her down. The rest of the journey was quiet but she still required some holding. Once back in school, the usual procedures were followed when restraint was used. The forms were filled in and copied. A letter went home to Kirstie's parents and the head of the upper school interviewed the teacher to check that he was all right, as he was quite shaken by the experience.

Ensuring the safety of the other students as well as your own personal well-being should be your primary concern. Remaining calm at all times is easier said than done but is also probably the most important thing you can do. Teachers who get emotionally involved and express anger fuel the situation as well as providing satisfaction for those students seeking a response. Training in positive handling procedures will give you the confidence and the skills to deal with students who get physically aggressive. Well-kept records of incidents and the action taken are essential for other professionals who may eventually take up the case. They also provide you with useful memory joggers if a student decides to challenge decisions made about them. Most of all, be realistic. Try to remain consistent and fair. Look for small changes in behaviour, as progress will not be immediate. Do not take things personally. Most teachers find it difficult to deal with students who have challenging behaviour.

SUMMARY

- Students with very challenging behaviour will have special needs that may be based on clinical causes or emotional difficulties.
- Correctly interpreting the causes of undesirable behaviour is important for developing suitable responses.
- Find out whether a student has a record of poor behaviour in other classes.
- Investigate the student's family history and home life and ascertain whether there has been a critical incident that could explain their behaviour.
- When there is no apparent reason for the behaviour, you could try using Dreikur's goal disclosure method.
- Asking colleagues for help is not an admission of failure. Not asking is.
- Use the knowledge and expertise of other professionals in seeking a solution.
- Stick to your behaviour plan even when the student does not seem to be responding. This will prevent you becoming emotionally involved. Remember it is the student who is making the choice, not you.
- Reinforce the idea that it's the student's behaviour you do not like, not the student themselves.

9 THE TOUGH CLASS

Much of this book has been about how to manage individual students who behave in particular ways that disrupt the rest of the class. The point of having a behaviour code is to ensure that the students know the rules and the expectations placed on them and that you will have suitable responses worked out in advance to deal with incidents when they occur. Dealing with a tough class is different to dealing with a difficult student. The difficult student tries to disrupt the lesson for the majority, whereas the tough class prevents the minority from learning.

Certain classes develop a reputation for being difficult. This could happen at any time in any school. Some staff are more aware and are able to prevent the triggers that cause it by careful planning, grouping, timetabling and by supporting colleagues when things start to go wrong. A difficult class is not a natural phenomenon. It arises over time because of the context, the mix of individuals in the group, and the staff who teach it.

A tough class will evolve from a few individuals who draw the majority in and muster them as a force against the teacher and the school. The story is about who is in control. Normally it is the teacher but sometimes this changes and the students take power. They call the shots, decide what happens, make the decisions and dominate the time and the space. When this happens the teacher retreats and finds they are in a very awkward and demoralising position that is difficult to reverse without the support and help of colleagues. Another position you may find yourself in is being given a group that already has a reputation for being tough.

WHAT MAKES A CLASS TOUGH?

A class can be described as tough when the behaviour of the students is so disruptive in its frequency and intensity that the teacher begins to feel a sense of failure. The teacher will suffer professionally by questioning their own ability. They will also suffer personally in their health. Typical symptoms will be related to stress:

- Inability to sleep well
- Loss of appetite
- Headaches
- Feeling tired
- Short temper
- Feeling demoralised.

After a while the teacher will look for ways of avoiding lessons with a tough group. They will feel they cannot face the group on some days and will ring in sick. On other days they will feel stronger and come in, only to be worn down by the class and then be off for several days afterwards. The teacher who does not get any support will only gain release when they give up and resign their post at the school. The teaching profession cannot afford this. Teachers commit four years of their lives training to do the job. When they qualify they are not experts. They are usually enthusiastic and have substantial theoretical knowledge of the work they will do. Their experience of the classroom and the students may be considerable and gained during a number of teaching placements but it may not prepare the graduate for tough groups. Therefore they need to be given a chance with proper support and guidance together with careful timetabling to reduce the risk of them coming up against a tough class. Suggesting that we all find it hard when we began our careers is not a convincing argument.

NO BEHAVIOUR CODE

One of the most common reasons for a class getting out of control is the absence of an explicit, detailed behaviour code. Taking over from a teacher who has not used a clear code can be a lottery. An aggressive teacher may have kept the class under control but the students would not have had the opportunity to take responsibility for their behaviour. The absence of a code may be due to the school not having a coordinated approach. Teachers would have had to make their own arrangements, resulting in a great deal of variation between classes.

If you find you are taking over a poorly established class that has got used to working without clear boundaries, you will need to be resolute in putting measures in place. Most classes will respond positively because they will probably feel insecure. Young people need and want clear routines and rules. There will always be a minority who will exploit the absence of order but the majority will feel safe and want a teacher who can show they are in charge.

The implementation of a behaviour code can be very hard work with classes that have had a weak teacher. They will be used to ignoring and even despising the teacher and need a very clear, assertive approach from someone who is not prepared to accept any cheek, rudeness or deliberate non-compliance. That does not mean you become aggressive or dictatorial, just determined to achieve your goal.

NEGATIVE VIBES

Students are very adept at picking up the vibes. They can tell whether or not you are having a good day. Some will even be quite sensitive and try to help. This awareness can be very destructive at times. Teachers who send out negative messages will find that they are being picked up. The long-term effect can be disastrous for the students and the teacher.

Negative vibes are not always blatantly obvious. They may be hidden away in the things you say and do. For example, a throwaway comment like this carries a message to the student that they are not able to remember something and so dense that even the most obvious point cannot penetrate:

'How many times do I have to tell you before it sinks in?'

Comments like this serve no purpose because they do not tell the student how they can improve. Be wary of making statements that sound final:

'I've had it with you lot.'

This implies that the teacher is not going to make any more effort or allowance and has given up on the class. They are also getting cross and frustrated, which reveals their own weakness. Describing the class as 'you lot' lumps them all together, which can be interpreted by some as unfair. The well-behaved students will feel they are being labelled and judged along with the less well-behaved. They will resent the punishment for something they haven't done and turn against the teacher. Making comparisons can also be dangerous:

'The other class have already started the next stage of this work.'

This can be very upsetting and demotivating for most students. The other class may be further on, but so what. This really says more about the teacher than the group. Teachers with two groups of similar ability will find they cannot help comparing them. The groups would probably progress at approximately the same rate providing lessons are not missed. Groups with students who have special needs may make slower progress, so the role of the teacher will be to get the pace right and keep the whole group moving forward. Individuals within the group may feel they are doing their best, therefore a blanket criticism does not help anyone as it is unspecific. Blaming the group merely highlights the differences and some may perceive it as a fault of the teacher rather than the students.

It can be incredibly irritating for a student when a teacher compares them to an older brother or sister:

'You're always getting into trouble. Why can't you be like your brother? He always gets his homework in on time.'

Comments like this are guaranteed to get the hackles up. Teachers may have these thoughts from time to time but they should keep them for the privacy of the staffroom. Actually saying them to a student will not yield any benefits, only fuel resentment. And here is another negative comment:

'I just don't understand why students in this class feel they have the right to talk during assembly. You know the rule. All the other classes can manage it.'

Worse still is the treatment of the class as a homogeneous entity rather than a group of individuals. There will almost certainly be students in the group who will not like being addressed in this way. They will be aggrieved by the unfair treatment and may react badly.

The heartening thought is that if students can be so deeply affected by a teacher's negative and destructive comments, perhaps positive comments could have a very beneficial effect. Teachers who have high expectations, talk up their classes to other teachers and give their students plenty of support will find they achieve much more. It is certainly worth trying and you have nothing to lose.

THE NEW STUDENT

New students often join schools part of the way through the year. In some schools this may be more common than others, so the staff become skilled in dealing with the changes. It can be a daunting prospect for a young person. They have left their school and a local community that was familiar to them, where they were known and accepted. Joining a new school brings new challenges. The first one is entering the building and going into the classroom. No matter how great the preparation, there will still be barriers for the student to overcome. Many schools set up buddy systems and link the new student to someone with similar interests. This is a good practice but the student still needs to establish themselves with the peer group.

Peer group membership creates a range of problems in schools. There will be hierarchies in every class and the teacher needs to manage and perhaps control them. Students take their places in the pecking order by their ability to communicate status and leadership qualities. Status can be conferred or appropriated according to strength, achievement and persuasive influence. For example a strong, well-built, powerful-looking student will be feared and admired. A student who is attractive and good-looking will be more readily accepted in a group than someone with a physical anomaly.

A student may exhibit an air of confidence through their dress sense, posture, language and turn of phrase. Such street credibility may place them centrally in the group as an okay person. Some may even be elevated to positions of movers and shakers whereas others will become members of the peer group. The losers are the ones who fail to get accepted and find themselves ostracised and on the outside of all the groups. They may eventually come together and be labelled by the others as misfits.

A new student trying to find their place will disturb the equilibrium within the group until they are accepted or cast out. They will be a novelty for a few days or even weeks as the rest of the class size them up. Some of the students may start to behave in ways that are out of character as they attempt to impress or dominate the new member of the class. The disruptions will become less frequent as the student gets accepted and finds their place. There are many strategies to prevent some of the disruptions:

- Allocate a desk and a group for them.
- Find out their interests and achievements and put them in touch with friends who share the same interests.
- Set aside special sessions for discussing their interests. Plan these sessions to ensure you know in advance what they are. Get the students to complete an interest audit of things they like doing, places they have visited and things they have done well. The appendices contain an audit form you can photocopy.

This information can be used to help you organise groups and plan lessons. Students may have a specific interest that you can incorporate into an activity to bring it to life. Drawing on their own experiences will ensure you are anchoring the lesson in their culture as well as providing them with a useful starting point to explore new things.

A new student will threaten existing friendship groups by challenging the leadership and putting pressure on relationships between the boys and the girls. A new girl can cause a lot of friction with boys, especially if she is popular and good-looking. Other girls will become jealous as the attention shifts from them to her and then the reprisals and niggling behaviour begin. Friendships will become strained and the seeds of bullying may be sown.

The teacher needs to be on the lookout for these signs and should be prepared to intervene as early as possible. Reorganise the seating, regroup students and keep an eagle eye on them, especially when they do not think you are looking; this will safeguard the vulnerable students who may become the target during the instability of the new student's arrival.

THE SINK CLASS

A tough class can arise for various reasons. It may be a good group that has been poorly managed or the result of thoughtless grouping, setting and timetabling. When a class has more than 10% of the students with special needs there has been an error of judgement in deciding the groupings. Placing a large number of students with special needs in one class may seem like a good idea, because their needs can be better served if they are together. Resources and staff can be concentrated in one class. Students attracting support can be grouped to make better use of the support staff assigned to them. The lessons can be planned to address their specific learning needs and the pace of the teaching can be adjusted to ensure all the lower-ability students understand the work.

The disadvantage is that although the lessons seem to be well staffed, in practice there is not always enough support time to cover every lesson. The lessons without support then become extremely difficult to manage for the teacher, and the whole group starts to lose out, culminating in behaviour problems. The profile of the group gets skewed towards the lower abilities and you lose the benefits of having a mixed-ability group. The group as a whole will eventually perceive themselves as less able. They will realise they are the group that is least likely to do well. They will not generate as many opportunities to engage with ideas as the more able groups. Their diet in the lesson could become simplified and even bland. The self-fulfilling prophecy of being the 'dunces', 'duffers', 'morons' or 'the thick class' will start to dawn on some of them and they may even use these labels themselves.

Self-belief blossoms in a positive class but will wither away and die when the teacher starts to label the students. Similar problems arise from setting and streaming. There are contrasting views on separating students by ability. Educationalists who argue for setting stress the need to focus on the ability range and present an argument based on common sense. The teacher who has students with a narrower range of abilities can plan tasks and activities that match their needs so that everyone is working on similar things. The hope is that it makes better use of time and resources. The most obvious disadvantage is that the students will make personal judgements about their own abilities based on the group in which they find themselves. This can be demotivating for those in the lower sets and also for the students in the top sets who cannot keep up. They start to see themselves as weak even though they may be in the top 20% of the year group of up to two hundred students.

Teachers of mixed-ability groups deal with the wide range of abilities by grouping or setting the students within the room. They differentiate the work for the groups. It does not take long before the students in the low-ability groups realise they are getting different, easier work. This can become a source of conflict if it is left to fester.

TEACHERS WHO ARE AFRAID TO ASK FOR HELP

Some teachers believe that when the class behaves well it is a mark of their success. This is fine when things are stable and the students are learning and behaving well. The danger occurs when things start to go wrong. The confident teacher will ask colleagues for help and then the problem will be shared. The confidence comes from the knowledge that the behaviour is the responsibility of the students and that they do not always make good choices. Teachers who believe this will be more ready to ask for help, because they do not feel their skills in managing the class are being questioned. Even the most experienced teachers get very difficult students they cannot deal with on their own. Teachers who feel they should manage every incident without help put unnecessary pressure on themselves. They will probably try to manage their class using an authoritarian style, which will inevitably result in challenges they may not be able to win. When that happens they will start to feel threatened and their doubts will grow.

TEACHING

The best way to avoid poor behaviour is with good teaching. Get the activities right, pace the lesson well, engage the students with interesting activities and an upbeat delivery, add your own enthusiasm for the subject and you will have cracked it. It sounds easy, doesn't it? But there are so many variables. Conscientious teachers know it and plan their lessons to reach this goal. Occasionally a teacher will find it is too much of a challenge and give up. They resign themselves to what they know rather than seeking help. Perhaps they are too afraid or too proud to ask, or perhaps they do not even realise their lessons are dull. Whatever the reason, poor teaching eventually leads to switched-off students. When this happens the problems start. There will always be some students who have their own personal difficulties and do not respond to even the best teacher. They will need very clear approaches to help them manage their behaviour.

Poor teaching causes all manner of problems. Individual students will become frustrated about the work for a variety of reasons. They may not be able to do it or the work may be too easy. It may be boring or made boring by a dull delivery. When this happens they will communicate their frustration by doing things that cause low-level disruptions. Some will do it in a way to test the teacher's response. They will try to find out whether the teacher can cope with their behaviour. An inadequate response will be the signal for them that the teacher is weak and ripe for systematic baiting designed to bring turmoil to the classroom. A ringleader may emerge at this point. He will orchestrate the disruptive activities and make comments outside the lessons that are designed to undermine the teacher.

Students can be merciless, so you need your wits about you when you are working with them. When they get a teacher in their sights they will go for the jugular. They will look for personal attributes they can exploit and these will form the basis of their comments. Protect yourself by preventing them having information about you. Follow these guidelines:

- Do not reveal your first name or where you live.
- Do not express your own likes and dislikes until you are confident with the class and feel you have control.

- Refrain from using obviously outdated expressions or expressions the students use.
- Project an air of confidence.
- Do not get into any conversations during lessons. Students will try to take in a weak teacher by showing some interest in something they have found out about them.

The ringleaders will be clever and select their followers carefully. They will pick students who are weak-willed and easily led or bold characters who share their view.

The process of undermining will spread quickly as impressionable young people, uncertain about themselves, gravitate towards a group to gain a sense of belonging. As more join the campaign, the low-level disruptions become more frequent. Here are some things they may try:

- Sitting in the teacher's chair
- Changing the computer settings and passwords
- Locking the teacher out of the room
- Going through the teacher's cupboards and drawers in search of personal possessions to abuse
- Calling the teacher by their first name
- Forgetting to address the teacher as Sir, Miss or Mr
- Deliberately ignoring the classroom code
- Making funny noises that are hard to trace
- Annoying students who do not join them in their disruptive activities
- Turning up for the lesson late or leaving early.

The teacher will become more aware of the incidents but find it hard to challenge the students because they will be very clever in concealing their activities. The rest of the class become the audience, spectators of a game that everyone enjoys except the teacher. When the teacher does try to challenge someone, they will deny any knowledge, seek the support of their peers and pass the blame to confuse and exhaust the teacher. Eventually the teacher will give up trying to challenge the students, because they never seem to catch the perpetrator and the daily occurrences sap their energy. They try to ignore the disruptions, but this merely gives the students licence to try harder.

Picture the scene; it is almost like something from *The Bash Street Kids* or *Please, Sir!* The teacher is desperately trying to teach but the class are not listening. Things fly across the room. Students get up and walk around and seem to be doing as they please. When the bell goes they get up and walk out, knocking books on the floor and overturning furniture for the poor teacher to tidy up before the next group comes in. Clearly the teacher has lost it at this point and the students do not want to know. They will become the teacher's nightmare class from hell. A victory will spur the students on and they will start looking for their next victim unless they are stopped. These students will be very good at rallying others around them to give them power and status. They will influence their peers to cause problems or to follow their lead in challenging the teacher. Their strategies will be quite covert.

THE TOUGH CLASS ACROSS THE YEAR GROUP

Difficult classes manifest in several ways. They may be particular to one teacher because there are problems with the relationship. Alternatively, most of the teachers taking the class may be experiencing difficulties. When this happens there needs to be a collective response to the problem. This is easier said than done, because a teacher may find it hard to admit they are having difficulties managing the class, as described earlier. Sometimes colleagues may suspect there is a problem and may be able to help. They may witness a teacher struggling or they may be called on a regular basis to help deal with students and begin to realise that something more is required.

Assuming there is the desire to help and support, the next step is to make enquiries among other staff who teach the group. This will enable you to decide which way to go in resolving the problem. If all the teachers are finding the class difficult to manage, call a meeting to discuss what is hard about them. List the reasons with examples. During the discussions, staff will start to name specific troublemakers. Draw up a list and try to identify the ringleaders. Record anecdotal evidence to inform your decisions on tackling the problems. It is tempting to believe the student is at fault, but consider other factors such as the subject, the timetable and the collective approach of the teachers, who may be inadvertently treating the student negatively.

Move to solutions by ascertaining whether any of the teachers are doing things that are working. An action plan will be required and should include these strategies. The plan will ensure that everyone is clear about the interventions to be used. Work will probably be required to develop a suitable behaviour code that can be shared across the year group. The teaching team may consider changing the groups and the lesson timetable. When the action plan is in place, set up meetings to interview the ringleaders. These meetings should always be attended by two members of staff. Pay attention to teacher harassment. If there is evidence of students harassing a member of staff, follow the procedures on page 163. All action plans need to be reviewed. Figure 9.1 (overleaf) shows the steps for dealing with a tough class across a year group.

WHEN ONE TEACHER FINDS A CLASS TOUGH

A different response is needed when just one teacher in a year team finds a class difficult. Knowing they are having difficulties is the first hurdle. Some teachers are afraid to seek help but the signs will be there. Two tell-tale signs are excessive noise coming from the room and the teacher looking anxious and stressed. Immediate assistance should be provided to alleviate the stress while longer-term solutions are devised. The following could be tried:

- Ask the teacher if it is okay to use one of the computers in the room because all of the others are in use, have crashed or have the wrong software. It could be a piece of equipment or a space in their room if there is no computer.
- Go in and relieve the teacher by telling them they have an urgent telephone call in the office.
- Send a message to the class with a list of students who you want to see in your room. These are the known troublemakers. It gets them out of the lesson and gives the teacher a chance to stabilise the rest of the class.
- Go in and ask the teacher if you can borrow some students from the class to help you do a job such as sorting out books, cleaning computer screens, resetting

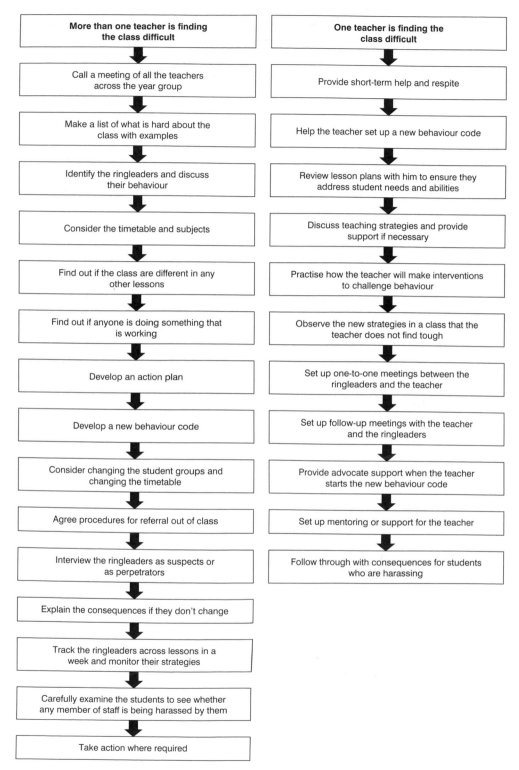

More than one teacher is finding the class difficult	One teacher is finding the class difficult
Call a meeting of all the teachers across the year group	Provide short-term help and respite
Make a list of what is hard about the class with examples	Help the teacher set up a new behaviour code
Identify the ringleaders and discuss their behaviour	Review lesson plans with him to ensure they address student needs and abilities
Consider the timetable and subjects	Discuss teaching strategies and provide support if necessary
Find out if the class are different in any other lessons	Practise how the teacher will make interventions to challenge behaviour
Find out if anyone is doing something that is working	Observe the new strategies in a class that the teacher does not find tough
Develop an action plan	Set up one-to-one meetings between the ringleaders and the teacher
Develop a new behaviour code	Set up follow-up meetings with the teacher and the ringleaders
Consider changing the student groups and changing the timetable	Provide advocate support when the teacher starts the new behaviour code
Agree procedures for referral out of class	Set up mentoring or support for the teacher
Interview the ringleaders as suspects or as perpetrators	Follow through with consequences for students who are harassing
Explain the consequences if they don't change	
Track the ringleaders across lessons in a week and monitor their strategies	
Carefully examine the students to see whether any member of staff is being harassed by them	
Take action where required	

Figure 9.1 *Who is finding the class difficult?*

desktops on computers, tidying sports equipment or moving furniture. This will enable you to talk on a personal level to individual students about what is going on in the room and why they are behaving that way.

These suggestions provide immediate support as a lifeline but will not solve the problems. Real solutions need to be found in the longer term. The teacher needs help to set up a new behaviour code and then to implement it. They need an experienced colleague to help them review their lesson plans to ensure they address the needs and abilities of the students. Teaching strategies that have been proven to work with the group should be considered and opportunities for the teacher to observe them in action should be given. Coaching the teacher in making successful interventions will also be very useful. The next step is to help the teacher to practise the interventions with a different class.

BULLYING AND HARASSMENT OF THE TEACHER

A group that becomes tough due to a slippage of the teacher's behaviour management skills may eventually be perceived as bullying and harassing. Bullying is a learned response and can be stopped. Teachers who find themselves under pressure in this way will be distressed, have low self-esteem and be afraid to challenge students who are harassing them. Students who are not challenged will feed off their success, grow stronger and continue. It is vital that a teacher in this position confides in a colleague and shares the problem as early as possible instead of bottling it up.

A senior colleague should be included at this point and should organise a class meeting with the teacher to tackle general issues of bullying. Use the session to address the following issues:

- What is bullying?
- Why do people bully others?
- What do you think they get out of it?
- How do you think the victims feel?
- How do the bullies feel?
- Have you ever been bullied before?
- How do you think it affects the victim's life?
- How can we help the victims of bullying?
- What can we do to stop bullying?

Once the class start to talk openly, ask them whether they think it is a game. If they try to say it is just a bit of fun, point out that it is certainly not fun being on the receiving end. This is a suitable time to start to be more specific. Explain that adults can be bullied by other adults and even by children. Give some examples to illustrate what you mean. Introduce the word 'harassment' and emphasise that teachers are human beings and deserve to be treated decently. Tell them that their behaviour in the lesson is a form of harassment and has to stop. Most of the students will not have thought that what they were doing was very serious. By the end of the meeting they will realise it is serious and they will know the consequences if they continue.

The class meeting should be set up to allow the students and the staff time to talk. Avoid letting the students just moan and vent their feelings about marking, lessons, homework, school dinners, etc. Avoid having the teacher talk at the students. Help the students to consider how the victim feels by getting them to empathise. Suggest they imagine the victim to be someone they know; it could be a brother, sister, mum, dad or friend. Explain to them that the victim has feelings, a life and a right to be treated with respect. Teachers are the same and have these needs too.

Bullying exists in a climate of fear and secrecy. The bully threatens the victim with reprisals if they try to tell the authorities. They will gain status if their peer group become aware of their activities. Their peers will probably become too frightened to intervene or they will turn a blind eye to what is happening. Furthermore, a student who bullies an adult will gain greater kudos from the peer group. If you find they are slipping into this situation, keep records of exactly what happened, including dates, times, places, names and lists of witnesses. Then try to get some help. Do not leave it until it's too late. If you feel a colleague is being harassed, offer support. Do not legitimise bullying by ignoring it.

PICKING OFF THE RINGLEADERS

A tough class will have its ringleaders. Identifying and confronting them through the official channel of a face-to-face meeting organised by the senior colleague is the best way to put a stop to their activities (Case Study 9.1).

Case Study 9.1 *Paul*

I was in my mid twenties and had been teaching for just over two years. I worked in a very large secondary school in a leafy suburb. The students were from predominantly well-off homes with parents working in business and the professions. The school had a good reputation and very good results. If you saw any of the students out of school, you would think they looked smart and well behaved. They were model students from a very successful school. The catchment area was in demand with a premium price on the houses. The school was over-subscribed and parents moved into the area to ensure the children got a place.

The school and the students were high achievers. If you flicked through the local papers, you would be sure to come across stories of their achievements. The sports team won their fair share of cups and trophies. Business partnerships between major international companies and the school promoted its outward-looking curriculum with work placements and bursaries. Staff also made links with schools in other countries and went on expeditions to South America and Africa to work with local communities. Its orchestras and teams would tour the world, providing fantastic experiences for the students. The school seemed to have everything going for it and I was proud to be part of it.

Behaviour in the school was good. A recent Ofsted report commented on how well it was managed, enabling the students to flourish and grow with the responsibilities they were given. The leadership team had tackled all the main aspects of pastoral care and developed policies for them. Prospective parents couldn't help but be impressed by the school's explanations of the student services. They went away thinking this was a school that really cared, where their child would be safe, secure and valued as an individual. Students leaving the school at the end of Year 13 were confident, well-rounded people ready to take their places in the community as leaders, movers and shakers.

I remember thinking how good the staff were when I came to look round before my interview. They seemed to be so dedicated and committed to their work. Everything I'd read in the prospectus, everything the head teacher had said, it all seemed to be happening. One point in particular struck me as very significant and laudable. The head had been asked a question about bullying by one of the parents and he had replied, 'We do not have bullying in this school. We treat the students fairly and in an adult way and expect them to act accordingly. We have a very detailed anti-bullying policy and every student attends an introductory session in Year 7. The head of year makes it very clear what will happen if anyone even so much as considers abusing the rights of others.' He had made it obvious that bullying was not tolerated in the school.

For a while, I was very confident that the school had got it right in practically everything. The head was right, there didn't seem to be any bullying going on that I could see. My first year was a happy one and I was really getting to enjoy my work. I had mainly Year 7 and 8 science groups with one first-year A level physics class. This year I was also given a Year 9 group and a Year 10 group. They seemed fine, although there were one or two students in the Year 10 class who were harder to manage, but I was confident they would settle down eventually.

I was probably a little too generous, because the students seemed to be distant and difficult to engage. There were about half a dozen who were very clued up about the work and I knew they would be a pleasure to teach. It is nice when you get some students who really seem interested and able to produce work of a high level. I was slightly in awe of them and found that it was hard to keep ahead of them to make sure they were challenged. They seemed to finish the work so quickly and to a very high standard.

Then there were the three guys at the back. They were in a different league. They would all get their GCSE grade C but were not showing signs of being very interested. Whenever I came into the room they were deep in conversation and would not break off and give me their attention until I started to get a bit cross. No, this group were a different kettle of fish to the ones I had last year. But I knew my stuff and felt confident we would get through the syllabus by the summer term. I just needed to keep ploughing on and not let a few spoil it for the rest of the class.

I have never been one to start bossing students around. They need to learn otherwise they won't get the grades. I must say, I don't like having kids in my class that don't want to learn. They waste everyone's time. I don't know why the head doesn't get all the ones who don't want to do well and put them into one class. I'm sure that would solve the problem of time-wasting and teachers like me could get on with my job of making sure the rest of the class do well. Anyway it's not up to me, I don't manage the school.

The autumn half-term drew nearer and the belligerent ones at the back were still dragging their feet. The sparky group were pushing ahead and I felt confident they were on target for A*s. The rest were also doing well. My problem was differentiating the work for the high-flyers. No matter what I gave them, they seemed to lap it up and finished it earlier than I thought. I noticed one of them starting to get restless and misbehaving. I put it down to a windy day but he continued the next lesson. He started to get a bit cheeky with me, which I didn't like. I suppose he could see I wasn't amused and seemed to be enjoying that, because he carried on.

I forgot about this over half-term and returned revived and ready, but I was not prepared for what came next. Each time I took the Year 10 group things got worse. The high-flyers seemed to have crash-landed. I couldn't get them to do their work. Whenever I turned my back, something happened and it seemed to come from their direction. Objects flew across the room, books fell off desks and sudden noises broke my concentration. I couldn't tell who was behind these incidents, so it was difficult to do anything about them.

On one occasion I was helping a group with an experiment when there was a crash and a whole load of glassware cascaded off the shelf. It landed on my desk, sending shards of broken glass over my coat and into my open briefcase. The laptop near the interactive board was covered in bits too. I was livid and prepared to take the culprit to task. A quiet student from the most able group volunteered an apology in such a way that it was hard for me not to accept it. He explained that he was trying to get one of the flasks down but it must have caught the others and unbalanced them. I knew he was lying but what could I do? I accepted his apology and got someone to go and get the caretaker. Out of the corner of my eye, I caught several of the high-flyers looking my way and sniggering together.

On another occasion the whole class seemed to have developed coughs, because when I tried to explain what we would be doing, a coughing epidemic broke out. I stopped to let them finish. Then when I tried to resume, the coughing started again. This went on for quite some time. Then they stopped and everything seemed quiet. I managed to get them started then a mobile went off. I tried to see who it belonged to but it stopped after two rings, so I couldn't really pin it down. I got everyone together and told them that all mobiles should be switched off. A few minutes later it happened again. I was getting rather cross now but I didn't know who was responsible, so I told them that if it happened once more they would all stay in over lunchtime.

No sooner had I finished and got them back to work than a phone rang. I knew I had to carry through with what I'd said, so I told them they would be kept in. When the bell rang, they all packed their stuff away and I was just about to tell them to stay put when two students at the back got up and started walking out. I demanded that they sat back down but they said they didn't have mobiles and I could search them if I didn't believe them. They said they weren't going to be punished for something they didn't do. I couldn't reach the door to stop them, so they got away. Before I knew what was happening, about ten more students got up and were saying the same thing. They barged past me and were gone.

I could see the high-flyers smiling but just staying put. 'You aren't just going to let them go are you, Paul?' I didn't like the way they used my first name. The expressions on their faces were sinister. 'Well if they're going, so are we, because we're not taking the punishment on our own.' And off they went. I knew I couldn't take much more of this. Several more lessons went by with similar incidents, further rudeness and downright insolence. I also started to notice things outside the class. My windscreen wipers were tampered with on several occasions. One of my tyres looked rather soft but was not punctured. Gum was put on my classroom chair and one of my desk drawers looked like it had been filled with water and then emptied. It was very wet and some of my books and papers were damp and the ink had run.

Eventually I decided to tell a colleague in the science team who had joined the school just before me. He advised me to make notes of the incidents then we took them to the deputy and discussed what to do. The deputy was very supportive and set up a series of meetings between me and each of the students on my list. I went away, worked out what I was going

to say and practised with my colleague. On the day of the meetings I started to feel nervous. I don't know why, because at last something was being done and I was hopeful. I sat next to the deputy and the first student sat opposite at the other end of the table.

The deputy opened by addressing the student in a very calm, serious and firm way. 'We called this meeting because I am very concerned about the kinds of behaviour in your class.' He went on to describe in detail the things the students had been doing. He made it specific, naming individual students whenever necessary. Then it was my turn. I explained to the student how his behaviour had affected my ability to carry out my job as the teacher. I looked the student straight in the eyes and expressed my feelings in vivid detail. I could see he was feeling uncomfortable and ashamed. I described how harmful his actions had been and the disappointment I had felt. He found it hard to look me in the eye but I faced him and made him do it. He had nowhere else to look except down. I finished by telling him I wanted the behaviour to stop.

I think my descriptions of the hurtful effects got through to him. I'm not sure it worked for all the others, but certainly most of them seemed surprised. The deputy invited him to speak and respond to what I had said. He explained that he hadn't realised it would do this much harm. Looking back, he could see that what they had been doing was serious stuff but he just wanted to have a bit of fun. They thought I was someone they could do it to without getting into trouble. The deputy reminded him of our right to teach and do our jobs without being harassed. He pointed out that a campaign as systematic as theirs was bound to have harmful effects on my feelings. It was bullying. There was no other way to describe it.

The deputy reiterated the school rules, especially the one on bullying. One of the other students tried to deny that they were bullying, but the deputy was forceful and said that bullying would not be tolerated. This student got abusive and one of the others remained silent and refused to acknowledge anything. The deputy handled them both very well by explaining this was their opportunity to account for themselves and it was up to them to use it. Getting aggressive or refusing to speak did not help them in any way. He asked the student what he would do to ensure I could teach the class and not have to endure any more of his disruptions and harassment. He then asked him how he was going to rebuild the relationship. It ended with the student apologising to me. The deputy concluded by stating again that the student would be expected to stop the bullying or face the consequences. He spelled out the consequences in no uncertain terms and made a date for a review meeting in two weeks' time. Then he signed and dated the notes, put them together and dismissed the student.

We had similar meetings with each of the students and I must say that through all of them I felt very supported and more confident knowing I had the backing of the deputy and the school. The reviews went ahead but really the problems seemed to stop after the first meetings. I can see now where I went wrong and have got some help in extending the most able students and also my classroom management style. The whole experience was a powerful one and not a part of my career I look back on with pride. I learned a lot from it and appreciate how the school handled the whole messy business. I'm a deputy myself now and have had to deal with bullying between students. The situations aren't identical but the methods are the same. The meeting with the bully and the victim works very well providing there is a structure and someone in authority to chair it. They can then stress the consequences and the need for it to stop. I haven't had to deal with a member of staff being bullied, because I can see how it starts and I've set up a very clear behaviour code. I have channels for referring the students when their behaviour starts to escalate.

CHALLENGING STUDENTS YOU SUSPECT ARE BULLYING YOU

Sometimes it is very difficult to identify who is doing the bullying or whether it is in fact bullying. This needs a different approach to actual bullying. Keep notes of things that happen and once you have your evidence, go to a senior colleague and set up a meeting. The pattern of the meeting is very similar to the one for actual bullying; the difference is what is said. The senior colleague begins the meeting using a phrase like this:

'We are interviewing a number of students about what has been going on in the maths lessons.'

(Replace 'maths' with the appropriate subject.) This will inform the student that a systematic investigation is being carried out. Specific examples of behaviour should be presented:

'Mr A has told me that some of the students, including you, have been deliberately ignoring him when he comes into the room. When he tries to call the class to attention they begin to hum and that lasts for about a minute. Then they stop and start laughing and jeering. Eventually Mr A is allowed to begin but the same thing often happens again later in the lesson.'

The student is given an opportunity to comment:

'What do you know about this?'

This lets the student know you are on to him but gives him a chance to explain what has been happening, especially if he has not been directly involved. Then the teacher is invited to explain how he feels when the behaviour starts and how it is preventing him from doing his job. Empathy is used to get the student to think about how he would feel if he were the teacher. The senior colleague concludes this part of the meeting by stating:

'No one deserves this kind of behaviour. It doesn't matter who they are, a student or a teacher, it is wrong and it will not be tolerated!'

Sometimes students feel that a weak teacher is an easy target, or a teacher with characteristics that are funny or quirky. The senior colleague answers any suggestion of this with:

'If you feel you are not being treated fairly or have a legitimate complaint, you either speak directly to the teacher, the head or me and we will listen to you.'

The meeting is concluded by reminding the student of the behaviour code and detailing the rights of everyone, including the staff, and the responsibilities of all to uphold those rights. Make notes of everything that is said during the meeting and then make a date to review the student's behaviour in two weeks. Note that no one is blamed. Empathy is used instead. It is a more neutral way of getting the student to think about the implications of the situation. The student will go back to his friends and talk about the meeting and they will know you are on to them.

BULLYING TEACHERS: A CONCLUSION

Serious bullying may need actual consequences and head teachers should not refrain from giving them when they are required. Here are three examples:

- Contact the student's parents
- Change the student's class
- Exclude the student.

These consequences should be used in the last resort and should only happen if the bullying recurs after the meetings. Prevention is best and there are several ways to do it. Figure 9.2 (overleaf) summarises them as a checklist. You could use it to check whether you are taking the right preventative measures.

TAKING OVER A TOUGH CLASS

Taking over a tough class can be a daunting prospect. Some might believe it is a rite of passage for the fledgling teacher, an initiation into a fraternity who have known the stresses and troubles caused by the occasional difficult class. When the staff in a school know there is a tough class, help should be on hand. It should not be an experience to be endured like running over hot coals. The tough class needs to be made normal again for everyone's good, but especially for the students. The solution is straightforward. It is what this book is all about, but it's not easy. It would be all right if you could just walk into a room and tell the class the rules, but getting their attention needs to come first. They will have become used to deciding when they will attend and when they will listen to the teacher. Cracking that will require help from colleagues, and so will getting enough time to show you are different from the other teachers they've had.

Checklist to Prevent Bullying

You plan and deliver lessons that are right for the student group ☐

You make the effort to get to know the student in and out of class in order to find out their interests and common ground ☐

Teaching is monitored to ensure the curriculum is delivered appropriately ☐

The school has safe confidential channels for disclosure where victims of bullying can seek support ☐

There is a school council that gives students the opportunity to air their views and contribute to the operations of the school community ☐

Regular class meetings are held to resolve difficulties and agree items to go to the school council ☐

Interventions are timely and follow an agreed procedure laid down in the behaviour policy ☐

Behaviour management is a whole-school procedure and individual members of staff are given guidance on how to carry it out ☐

Figure 9.2 *Checklist to prevent bullying*

THE ADVOCATE TEACHER

An advocate teacher can be used to help teachers who are being harassed as well as new teachers taking over a difficult class. It depends on the school recognising two things:

- New teachers will need support during the early weeks while they are establishing themselves with their classes.
- All schools have classes that could become difficult if they are not managed carefully.

Senior managers need to identify any potentially tricky classes that a new teacher has on their timetable before starting in the school. The subject team are then contacted and asked to meet with the new teacher to plan the first term. They will help the teacher plan the lessons for the first two weeks and help them with resourcing. This will ensure the teacher is prepared and supported for starting in the school. The advocate teacher should be a more senior member of the team who knows the class well and holds some authority in the school; they should introduce the new teacher to the class.

Introductions

The advocate teacher arrives at the lesson and makes sure the students line up and enter the room in an orderly fashion. He moves to the front of the class in the centre of the room and greets them. The new teacher takes his place at the side of the room and attends to what the advocate teacher is saying. He does not look at the class. His focus is on the front, like the students'. This maintains the advocate teacher's authority. The advocate teacher then says:

'Good morning. As you know, Mr Clark left us last term and Mr Smith has joined us to take his place.'

He maintains the students' attention and says nothing about the teacher's past experience or the poor behaviour of the class.

Handover

The advocate teacher then turns to the new teacher and signals to him to move to the centre of the room at the front, where he introduces himself:

'Good morning, I am Mr Smith and I will be taking you for science this year.'

The advocate teacher moves to the side and maintains his attention on Mr Smith, listening intently to his introduction. He does not look round at the class. His body language is open and he shows interest in what the teacher is about to say. The handover is seamless and the movement of authority occurs without question. The advocate teacher needs to send out the right signals at this crucial time. He is there to introduce the new teacher, not to be his bodyguard. The students need to feel that both teachers are working together as equal partners and not detect any signs of seniority. They must see the new teacher in front of them as an experienced professional who knows what he is doing.

'I am pleased to have been asked to come and work at this school. I have taught in a number of other schools and am looking forward to working with you.'

A confident delivery will settle the students and ensure they do not try to test you on the first day.

Behaviour code

The advocate teacher should sit or stand in a relaxed way during this time. He should avoid surveying the room and fixing any potential troublemakers with a glare that says, 'I know what you are capable of and I am watching you.' Nor should he stand, arms folded, facing them like a bouncer outside a nightclub. The teacher briefly explains the behaviour code and takes any questions then begins the lesson. Any chatting, lateness or minor disturbance that occurred during the introduction should be dealt with assertively by the new teacher. Once the students are engaged in the tasks, both teachers use correction and praise when it is needed. This communicates the message that they are working together and team teaching.

Ending

The class comes back together at the end and the new teacher takes up his position at the front. The advocate teacher returns to the side of the room and gives him his full attention. His style remains relaxed and he appears interested in what conclusions the teacher will draw. His attention channels the attention of any students who are looking at him. They follow his eyeline towards the teacher at the front. After the plenary, the homework is set and the reminders are given about leaving things tidy. The teacher thanks the class and dismisses them. The presence of an advocate has given the teacher a window of calm and order to establish himself with the class. His presence has also given the teacher the confidence to concentrate on his teaching rather than worrying about the behaviour. This, together with a well-planned and resourced lesson, has led to a good experience for both the teacher and the students, perhaps the first they've had for a while.

Next lesson

There are several ways to manage the subsequent lessons. The advocate teacher could arrive at the same time as the teacher, enter the room and sit at the same place at the side. He observes the teacher's performance during the whole class and plenary parts of a lesson and makes notes in the same way as an inspector. During the tasks, he assumes the team teaching role as before. This provides a presence in the room but allows the teacher to remain in charge.

The other way is to drop in and have a chat about something. The students will have begun their tasks, giving the teacher freedom to have a visitor. This way should only be used if the teacher and the advocate feel confident that things are going well. If the class is really tough, the first method is preferable, at least for several more lessons until the teacher has properly established himself and the students have settled into their new routines. The test for this is the number of disruptions and how they are handled. The new teacher should feel that disruptions are being handled well and the students are responding by accepting the consequences. The acid test will be when he has to give a consequence without the advocate in the room.

ADVANTAGES OF THE ADVOCATE APPROACH

- The new teacher feels supported by a team of colleagues from the first day and in the future will not feel afraid to ask for help.
- The teacher will get a good start with the class and have a chance to establish himself knowing the advocate is there to help if things start to go wrong.
- The team will show the teacher how lessons are planned in the department and set the teacher on the right road with a couple of lessons planned collaboratively at the start.
- The students in the class will accept the teacher more easily if it is done through the advocacy of another teacher they already know.
- The new teacher will be directed to plan in detail the lessons and the behaviour code and the routines within the class such as lining up and entering the room. The advocate will be responsible for showing the teacher what is required rather than just assuming they know. Where the new teacher obviously knows what to do, the professional courtesy is to reach an appropriate agreement. The spirit is not one of patronising the new teacher but of ensuring they feel supported and free to ask for help.

INDUCTION PROGRAMMES

Schools without these systems would do well to consider them when planning their induction programmes. They should be incorporated into a whole-school approach for managing behaviour, the subject of the next chapter.

Summary

- Tough classes come about for a variety of reasons, including a teacher's classroom management skills.
- A class may be difficult for all the teachers in a year group or just one or two of them.
- Immediate interventions should be made. The ringleaders need to be identified and then meetings arranged between them, the teacher and a senior colleague.
- Empathy should be used to help the perpetrators get an idea of what the teacher feels.
- Students should be made aware of the consequences if they continue to disrupt the lesson.
- Class meetings can be used to try to resolve problems between students and the teacher.
- More experienced teachers should support the teacher in distress by helping them plan their lessons, acting as an advocate to give them a chance to change things in the room, and providing moral support.
- When taking over a tough class, the school should provide a programme of support that enables the new teacher to establish themselves with the class under the wing of an advocate teacher.
- The school needs to have channels of communication for the victims of bullying. These channels should include staff and students.

10 THE WHOLE-SCHOOL APPROACH

The whole-school approach is the most important factor in managing behaviour. Clear systems operated consistently and fairly by assertive staff will minimise problems and will lead to students taking responsibility for their own behaviour and making the most of their time at the school. The problems occur when there are no agreed procedures. Teachers start to interpret the rules in their own ways, set up their own behaviour codes and respond to inappropriate behaviour in different ways. This eventually leads to confusion. This book provides guidance on managing behaviour for individual teachers. However, it is best used as a resource by the whole staff when devising a unified school behaviour policy. Consequently, this final chapter is the most important.

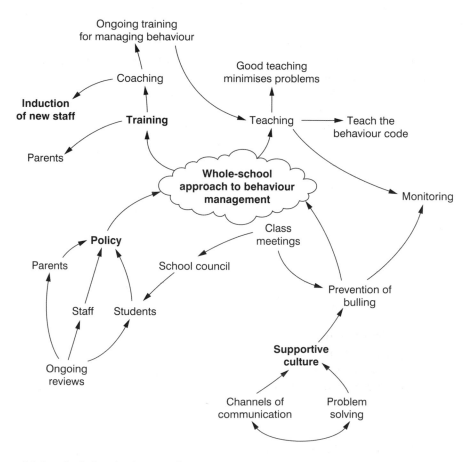

Figure 10.1   *A whole-school approach*

A whole-school approach has four key areas:

- Policy
- Training
- Induction
- Support.

They are interlinked and provide the cornerstones for building a management system that reaches into every aspect of school life. Figure 10.1 shows how each area contributes to the overall plan. This chapter looks at how to draft and implement a behaviour policy. It will take you through the steps to produce a document that will encapsulate the school ethos on behaviour management and outline the practices to use on a daily basis.

STEP 1: GETTING STARTED

The policy is a very important document. It communicates the ethos behind the school's approach and describes how it will be translated into practice. It can only be effective as a working document if everyone contributes. There are several ways to achieve this:

- Hold meetings to agree practices.
- Involve students in drawing up the behaviour code with rewards and consequences.
- Circulate drafts for comment.
- Provide special lessons for the students to learn the code.
- Train the staff in how to use the code.
- Invite parents to contribute to the annual review of the code.

STEP 2: ESTABLISHING THE RULES

The senior managers need to take a lead by producing a draft for discussion by the whole staff. At the end of the session, the staff should have reached an agreement so the actual practices can be formulated. A positive management ethos should include these three ideas.

Rights
The policy protects individual rights and makes that aim the responsibility of everyone.

Behaviour not the person
The underlying belief will be that everyone is capable of changing. A person who behaves inappropriately has the power to choose. It is the behaviour that is disliked not the person. They are in control and not perceived as a victim. This also prevents teachers labelling students as bad.

Responsibility
The use of choice places the responsibility with the student. It is up to them to make good choices. The aim is to help the students manage their own behaviour.

STEP 3: THE PRACTICE

It will take several sessions to bring together all the ideas and reach agreement on the practices the staff will use. The senior team need to agree the basic rules that will apply across the school. These rules are then discussed with the staff so they can see the difference between rules and directions. Individual teachers then work alone or in groups to write up the directions for the routines that operate in the school, but they do not form part of the policy. Teachers also take the plan to the students to gather their suggestions about rewards and consequences. The senior team should work out the hierarchy of responses, indicating when a student should be referred on to the next stage. They should also devise a means of recording incidents and a way of tracking them in the referral process. The following guidelines should help the staff clarify their practices.

Rules

Rules need to be fair and easily understood. They should be written as dos and don'ts wherever possible. The rules should stem from the list of basic rights.

Interventions

Teachers should consider how and when to make interventions. The policy should state clearly that all staff will be trained to be assertive and make interventions in a non-confrontational, detached and unemotional way.

Rewards

Students and staff should have discussions and agree on some realistic rewards; these rewards are then listed with an explanation of how they will be given.

Consequences

Consequences should be carefully considered by everyone concerned. Governors may also need to be consulted to ensure that everyone agrees on the consequences, how they will be given and who will make the decisions to give them. The use of more serious sanctions such as internal isolation and exclusion should be described with care; state clearly that government guidelines will be followed.

Stages of response

Where no guidelines exist, staff may refer students to senior colleagues for minor incidents. Alternatively, they will refer incidents straight to the head teacher and miss out the head of year and key stage manager. The policy should describe the stages, list the gatekeepers and outline the reasons for the referral. A report form should follow the student right through the referral process and be signed by each gatekeeper who has an input. Once the consequence has been completed, the form should be returned to the teacher so they are aware of the outcome. Then they put it in the student's file. Teachers who refer a student to a more senior colleague sometimes do not know what happens to them, so this system keeps everyone informed.

Records

Incidents that occur in the class should be recorded. Teachers should have a simple tick sheet to use during the lessons for recording verbal warnings, time-outs, one-minute detentions, etc. These record sheets should be kept and used when writing individual education plans and personal support plans.

Wider issues

The policy should show the links to other areas of school life. Make reference to other policies so that you demonstrate a unified management process.

PSHE

Personal, social and health education (PSHE) is one of the most obvious links. The PSHE curriculum is concerned with personal development in its broadest sense. It provides the teachers with opportunities to tackle behaviour alongside the other responsibilities needed to become a knowledgeable, well-adjusted citizen. It also offers space to engage with emotional intelligence (Goleman, 1996), arguably an important skill for success in adult life as it puts you in control of your own emotions and makes you sensitive to those of other people. Emotional intelligence provides a good foundation for managing undesirable behaviour that could stem from feelings of anger, frustration and aggression.

Teaching and learning

The teaching and learning policy will set out the school's ethos and make the link between interesting lessons and good behaviour.

Induction

The school's induction programme will prepare new staff for the work they will do. Give careful consideration to the ways the staff do things and outline training in the policy. Highlighting the provision of a mentor, the level of support given during the first lessons, etc., will communicate to everyone that proper support is available.

Student involvement

Describe the involvement of the students in behaviour management. It is a regular ongoing commitment of reviewing the code and the procedures. This gives the student body a role in the school's management and ensures the leadership team remain informed on the day-to-day operation of the system. Regular class meetings and school council meetings are the forums for these discussions; any recommendations are forwarded to the relevant senior managers.

Parental involvement

Parental involvement is a vital part of any behaviour plan, and parents will be pleased to see they have been included in the policy. The methods of involvement should be described and could include their input to the annual review of the plan together with training sessions for those parents who want to improve how they manage behaviour at home.

Harassment and bullying

Refer to the anti-bullying policy. Briefly summarise the school's approach plus the main methods it will use, such as mentors and the buddy system. Stress the school's climate of openness and its supportive nature.

STEP 4: TRAINING

Training is at the heart of the policy. Good training will ensure that everyone concerned knows their role and the expectations placed on each individual. Staff who are trained will feel confident they can carry out their role in accordance with the policy guidelines. These will probably be the main areas of training:

- Induction for new staff
- Teaching the behaviour code to the students
- Helping parents improve their behaviour management skills
- Refresher sessions for all staff using problem solving.

Training in behaviour can be great fun as well as extremely productive. The school can organise its own training or bring in a specialist to facilitate the sessions. This largely depends on how individual schools like to go about it. The advantage of a specialist is that they know what works well and what doesn't. For schools wishing to do it themselves, the following model may be useful.

The case study model

The staff are given several scenarios like the ones featured in this book. They then work in small groups or pairs to discuss how they would deal with the incident. Their target is to suggest strategies that could be used. The facilitator should provide some generic guidelines before the groups begin. Here are some things to remember when considering interventions or responses:

- Offer choices.
- Either respond or tactically ignore.
- Use rule reminders.
- Redirect the students to the task.
- Do not respond to secondary behaviour.
- Do not provide a show for the rest of the class.
- Begin interventions at a low level and only move to a higher level if this does not work.
- Keep consequences and rewards in proportion and linked to the behaviour.
- Dislike the behaviour not the student.
- All behaviour is a communication.

The groups should write brief notes on their recommended responses to the case study. They could be asked to describe how *not* to respond to the incident. This allows them to focus on the potential pitfalls. The whole staff could be given the same case study, or each group could be given a different case study and then swap case studies at a convenient time. The facilitator's job is to gather up the notes and responses to each case study. These can be written up and gradually turned into a school manual on behaviour management. Wright (1988) is a rich source of case studies. This is a highly successful method for staff development. Staff enjoy the sessions because they can actively engage with the problems, devising new strategies and reviewing current practices at the same time. The end result is a very useful handbook for any teacher to use.

Input as well as output

Good training needs input from someone with experience for staff to feel they are gaining new skills and knowledge. It can be very frustrating to find you're on a 'do-it-yourself' staff training course. Senior staff offering training in behaviour management need to look at the school and judge the needs. It will be a fruitless exercise giving staff case studies if they do not have enough experience to generate workable ideas. Schools that have developed behaviour codes along the lines of this book will gain a great deal from case study training. Schools that are just starting on this road should consider bringing in a specialist to help staff think through their ethos and produce a policy. From this they can work on practices and test them using the case studies. Wherever your school has reached, I wish you good luck and I'm sure you'll enjoy the rest of the journey.

Summary

- Consistency is vital so the students know what to expect.
- Every school should have a behaviour policy that clearly sets out its behaviour management methods and the ethos which underpins them.
- The methods should be clear, staged from low-level incidents dealt with by the teacher to high-level incidents that require action by the head teacher and the governors.
- The behaviour policy should be simple and practical so that the newest or most inexperienced adults can use it.
- Devising a whole-school approach should include all staff, students, parents and governors so the behaviour policy is owned by everybody.
- Special lessons should be timetabled so that students can be taught the behaviour policy at the start of the school year, and refresher sessions should be scheduled during the year when required.
- New students will need to be taught the behaviour policy.
- New staff should be trained in how to use the behaviour policy during their induction.
- The behaviour policy should be reviewed half-termly at the beginning and then annually in the policy review cycle.
- A serious breakdown in behaviour should prompt a review of how it was handled and the effectiveness of the behaviour policy; check for flaws or omissions that need addressing.
- Form partnerships with other schools, pupil referral units and external agencies such as behaviour support and the educational psychology service for support in creating and developing the behaviour policy.

CONCLUSION

While I was researching and planning this book it became obvious that there is far more to managing behaviour than just setting up a behaviour code. My questions led me to the work of Daniel Goleman (1996). He argues that there is more to intelligence than the academic intelligence quotient (IQ). The brain functions on several levels. The amygdala is a small area of the brain that controls our emotional responses and was a major force in helping our ancestors to survive in a dangerous world of predators, where food had to be hunted or gathered. The intuitive judgements made by the amygdala could have meant the difference between life and death for humans up to about a thousand years ago. Since then massive technological advancements have changed our world and our lifestyles. Those split-second decisions based on experiences gained in the early years of childhood and filed in a muddled way could now mean that we do something we may regret later. They are devoid of the rational thoughts of the cortex that could tell us to stop and consider what might happen if we went for other options.

Goleman describes one group of primary school boys with above average IQs. They were not doing very well in their academic work, so neuropsychological tests were carried out and revealed that the boys had impaired cortex functioning. They were impulsive, anxious and often got into trouble. It was believed they had faulty prefrontal control over their limbic urges. Their lack of control over their emotional life placed them at highest risk of failing academically and of getting involved in crime, alcoholism and drug abuse. I am sure you will recognise students who exhibit these tendencies in the classroom. The worry is that not enough is done to help students take control of their emotions and the results become obvious at school and in later life.

We teach the National Curriculum subjects but we need to go further to make sure every child is taught how to control anger and resolve conflicts positively. If we leave this to chance, we risk missing the opportunity given us by the slow maturation of the brain. Once a child reaches adolescence the pathways become harder to access and there is less chance of harnessing and controlling those urges. Catching children early and teaching them how to behave is the first step. However, we will be leaving the job unfinished if we do not try to teach them how to manage those times when they see red mist and how to control their emotions when their primitive amygdala kicks in.

As educationalists, we need to put pressure on the policy makers to consider more recent research into how the brain functions and to broaden their view of human intelligence. A different perspective needs to be adopted on what is required for an adult to function efficiently as an individual, a member of a community and a useful employee. If Goleman is right, we should be helping our young people to develop the qualities of self-awareness, impulse control, persistence, zeal and motivation, empathy and social deftness. Maybe this will bring a significant reduction in the problems teachers experience with students failing to behave appropriately. In the meantime they need strategies that are effective. I hope this book will help you develop them so that your classes will be well managed and you have no need to shout.

GLOSSARY

assertive style
An assertive style is a teaching style that depends on a way of speaking and acting. Assertive teachers do not need to shout or use threats. They assert themselves in the way they say things.

attention seeking
Some students crave attention and will misbehave in order to get it.

choice
Offering choice is a means of placing the responsibility with the student. They have to decide.

consequence
All actions have consequences. Teaching students to understand this is one of the keys to successful behaviour management.

cooling off
Sometimes students need time to calm down and think about their actions. If they are given time, they may change their position and show you they have realised where they have gone wrong.

deferred consequence
A deferred consequence is a consequence that happens at a later time. The student will know they have got a consequence but will not receive it until later. Giving a red card is a signal that a deferred consequence has been issued and will need to be paid back later.

direction
The teacher gives a direction. A direction applies to specific activities whereas a rule applies all the time.

golden time
See motivational time

hierarchy of responses
A hierarchy of responses is a range of responses used by a teacher. The teacher begins by using low-level responses for minor disturbances, but the response level is increased if the student persists or the incident escalates. Ultimately the teacher will call for assistance from a senior member of staff if the student's behaviour becomes unacceptable.

intervention
An intervention is a teacher's response to a student's behaviour.

modelling behaviour
The teacher may model or show how they want the students to behave by doing it themselves. For example, a teacher may model good manners such as saying 'please' and 'thank you'.

motivational time
Motivational time is time that students can earn by behaving well. It may be earned by individuals or the class as a whole. It is also known as golden time.

off task
Students are off task if they are not following directions and not doing what the teacher has told them.

over-servicing
Teachers who respond or get involved in secondary behaviour (*q.v.*) will over-service the incident and possibly fuel it. When a student begins to misbehave, the teacher should redirect them with the minimum of fuss. Students who are looking for attention will try to draw in the teacher with their demands.

positive reinforcement
Praise positively reinforces the desired behaviour. Any form of reward will do this.

primary behaviour
Primary behaviour is a student's first response to a situation. The teacher should deal with undesirable primary behaviour.

redirect
When a student goes off task, the teacher's response should usually be to get them back on task. This is done by redirecting the student to the work and offering help.

repair and rebuilding
After a teacher has given a student a consequence and they have served it, a period of repair and rebuilding is needed to help the student realise that everything is now okay in their relationship with the teacher. This will enable the student to see that inappropriate behaviour is unacceptable but that the teacher does not dislike them as a person.

responsibility
In a culture of rights, everyone is responsible for protecting the rights of others.

rewards
Extrinsic rewards such as stickers, certificates and motivational time are earned by doing things well. Intrinsic rewards are the feeling of doing something well or knowing you have won a race.

rights

A right is a basic entitlement of everyone within the group. Rights enable each member of the group to enjoy certain freedoms without hurting others or being hurt. Rights need to be agreed and defended by everyone.

rule

A rule is an absolute limit of behaviour within the group that applies at all times in the school.

rule reminder

A rule reminder brings the attention back to the rule that has been broken. If a student does not follow directions, the teacher will have to intervene. They will point out where the student did not follow the directions and remind them of the rule.

secondary behaviour

A student who has behaved inappropriately will often shift the emphasis away from their initial behaviour to secondary behaviour. For example, they may say that a teacher is being unfair and try to draw the teacher away from the initial behaviour on to the teacher's alleged unfairness, which is the secondary behaviour.

tactical ignoring

A teacher may deliberately ignore a student who is behaving inappropriately but they will highlight a student who is giving the behaviour they require. This will demonstrate to the other student what they need to do without having to reprimand them for not doing it.

take-up time

Some students require longer to process a direction than others. When a teacher challenges a student, they may allow some time for the student to think about their behaviour and decide how to put it right.

timed intervention

A timed intervention is a period of time that a student may take away from the school at a learning support unit. It is used to help the student work on their behaviour so they can return to the school and cope with working in a classroom.

time-out

Time-out is a period of time away from the class, either in the room or out. There may be a special desk in the room for this and the students go to it for a fixed period of time, usually one to five minutes. If they can behave, they are allowed to resume their place in the class.

warning

The teacher will give warnings before giving a consequence to allow the student an opportunity to put right their behaviour. The warning allows the student to think about what they are doing and make a choice. This places the responsibility with the student and removes the excuse of being a victim. Victims do not usually have choices.

REFERENCES

Ayers, H., Clarke, D., Ross, A. and Bonathon, M. (1993) *Assessing Individual Needs: A Practical Approach*. David Fulton, London.

Bennathan, M. and Boxall, M. (1993) *The Boxall Profile: Handbook for Teachers*. Association of Workers for Children with Emotional and Behavioural Difficulties, London.

Canter, L. and Canter, M. (1992) *Assertive Discipline: Positive Behaviour Management for Today's Classroom*. Lee Canter Associates, Santa Monica CA.

Department of Health (2000) *Framework for the Assessment of Children in Need and Their Families*. The Stationery Office, London.

Dreikurs, R., Grunwald, D. and Pepper, F. (1982) *Maintaining Sanity in the Classroom*, 2nd edn. Harper & Row, New York.

Goleman, D. (1996) *Emotional Intelligence: Why It Can Matter More than IQ*. Bloomsbury, London.

Maslow, A. H. *et al.* (1998) *Toward a Psychology of Being*. Wiley, Chichester, W. Sussex.

Rogers, B. (1994) *The Language of Discipline: A Practical Approach to Effective Classroom Management*. Northcote House, Plymouth.

Smith, A. (1996) *Accelerated Learning in the Classroom*. Network Educational Press, Stafford, Staffs.

Willis, P. (1977) *Learning to Labour: How Working Class Kids Get Working Class Jobs*. Gower, Aldershot, Hants.

Wright, D. (1998) *Managing Behaviour in the Classroom: Practical Solutions for Everyday Problems*. Heinemann, Oxford.

BEHAVIOUR LOG

Class ....   Date ....

Name	Verbal warning	Yellow card	Red card	Consequence given

STUDENT PROFILE:
QUESTIONS TO ASK THE STUDENT

Name ....   Date of birth ....

What is your name?	
Do you have a nickname? Who is allowed to call you it?	
How old are you? (Leave blank if s/he won't answer)	
When is your birthday? (Leave blank if s/he won't answer)	
Where do you live? (Leave blank if s/he won't answer)	
What is your phone number? (Leave blank if no answer)	
What school did you used to go to? (Leave blank if no answer)	
What do you do at home?	
What do you most like to do?	
What time do you have to get up in the morning?	
What do you have for breakfast?	
What time do you go to bed at night?	
What is your favourite food?	
What is your favourite TV programme?	
Do you support a football team? Which one?	
Do you play any sports, e.g. football, cricket, basketball?	
What other sports do you like to play?	
Do you go to watch a film or football with your mum or dad?	
What do you most like doing with your mum?	
What do you least like doing with your mum?	
What do you most like doing with your dad?	
What do you least like doing with your dad?	
What are your favourite items of clothing?	
What clothes do you hate wearing, if any?	
If you were shipwrecked on a desert island, what would you like to have as a:	
Food	
Game	
TV programme	
Film/DVD	
Possession	
Which person would you most like to be with you on your island if you were shipwrecked?	
Which person would you never want on your island with you? It can be anyone you know.	

Name ....
Day ....
Date ....

Morning	No warning	Notes
8.45–9.00		
9.00–9.15		
9.15–9.30		
9.30–9.45		
9.45–10.00		
10.00–10.15		
10.15–10.30		
10.30–10.45		
10.45–11.00		
11.00–11.15		
11.15–11.30		
11.30–11.45		
Total (12 possible)		
Afternoon		
11.45–12.00		
12.00–12.15		
12.15–12.30		
12.30–12.45		
12.45–1.00		
1.00–1.15		
1.15–1.30		
1.30–1.45		
1.45–2.00		
2.00–2.15		
Total (10 possible)		
Total for day		(22 possible)

Name ....
Day ....
Date ....

Morning	No warning	Notes
8.45–9.00		
9.00–9.15		
9.15–9.30		
9.30–9.45		
9.45–10.00		
10.00–10.15		
10.15–10.30		
10.30–10.45		
10.45–11.00		
11.00–11.15		
11.15–11.30		
11.30–11.45		
Total (12 possible)		
Afternoon		
11.45–12.00		
12.00–12.15		
12.15–12.30		
12.30–12.45		
12.45–1.00		
1.00–1.15		
1.15–1.30		
1.30–1.45		
1.45–2.00		
2.00–2.15		
Total (10 possible)		
Total for day		(22 possible)

Name ....
Day ....
Date ....

Morning	No warning	Notes
8.45–9.00		
9.00–9.15		
9.15–9.30		
9.30–9.45		
9.45–10.00		
10.00–10.15		
10.15–10.30		
10.30–10.45		
10.45–11.00		
11.00–11.15		
11.15–11.30		
11.30–11.45		
Total (12 possible)		
Afternoon		
11.45–12.00		
12.00–12.15		
12.15–12.30		
12.30–12.45		
12.45–1.00		
1.00–1.15		
1.15–1.30		
1.30–1.45		
1.45–2.00		
2.00–2.15		
Total (10 possible)		
Total for day		(22 possible)

HOME PROFILE:
QUESTIONS TO ASK PARENTS

Name of child ....   Date of birth ....

How is s/he at home?	
Does s/he respond to your directions, requests, desires?	
Does s/he show s/he cares about your feelings?	
Does s/he respond to anyone's authority?	
Does s/he go out?	
With whom?	
What does s/he do out?	
Does s/he come back at the time s/he is told to?	
If s/he is told to stay in, what does s/he do?	
If told to go to his/her room, what does s/he do?	
Where has s/he got in to trouble most? Home, school, out?	
Describe the trouble s/he has been in?	
Were there any other children involved?	
Who were they?	
Do they have a reputation?	
Has s/he ever been in trouble with the police? If so, how?	
What are his/her main treats at home?	
Does s/he get pocket money?	
Has s/he any way of earning money at home/or a job?	
What is s/he like with his/her brothers and sisters?	
Who chooses what TV programmes to watch?	
Who chooses the meals?	
Describe meal times: seating, order of serving, etc.	
Does s/he go and get food from the cupboard?	
Are food and mealtimes an area of conflict? If so, how?	
Do you feel s/he dominates you and your life?	
Do you get time away from him/her?	
How do you feel towards him/her?	
How do others in the home feel about him/her?	
On a scale of 1 to 10 (10 = most) how happy would you say s/he is at the moment? Can you explain your reasons?	
On the same scale, how happy are you about your relationships with him/her at the moment?	
If you could change things, what would you change and why?	

There's No Need to Shout: The Secondary Teacher's Guide to Successful
Behaviour Management © David Wright, Nelson Thornes Ltd, 2005

Never, never, never give up

Winston Churchill

You are now entering a

NO

PUT-DOWN

zone

There's No Need to Shout: The Secondary Teacher's Guide to Successful
Behaviour Management © David Wright, Nelson Thornes Ltd, 2005

PROBLEM SHEET

Name .... Class .... Date ....

I am upset because	Other people involved	This is what I said
This is what they said	This is how it happened	This is what I will do to fix things

STUDENT INTEREST AUDIT

Name .... Form ....

Best friend's name	Age	This school Yes/no
....	....	....
....	....	....
....	....	....
....	....	....

My favourite music   Album   ....
Group   ....
Music style   ....

My favourite film or DVD   ....
My favourite TV programme   ....
My favourite TV channel   ....
My favourite game   ....
My favourite food   ....
My hobbies include   ....
The person I most admire is   ....
Reason   ....

The job or career I would like when I leave school is

....

If I were marooned on a desert island, I would want to take the following

Book   ....
Food   ....
Person ....

What my teachers did last year that I enjoyed the most

....

What my teachers did last year that I liked the least

....

If I could change one thing about school to make it better, it would be

....

TO TEACH
IS TO LEARN
TWICE

Joseph Joubert

INDEX